Pisgah Press was established in 2011 to publish and promote works of quality offering original ideas and insight into the human condition, the realm of knowledge, and the world around us.

Copyright © 2020 Mort Malkin
Published by Pisgah Press, LLC

Printed in the United States of America

Book & cover design: A. D. Reed, MyOwnEditor.com
Cover image: Eye idol, early Tel Brak, circa 5000 to 4000 BCE.
Author's collection; used by permission.
Index prepared by Nancy Gerth (www.nancygerth.com)

All rights reserved. No part of this publication may be reproduced, stored in a retrieval system, or transmitted, in any form or by any means, electronic, mechanical, photocopying, recording, or otherwise, without the prior written permission of Pisgah Press, except in the case of quotations in critical articles or reviews.

Library of Congress Control Number: 2021931636
Library of Congress Cataloging-in-Publication Data
Malkin, Mort
Homo Sapiens: A Violent Gene?/Malkin

Includes references and index

ISBN-13: 978-1942016618
Philosophy/Political Science/World History

First Edition
April 2021

Homo Sapiens: A Violent Gene?

Mort Malkin

ANTHROPOCENE

In but a single lifetime, my
own, Planet Earth has changed — melting
glaciers, rising seas, Maine's North Woods

not a cool respite in summer.
The Great Ponds warm early, ice-out
promptly in May, every year now.

The Globe around, a sudden new
Age — the Anthropocene — dire and
tenebrous as a volcano.

Introduction

Chapter Why

Americans are proud of their culture and their position as the only superpower in the world. Some even see it as a responsibility to preserve order in the world. They also believe that war is a practice that goes back to the time that mankind first appeared on earth. War is thought to be in our genes and, thus, will always be with us.

That most Americans hold these beliefs is confirmed in formal and informal surveys. There actually is no debate. Those who are certain that human nature is one of violence have already made a decision—no discussion needed.

As you may suspect, a gender divide of sorts exists. Most women feel that humans are peaceful and cooperative, if not caring. Businesswomen, often competitive in their daily activities, will reply almost reflexly with "Violent." American men are ... well, American men.

Respondents who say that war has always been and evermore shall be so, give a variety of reasons:

- War is part of human nature.
- Men were hunters and lived largely on meat from the animals they killed. So they are naturally violent.

- Testosterone makes men aggressive and violent; although it's generally the older men, with presumably lower testosterone levels, who send the young to fight wars for them.
- Men are crazy, but men are in positions of power to make war.
- When women get into power, they feel they must act like men.
- Some men get a thrill from killing, and war gives them a chance to do it legally.
- War has existed since the beginning of mankind, and so there will always be war.
- To speak of peace is political and controversial, and "I'm very conservative."
- There are evil people in the world, and the only thing they understand is force.
- People would become bored without war.

Even the great ethologist Konrad Lorenz proclaimed in his book, *On Aggression*, that human aggression was universal, and our biology determined that the human race will never escape violence.

The present day media encourages this perception of violence and war as pervasive in society, and as everlasting. Besides, diplomacy, peace, and contemplation do not sell ad time and space. Cooperation is minimally better at bringing in ad revenues.

Corporate CEOs, the engineers of capitalism, live by the watchwords, "Nice guys finish last." They are driven by avarice, and many of them are not averse to ruthless business behavior if it's not blatantly illegal.

If, however, mankind were really so preoccupied with war, we would know only the negative emotions that are brought forth with war: hatred, xenophobia, otherness, revenge, greed, exaggeration and rationalization if not outright lying, vanity, and pride. Yet, there is a spirit of fellowship and cooperation in the land. In many other countries that we consider foreign, there is a long tradition of hospitality, even toward non-governmental American visitors. Perhaps our perception of war being part of man's nature and its inevitability need rethinking. Until we believe that cooperation, not violence, is part our genome, we will not have peace in the world.

To help along with the reality check, let us cite a few nations with a long history of peace:

- Iceland has had no war for about 700 years, and has no standing army for that matter.
- Switzerland has maintained neutrality through much European warfare for 200 years.
- Sweden has a policy of non-participation in military alliances during peacetime, and neutrality during times of war between other nations. Sweden has been at peace since the early 19th century. Yet it was not always so. In the time of the Vikings, Swedes practiced violence throughout Europe and were widely feared.
- Another 20 or so countries have each had over 100 years of peace.
- Costa Rica abolished its army & navy in 1949, in spite of US badgering and bribery.
- War, it is agreed by most disciplines studying evolution, is cultural and not genetically determined. Cultures can change, and have, in less than a generation.

The great majority of ordinary people deal with conflict

in daily life without resorting to violence, let alone having a war over it. To quote Rabih Alameddine, "At the heart of most antagonisms are unreconcilable similarities."

The last chapter in this book reviews many brutal and barbaric practices of civilization over the last 5,000 years which are now out of fashion. All of them—such as slavery, burning witches at the stake, and the like—were once thought to be changeless, but now thought of as cruel and inhuman. So, why not war?

Actually, war has already been abolished in 1928 with the signing of the Kellogg-Briand Pact, also known as the Pact of Paris, by some 60+ nations. The United States, with Frank Kellogg the Secretary of State at the time, signed the Pact and the Senate ratified it by a vote of 85 to 1. It still stands as the law of the land. War was/is declared illegal. The Kellogg-Briand Pact makes no exceptions — not for just wars, not wars to preserve the dollar as the reserve currency for oil transactions with OPEC countries, nor because "it will be only a short incursion and over in a matter of days."

The Geneva Conventions have attempted to place limits on war—matters such as forbidding the torture and killing of prisoners, providing medical care for the wounded, and protection of civilians. The Fourth Treaty of the Geneva Conventions was agreed to in 1949. It stipulated the several inhumane practices of war as War Crimes. Such satire! The Kellogg-Briand Pact already branded war, itself, as criminal.

In the following chapters we will ask the assistance of the sciences of archaeology, evolutionary anthropology, genetics, chemistry, primatology, and other disciplines, to ask whether we were war-like for our first 190,000 years when we existed as hunter-gatherers and the last 90,000 years of that time when our brains/thinking had become conceptual and our genome was established. The archaeological record shows that cooperation rather than violence is in our genetic nature. We will also see that mankind can live together peacefully and settle disagreements in ways that don't involve war and violence.

Let us remember Lydia Sicher, the German WW I physician who observed "Wars are inevitable … as long as we believe that wars are inevitable. The moment we don't believe it anymore, it's not inevitable."

> As primates
>   are the highest form
> of life, I wonder if
>
> it's about
>   opposable thumbs,
> or vocal cords, or minds
>
> that thrive on
>   signs and symbols. Some
> say: it's not the ways we
>
> live, but how
>   we contend, each with
> each, that makes us Us. They
>
> point to all
>   our glorious wars. I
> offer them: bonobos.

No accounting for opinion,
be one of professorial
renown who admits to global

heating, but not our part in its
cause. As climate eludes logic,
science and romance can't relate —

yet, our genes invite alliance,
even nurturing and kindness.
All of which brings us back to love.

Contents

Chapter 1	*Homo sapiens*: A Violent Gene?	3
Chapter 2	The Mesolithic and Neolithic Periods	11
Chapter 3	The 4th to 2nd Millennia BCE — The Early Cities and the Beginning of Conflict and War	21
Chapter 4	War in the Near East and around the World: The Neolithic Period until Today	31
Chapter 5	Peace Heroes, Peace Victories Brief Summation	45
Chapter 6	Peace Heroes, Peace Victories: The Renaissance to the Modern Era	101
Chapter 7	Peace Heroes: The 20th Century to Today	139
Chapter 8	Human Aversion to Killing	223
Chapter 9	Resolutions of Conflict	231
Chapter 10	The Tradition of Cooperation and Caring	255
Chapter 11	Social–Cultural Evolution	263
References		275
About the Author		279
Index		280

Acknowledgments

The first person I need to thank is Melissa Malkin Weber, the chief of my support team whose all-around assistance and encouragement have been invaluable. My family, both East and West coasts, has been supportive of my writing, both prose and poetry. Melissa also introduced me to Pisgah Press and to A.D. Reed, its founder and editor-in-chief.

It was Leigh Merinoff who started me on the entire journey to develop the book with a generous grant to do the research and gather a few dozen key references. I'm also very grateful to Christine San José, who more than once encouraged me to continue the manuscript when I would have given up. She has also been a valued historian of the UK for several sections.

Indexer Nancy Gerth deserves a sincere thank you for her professional, detailed work—and for tolerating the author's idiosyncrasies and perfectionist nature.

Finally, I thank all those who read this book with an open mind, take its ideas to heart, and join in the ongoing mission of achieving more peace in our world.

Homo sapiens: A Violent Gene?

Cro-Magnon Man ...

... aware of himself, as alpha
and omega chimps must be;
Homo sapiens woman so
loving as she tends her child,

much the same as mother whales;
and elephants grieve as much
as we do. A Paleo day
chanced by with songs and stories,

images held firm from sun
to dark cave recesses where they
would be recorded by torchlight —
sensibilities we still feel.

Peace hath her victories, no less renown than war.
—John Milton

Chapter 1

Homo sapiens: A Violent Gene?

People of all political persuasions agree that war has always been with us and always will. Consensus has it that the best we can do is keep it down to a low growl by negotiated agreement where possible, and by limited military action where not. It is argued that because *Homo sapiens* made a living as a hunter-gatherer and used such weapons as spears and atlatls and bows and arrows, natural selection marked us with an innate proclivity toward violence.

This view seems too simplistic. Let's see what the archaeological record really says.

The Birth of Modern Man

The human race, *Homo sapiens*, has been around for some 200,000 years. For the first few millennia, the population was minuscule, and the rate of increase was nonexistent or minimal. It is estimated that it took 50,000 years to reach a breeding population of 10,000, and still *Homo sapiens* was in danger of extinction.

Homo sapiens was a gracile animal that had few weapons to defend himself and the band, and few for hunting. He was not as strong as a Neanderthal, or even as a half-his-weight chimpanzee. He had no rapier canines or sharp claws. He could not run very fast. It takes a trained track athlete to run a four-minute mile, or 15 m.p.h. Most four-legged animals can beat that speed.

During that first 100,000 years of hunting and gathering, the men hunted in ones and twos, and not very successfully. The women would form gathering parties, wherein a trusted sister or aunt or grandmother would care for or watch over the small children of a number of mothers, who could then join the workforce for a few hours. Human children did not grow into self-sufficient adults for 14 to 16 years. For the first year or two they couldn't stand upright, as remains true today. Thus, the women were cooperative among themselves, and with the men in gathering, as well.

At more or less 90,000 to 70,000 years B.P. (before the present), the men started to copy the women. They began hunting more cooperatively, in groups, and became more successful in bringing back larger animals to share with the whole group, clan, or tribe. It took active cooperation for the hunters to carry a 150-lb deer any distance back to the gathering.

Along with cooperative hunting came chemistry, not known to the hunters but apparent in its effects: Vitamin B3, nicotinamide, is present in cured and slow-cooked meat. That B3, added to flavonoids and other phytonutrients from berries, fruit, and leafy greens, acts on developing as well as adult brains to promote new synapses and connections between various centers of the brain, especially the cortex, hippocampus, and hypothalamus.

Those changes in the chemistry of the brain enabled the development of complex conceptual thought—cause and effect, a sense of past and future, awareness of the thoughts and subtle emotions of others, and empathy.

Let us call it the "Conceptual Brain," and the time of our second hundred millennia the "Second Coming."

Many artifacts have been found from the Upper Paleolithic Period, between 60,000 and 12,000 BP, a long era during which we were still hunters and gatherers. These stone, bone, and ivory artifacts provide us with important insight into the cognitive and psychological nature of the species. This second coming of *Homo sapiens* was skilled in using imagination, analogy, and symbolic thought; could weigh the different outcomes of different scenarios; had a strong sense of self-awareness; understood the concept of motivation; and exhibited a high degree of social intelligence. The genes that guide our behavior today were defined during this time. This new-found genome enabled the species to survive and slowly increase its numbers through times of adverse weather and hostile environments, including such threats as huge cave bears, hungry lions, wooly rhinos that could trample a hunter into a blood spot, and no antibiotics to combat infections. Geneticists have estimated that on the basis of present-day nuclear DNA variation, the *Homo sapiens* population during the early Paleolithic Era is estimated to have comprised fewer than 100,000 individuals, while the variation in mitochondrial DNA predicts a human population of only 10,000, a population dangerously close to the lower limit for survival of the species.

Although *Homo sapiens* did not have the physical attributes of sharp horns, large canine teeth, lethal claws, or speed afoot to be good hunters or to defend themselves against predators, they were clever and could use tools and fire, they had imagination and foresight, and after the Second Coming they could act in concert. Anger and violence against perceived disrespect of a fellow hunter, for example, would result in a failed hunt. They and their families back at the camp would have to subsist on a diet of edible weeds, roots, and berries. Any violent individuals were generally ostracized, and such natural selection ensured that their genes would not be passed on. Intraspecies violence would have left the small populations of this new species of *Homo sapiens* at risk of extinction.

The other half of the human genome was contributed by the Paleolithic women—the gatherers. Not only did they gather wild edibles, they bore responsibility for rearing the children, a multiyear process. The survival of the species depended on those women's skills in nurturing and their kindness of spirit. In addition, Paleolithic women had some help from the hormones of pregnancy and lactation. Pregnancy may have lasted only nine months for each full-term baby, but lactation often continued for three or four years, during which time prolactin and oxytocin levels were elevated, resulting in peaceful and mellow demeanor. Over the long term, this pleasant nature would have been instilled socially.

Compassion is the diametrical opposite of violence. To this day women with a penchant for physical violence are an exception. Recent research comparing men's and women's physiological and emotional response to danger shows that men react by fight or flight, whereas women gather together to express their fears and work out their best defense. A violent nature among women would have been a disadvantage to the species.

Moreover, we know that personality and the proclivity for peace or violence are determined by many factors, including multiple genes, our many experiences as children and adults, and situations and the playing out of events. War or peace cannot be attributed to a single gene for violence or one for pacifism. Rather, environmental and social influences are more compelling drives in determining human behavior. Most archaeologists feel certain that the hunter-gatherer bands of ten to thirty individuals, as existed in the Upper Paleolithic, were egalitarian in their social-political structure. Evolutionary anthropologists, sociologists, and psychologists agree that small, egalitarian communities exhibit little violence.

The basic cooperative, sharing nature of paleolithic mankind is evidenced by collections of stone cutting and scraping tools found at sites along with different kinds of animal bones. The hunters/scavengers must have carried animal prey back to base camps to share and prepare for eating among the entire group.

Further insight into mankind's basic character can be gained by examining the cave paintings and relief sculptures at Altimira, Chauvet, Lascaux, Niaux, Pech-Merle, Dolni Vestonice, and many other caves and rock shelters in France, Spain, Italy, Germany, Moravia, and Russia. The Upper Paleolithic artists throughout Europe represented animals of their time—bison, horses, mammoths, antelope, reindeer, ibex, wild cattle (aurochs), wooly rhinos, musk oxen, owls—as majestic beasts. Cave bears were shown occasionally, but in non-aggressive postures. At Chauvet, there are a few images of rhinos, one painting showing two angry rhinos charging each other.

With rare exceptions, violence is not depicted. Rather, the paintings and sculptures often seem an expression of reverence, frequently created in sanctuary-like spaces in the inner recesses of the caves. Further, the animals were mostly herbivores: horned, hoofed beasts. The few lions depicted appeared more like portraits than as hunting carnivores. The same is true of the small sculptures, drawings, and models on bone, antler, ivory, rock, and clay—the portable art found in shelters and camps across all of Europe. Among all the representations of animals shown on these small pieces, violence is not seen. The closest is the depiction of three lions shown running in an engraved drawing.

One of the rock shelters at Valitorta in Valencia contained a painting of a hunting scene, with four hunters wielding bows with arrows facing a group of charging deer. But this is is from the Neolithic rather than the Paleolithic period. In Bhimbetka, Madhya Pradesh, India, a war scene is depicted with two helmeted warriors wielding sabers and shields. This painting is dated even later, from the "historical period."

Additionally, from across Europe and and Asia there have been found between 200 and 300 figurines and amulets representing the human female, many of them pregnant. These small sculptures in limestone, clay, ivory, and bone were

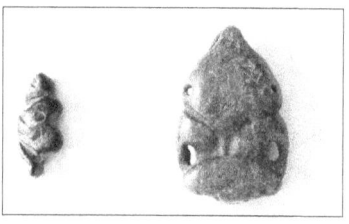

Two amulets of pregnant women, @5000 to 4000 BCE.

discovered at sites separated both temporally and geographically: Willendorf, Galgenberg, Dolni Vestonice, Petrkovice, Kostenki, Lespugue, Balzi Rossi, Brassompouy, and elsewhere. Many are works of art in their own right, whatever their original purpose. They are generally described as Venus figures and are often interpreted as fertility carvings, offerings to insure successful pregnancies. In contrast, sculptures of male figures are rare. The Venus figurines may have been meant to glorify women, as icons for goddess worship, pleas for healthy pregnancies, or art for art's sake. Whatever the reference of each, they tell us of Paleolithic cultures in which procreation, nurturing, and art—not violence—were the main concerns.

At the base of a cliff near Toulouse, France, a piece of mammoth ivory depicting a pair of deer was uncovered. It is dated to 13,000 years ago. The well-executed carving must have taken many days of work, and the skills of the hunter-gatherer artist must have been developed over a period of time. The same is true of an earlier sculpture of a lion-headed man carved out of mammoth ivory, found near Hohlenstein in Germany and dated to 40,000 BP. It is estimated to have taken a couple of months of full-time work during daylight hours to complete. These artists must have been looked after by others of the hunter-gatherer camp for their food and clothing needs. Archaeologists are in agreement that all the artworks of the ancient painters and sculptors presume cooperation among the group members, not conflict and violence.

In the same Upper Paleolithic period, *Homo sapiens* became skilled tool makers, adept at using wood, stone, bone, and antler to craft their implements. While there is evidence of wooden spears being used for hunting, the stone tools found in abundance included predominantly blades, scrapers, hand axes, cleavers, and points—tools for cutting meat, breaking into bone marrow cavities, and preparing hides. The points were predominantly shaped for use as awls, compared to relatively few designed as spear points. After 15,000 BP or so, sling-thrown stones were used in hunting, and atlatls were invented for throwing spears further and faster. Soon after, bows and arrows were imagined, designed, and created.

One might conclude that such early technology was bringing hunting and violence into greater alignment. By that time, large animals were the preferred game, and it took more than one or two hunters to bring down a giant antelope or a mastodon. Cooperation among the several members of a larger band of hunters was needed, and the large bones of such animals found at human campsites of the Upper Paleolithic are proof that the hunts were successful. Ipso facto, cooperation must have been the first rule of hunting. And, back at the campsite, the women gatherers who contributed half the genome were peaceful, amiable, and nurturing of the children.

A pair of evolutionary anthropologists did a recent extensive review of the archaeological record of the hunter-gatherer period of *Homo sapiens*. They report on over 400 sites and describe 2,930 human skeletons. Only five dating from the Paleolithic Period showed possible evidence of human violence. Five in all those millennia!

A putative violent gene is not much in the archaeological record of the Paleolithic period, the time when our genes became established.

The first flutes ...

... fashioned of
    the hollow bones of vulture wings,
forty thousand years ago,

never were a call to
    arms, only for music making,
dance, and sociality.

Millennia on, through
    reeds and keys, 'twas always one with
the glorious art of peace.

Chapter 2

The Mesolithic and Neolithic Periods

Let's look further at the archaeologic record. The late Paleolithic (or early Neolithic) has been termed the Mesolithic Period. Many settlements or villages dated to this time have been excavated throughout Europe, Asia, and Africa.

Occasional individual graves contain skeletons showing evidence of violence—embedded stone points, skull fractures, or "parry" fractures of the arm, but one in particular—the Jebel Sahaba site at the border between Egypt and Sudan—is an early mass grave (denoted "cemetery 117"). It is dated to about 13,000 BP and contains the remains of 24 female skeletons, 19 males, and 13 children, 40 percent of them showing evidence of violence. The first war? War is generally carried on by males, and this mass grave may represent a conflict that we can no longer define.

Moreover, among the many sites of the Mesolithic interim period excavated, it is the only one that shows multiple killings. A few smaller multiple graves have been found in Spain, Germany, and Austria, but are dated later, from to 7,000 to 5000 BCE (Before the Common Era), well into the Neolithic.

Military historians also point to earlier embedded stone points in skeletons as evidence of the violent nature of mankind. They may neglect to say, however, that early skeletal finds of such violence are rare in the first 190,000 years or so of the existence of *Homo sapiens*. Only five or six instances, whether by accident or intent, were found among over 3,000 human skeletal remains in more than 400 sites excavated in the entire Paleolithic Period.

Among the usual reasons for war—population pressures and scarcity of resources—neither was the case in hunter-gatherer times. Raids to kidnap women, another possible reason for warfare, can be ruled out in light of the hundreds of small sculptures of women discovered, often pregnant, and many carved quite artistically. Violence appears to be furthest from the minds of the sculptors in the Upper Paleolithic.

The Neolithic Era

About 12,000 BP, mankind learned to cultivate wild grains as well as some fruits and vegetables. Some individuals with more nomadic inclinations domesticated sheep and goats. As the climate cooperated, the Holocene Epoch began, and the Neolithic Period came into being. In many places around the human-populated world, especially the fertile river valleys of the Near East, South Asia, and East Asia, farmers raised more food than their Paleolithic ancestors could ever gather. The herders' animals supplied milk, cheese, meat, and skins. They produced surpluses of all these products, vegetable and animal, which could then be stored or traded. The grain—at first, barley and wheat—gave rise to beer-making.

Civilization was on its way. As settlements grew into villages, craft workshops were set up using the local natural resources. In river valleys, clay was used to make bricks for buildings, and the craft of pottery was developed for making containers to store food. Various inhabited regions offered sources for wood, stone, and precious stones used to make jewelry. Trade was a natural, almost inevitalbe, development for widespread exchanges of food, raw materials, and finished goods.

Excavations in Eastern Europe, the Balkans, Turkey, the Levant, Iraq, Syria, Iran, Pakistan, China, Japan, and other locations have found numerous Neolithic settlements. Discoveries at each give us some idea of life at the beginning of the agricultural revolution.

In Gobekli Tepe, in eastern Anatolia, a large temple complex was uncovered, as were megaliths carved with images of birds and animals. Jericho in the Levant has been excavated extensively, though some contention still exists as to the purpose of its walled structure and the life of its early inhabitants. (See p. 47 for more on Jericho.) Qaramel in Syria, dating to the mid-11th millennium BCE, is one of the earliest settlements. Inhabitants of Hacilar in southern Anatolia, dating to 7000 BCE, cultivated wheat, barley, and lentils, and produced pottery. Many small statues of the female figure, including a mother goddess (or possibly a mistress of animals) seated on a leopard, have also been found there.

Nearby, Catal Huyuk was a very large settlement which was first occupied about 7500 BCE. It differed from other early villages/cities in its social structure and is described below. In Cayonu, eastern Anatolia, a large settlement dating to 7000 BCE was excavated, uncovering several figurines of female form. Metsamor, Armenia, also first settled about 7000 BCE. Interested in astronomy, the inhabitants created cosmic observatories of great liths long before Stonehenge. Also found there were obsidian instruments and tools that might have been used in the observatories. At later levels, metal processing workshops with furnaces were discovered, the earliest in the Near East.

Numerous other sites also date to approximately 7000

BCE. Discovered at Jarmo in northern Iraq were obsidian, bone tools, beads, and stone stamp seals. Hassuna in northern Mesopotamia contained pottery at its earliest levels, and its red slip decoration was exceptional: female figurines were sculpted, and stone stamp seals were carved. Excavation of Sesklo in Greece uncovered pottery and statuettes of female figures. And in central Iran, at Tepe Sialk, examples of advanced pottery with beautiful decoration of animals and plants were found, as well as a large number of stone tools. Silversmithing was an early signature craft.

A picture of life among the people of Eastern Europe in the mid- to late-Neolithic Period is especially concerned with religion, generation of life, and renewal.

Dating to one-and-a-half millennia later, around 5500 BCE, is Samarra in northern Mesopotamia. There mud bricks were used for construction, figurines of birds and animals were sculpted, and stone seals were incised.

Mehrgarh in Pakistan was a very early settlement, long before the Indus Valley civilization of Harappa and Mohenjo daro. Terra cotta female figure sculptures were much in evidence.

The Jormon culture of Japan was making pottery at the Sannai Maruyama site as long ago as 10,000 BCE. The people there still hunted, fished, and gathered seeds and nuts. In the later Jormon periods the sea was the major source of food. The long-lived culture was eventually displaced during the 4th century BCE by the North China Yayoi culture, which exhibited strict social stratification, did large scale rice farming, and made use of iron technology. The Jormon people, despite their hunter-gatherer life and a simple social order, built planned settlements of hundreds of buildings and developed advanced pottery skills. Their development of technology encompassed not only ceramic craft but also basket weaving, the use of bone needles, and the making of sea-worthy bark vessels and wooden paddles. They also engaged in long distance trading, as evidenced by the artifacts of obsidian, amber and other exotic minerals discovered in Jormon excavations.

Cucuteni-Trypillian Culture

Across a wide area of Romania, Moldavia, and Ukraine, the culture included over 3,000 settlements, villages, and towns. The largest occupied between 600 and 1,100 acres, from the years of 5000 to 2800 BCE. These *Cucuteni-Trypillian* sites provided a trove of female figurines and characteristic pottery vessels decorated with feminine designs such as V shapes, triangles, and spirals, but no weapons of human conflict. Many other eastern European Neolithic sites have also been excavated with finds of hundreds of female figurines and other sculptures associated with animal symbols of fertility—birds, snakes, sows, butterflies, deer, and bulls—and pottery vessels decorated with designs associated with regeneration.

Few male figures have been found. Tools that could be used in farming, hunting, and fishing were among the artifacts, but no weapons meant for raids or war. There was no evidence of fortification and no depiction of bound or slain prisoners.

The people of this culture were engaged largely in subsistence farming, animal domestication, ceramics, and textile crafts. It was a peaceful, cooperative society with many settlements and showing no signs of social stratification or privileged class.

Two larger settlements in western Asia during the Neolithic deserve special mention: Jericho in the Jordan River valley of the Levant and Catal Huyuk in southern Turkey.

Jericho was settled in the 9th millennium BCE, the *Natufian* period. As the settlement grew into a village and eventually to a city, the inhabitants built thick, high walls. Such an enormous building project would have required a high level of social organization and cooperation in the service of a common goal. The lifestyle was simple and agrarian—inhabitants became adept at growing wheat and storing it in the dry season.

Pottery came late. Despite the massive walls, there is no evidence of preparing for armed conflict. Indeed, a serious theory holds that they were built for flood control, not as fortification. It seems more in keeping with the kinds of Natufian artifacts that have been found—stone and bone tools for farming, food preparation, and making clothing. They include microlith burins, sickle blades, spatulas, palates, mortars and pestles, and awl points.

One exception in a nearby site is a projectile stone point that was discovered in a vertebra of a skeleton found in a cave in Israel. Long-distance trade is evidenced by finds of obsidian, which could have only come from Anatolia, and cowrie shells which the Jerichovians used for such trade. The tower at Jericho, once thought to be for military purposes in conjunction with fortification walls, has more recently been the subject of different interpretations. One theory holds that it was a symbol of prominence; another that it was for the storage of grain; and finally, that it had the cosmological function of lining up with nearby Mt. Qarantal and the setting sun on the longest day of the year. The last explanation seems most valid. All told, the evidence suggests a farming community living simply and peacefully in a prime location with fertile soil, a pleasant climate, and adequate water. No storage of weapons of war that would be expected with fortification walls were found.

Catal Huyuk in south central Turkey was first established about 7500 BCE and grew larger and more prosperous until shortly after 5000 BCE, when it was abandoned for unknown reasons. The wall paintings and carvings were mostly of women and their attributes, leopards. One striking example is an ample woman seated on a throne between two leopards. She is thought to represent a mother goddess. Catal Huyuk was a city of shrines, but no animal sacrifices were required to please the deities. Instead, small bundles of grain were left on the altars.

Creating jewelry of obsidian, many figurines of women, and textiles of complex designs occupied the inhabitants. Warfare was unknown. Catal Huyuk had no defensive walls, and yet there is no archaeological evidence of military attack or plunder. Many archaeologists and art historians are certain that the city-state was egalitarian and matrilinear.

Ceremonial Places

Neolithic humans in Great Britain and central Europe built henges, or roundels, surrounded by V-shaped ditches. Stonehenge is well known, but there are a hundred or so other sites in Britain and many in central Europe, especially in the Rhine to Danube basins. The ones in continental Europe had various overall shapes—oval, triangular, or rectangular, and were surrounded by ditches and, often, palisades, but the purposes appear to have been the same as the roundels—religious, ceremonial, and related to the seasons.

The large ones and those with large stones, at least, must have been a joint effort by several clans or settlements; and so, each was meant as a commons for collective purpose. They were set out aligned with the four cardinal directions as solar observatories to determine the annual solstices and equinoxes. These ceremonial places would have been used for rituals, seasonal rites, and festivals. Excavations have found vases, flints, figurines (both animal and human figures), and also animal bones that would have been from sacrifices to deities.

Large auroch horns at some have been interpreted as symbolic of the goddess of death and regeneration.

These ceremonial places are another example of the cooperative nature of the human primate. The sites show no evidence of fortifications, weapons, storage, or even having been living quarters. Rather, religious rites, celebrations, and harvest festivals are the likely purposes. Peace, it seems, was the state of the world in the Neolithic period.

Stamp and Cylinder Seals

In Mesopotamia, the need for identification of ownership of goods, whether placed in storage rooms or shipped for trade, brought the invention of seals. Small stones were drilled so they could be worn on a string. One surface was flattened and carved with a distinctive design that could be stamped onto a clay wrapping. Writing had not yet been invented, but the patterns tell us something of the mindset of the seal owners at various historic times and places. Seals began to be used in the late 7th millennium BCE, and their use was continued throughout the Near East for almost 8,000 years in a variety of distinctive forms. Many, many seals have been found in excavations, and archaeologists have catalogued the seals and made glyptic art into an academic field of study.

Stamp seal, two deer facing backward, @3500 BCE

The people of the early Neolithic were occupied with growing, processing and storing food; making seals for the establishment of ownership; engaging in long-distance trade; and appealing to the gods for fertility of the land and the family.

Little or no evidence of warfare, the wholesale manufacture

of weapons or their use, or the destruction of villages has been uncovered.

During the early Neolithic in the Fertile Crescent, the Amuq and Halaf periods, the first seals were carved in geometric designs such as criss-cross or dotted patterns. There were no images of spears, arrows or maces, though they would have been easy enough to execute. Later, during the Uruk period, seal carving became more imaginative, showing birds, fish, and terrestrial animals. The creatures depicted were principally horned quadrupeds such as antelope, ibex, and cattle, only rarely a carnivore. More rare were human figures. After examining a few thousand Neolithic stamp seals, I have seen only one showing a figure holding a bow in each hand. A two sided seal, the reverse side shows a deer. The bow was probably meant for hunting.

At the end of the Neolithic, the Jemdet Nasr period of 3100 to 2900 BCE, cylinder seals were invented. The small cylinders could be carved around the circumference so that when the stone was rolled on damp clay it produced a continuous frieze in bas relief. The earliest cylinder seals displayed geometric designs, some representing eyes, others schools of fish, yet others mountains.

Two early cylinder seals, brocade pattern; Jemdet Nasr period, @3000 BCE

Another type, tall cylinders known as brocade seals, featured repeating symmetrical patterns. Next came short cylinders of eagles, scorpions, and running antelope, and then women at pottery work or weaving. Also in the Jemdet Nasr period, the shapes of

Three eye idols, early Tel Brak, @5000 to 4000 BCE.

some stamp sealstones were carved to resemble animals—occasionally lion heads, but predominantly recumbent sheep and cows—with the flattened surfaces usually incised and/or drilled to represent simple shapes of leaping small animals or water creatures.

The semiotics of seal carving during the Neolithic, from its beginning until the era of the cities of the Bronze Age, show little penchant for violence. Trade seems to have been preferred over might makes right.

The Neolithic, so named for its highly sophisticated stone work, also provides archaeological evidence in the polished stone scepters and mace heads that have been found at a number of sites. These finely finished implements show little wear or evidence of use in warfare. It is thought that they were for ceremonial and ritual purposes.

A number of papers and books have documented a few excavation sites—northern plains of the United States, British Columbia in Canada, Nubia in Africa, Ukraine, France, Algeria, and a few others—where evidence of assault or violent death has been found. These sites have been dated to the Neolithic period, not the Upper Paleolithic when the human genome was established and fine tuned. That *Homo sapiens* is capable of violence and murder—especially after the beginning of crop cultivation and pasturing of animals, the growth of cities, and the rise of empires—is well recorded by all historians. At any rate, it is universally accepted that human behavior is far more complex than a simple nasty gene that increased the likelihood of violence and war, or a more pleasant one that led to peace and cooperation.

The thesis presented in this book presents a refutation of the argument that we are programmed for violence, because our genome was formed in the hunting-gathering times of the Upper Paleolithic. We were largely peaceful and cooperative when our genome was defined, from 70,000 to 12,000 BP.

Next, let us see what human life was like in the civilizations of Europe, Africa, and Asia during the 3rd millennium, the era of the first cities, and the time of the first wars.

> An octopede knows no bones,
>   but can use its flex and squeeze
> to go from A to B, to
>
> find a home whose owner moved
>   out of town. The odd creature
> thinks us queer, whose brain can't
>
> grow within the limits of
>   an ossamine case, and needs
> to breathe in air above water.

Before stylus sticks
were used for writing,
metaphors were shaped

   as images on
walls of caves to tell
of great bison in

   the lives of hunters,
magnificent stags
of the Asian Steppe,

   metaphor in the shape
of Earth Mothers, carved
in stone full round — all

   callings early in
the lithic age, gifts
of the timeless Muse.

Chapter 3

THE 4TH TO 2ND MILLENNIA BCE—THE EARLY CITIES AND THE BEGINNING OF CONFLICT AND WAR

Central Asia

It is now generally accepted that the earliest horse domestication took place in Central Asia north of the Caspian Sea on the Asian Steppe of the Volga and Ural River basins at the beginning of the 5th millennium BCE. Excavations in Russia have found that the majority of animal bones in sites dated to the first half of the 5th millennium were of horses. The culture of pastoralists, sometimes called Kurgans (or the Yamna, or early Maikop) used the domesticated horse for meat, hides, milk, and transportation. Over the next few centuries, horses were trained for riding, as evidenced by the discovery of horse cheek pieces made of antler in excavations of late 5th-millennium sites in the Dnieper basin. The pastoralists comprised several different tribal groups and clans, but they all employed similar burial practices, imposed a patriarchal social structure, and had a similar religious identification with sun, sky, and thunder gods, as well as horse breeding and a pride in weapons.

By the mid-5th millennium BCE, the first wave of immigration moved west into the Dnieper Valley and eastern Black Sea region from the Caspian-Pontic Steppe. Despite the differences between cultures—the Asians were pastoralists and the Cucuteni-Trypolye villagers were agriculturists—they apparently coexisted without much conflict. They traded with each other and there was also a small amount of cross-cultural exchange. Excavations of the Cucuteni culture settlements found few weapons and no hill forts, even in the mid-5th millennium BCE.

By the mid-4th millennium, a second wave of immigration from Central Asia took place. The pastoralists were an aggressive, patriarchal society whose tool kit included flint daggers, arrowheads, spears, and hafted axes. By then, alloying of copper with arsenic or tin to produce bronze had been discovered—ideal for weapons. Mounted on horses, the new immigrants became ever more aggressive and capable of violence. It is easy to see a parallel with today and how aggressive some people become when they get behind the wheel of a car. The immigrants from Central Asia extended their presence across Ukraine, along the Danube, and into Yugoslavia, Romania, and Bulgaria. With that second wave of immigration, many of the older Neolithic cultures were relocating their villages to more defensible locations—high river banks and hillsides—where they could build protective walls and ditches. Many villages of the old agriculturalists—Cucuteni, Varna, Karanovo, Vinca, and others—moved farther west and north.

A third wave of immigration, just after the turn of the 3rd millennium BCE, extended the presence of the Indo-Europeans into most of western Europe. The extent of their influence is seen today in the many languages, which linguists agree are Indo-European based. The Caspian-Pontic region was not only the birthplace of many known languages, but also of a warrior culture. It should be emphasized that the violence was cultural, not genetic—our genes were well established in the Upper Paleolithic Period several thousand years before.

Egypt

The earliest organized warfare, most archaeologists agree, began in Egypt at the very end of the 4th millennium BCE, in predynastic times. A famous artifact, the Gebel el-Arak ivory-handled knife, dated to about 3200 BCE, depicts pairs of men in combat and, in the bottom register, boats engaged in a sea battle. Later in the predynastic period, King Scorpion was the ruler of Upper Egypt. For some Egyptologists, Scorpion's elaborate mace-head and a few references from subsequent kings are sufficient to say that he was a military leader. But the mace-head, bearing a scorpion and the standing figure of the king with a hoe digging out an irrigation channel, was probably ceremonial. Others have concluded that the mace-head, never intended for use as a weapon, was crafted to signify kingship and the celebration of an agricultural achievement.

After Scorpion's time, the first Pharaoh of the first Dynasty, Menes, "unified" Upper and Lower Egypt, by force of course. Thus, warfare officially began about 3100 BCE. Narmer, another first Pharaoh, was probably the same individual. We know of Narmer because of his beautiful slate palette that was recovered at excavation. The palette, artistically engraved on dark green slate, shows the King smiting an enemy with a mace. It is uncertain where Aha, yet another first Pharaoh, fits the history. Be that as it may (or may not), the Narmer palette is dated to the Proto-Dynastic era, about 3100 BCE. A modern poem by the author (M.M.) tells a story of Egypt at this time.

> **Pharaoh the First**
>
>   Pharaoh the First
> his name Aha,
> the city This, near
>
>   Abydos. There
> he prepares for
> a ghostly season
>
>   of the Nile. First
> Dynasty, then
> Second, Third, and on
>
>   through twenty-eight
> centuries, till
> hieroglyphs give in
>
>   to alphabet,
> and books collect
> at Alexandria.

After the early Dynasties and through the Old Kingdom period, violence and war continued on a fairly regular basis. A few of the highlights: Pharaoh Den of the First Dynasty embarked on a few military expeditions to the east and, in celebration, had a stone seal carved showing the King smiting an enemy with a mace. King Sneferu of the Fourth Dynasty carried out military campaigns into Nubia to the south. Under Pepi I of the Sixth Dynasty, commander Weni led five invasions of Palestine. In one, he landed troops on the shore from a ship, a first in naval history. Pharaoh Merenre, Pepi's son, commissioned Governor Harkhuf to lead trade expeditions into Nubia, but the later missions needed a military escort.

The first true Peace Heroes of Egypt appear in the New Kingdom in the 2nd millennium BCE: Hatshepsut and Amenhotep III. See chapter 5, Peace Heroes and Peace Victories, for more details of their rule.

Sumeria

In Sumer, the violence of war had its beginnings in the Early Dynastic period, but not for the first few centuries. Beginning about the 29th century BCE, many changes and advances were wrought, such as the alloying of copper with tin to produce bronze; the invention of a base-60 number system; and cuneiform writing. In this earliest period of Sumerian history, cities grew in size and prosperity as a result of productive agriculture and trade, and the duties of each city's first citizen, the *ensi*, were only religious and administrative. In the workshops, the cylinder seal carvers of the Early Dynastic preferred the artistic style of crossed animals standing on their hind legs, often lions attacking stags. It was a preview of politics in centuries to come.

The first major artifact that glorifies war is the famous Standard of Ur, found in the excavations of the royal cemetery of Ur. On one side of the Standard, we see soldiers in helmets carrying short swords, spearmen, four-wheeled chariots, and trampled enemy soldiers. Several naked and bound prisoners are being led before the king. On the other side we are treated to a celebration scene with seated figures holding cups to toast the king, and examples of the bounty of the earth—domesticated animals, fish, and bags of grain. A musician playing a lyre and a singer are also represented.

By the mid-25th century, Eannatum, the ensi of Lagash, decided to think expansively and took the title Lugal. Lagash and Umma had quibbled over some boundary lands from time to time under previous leaders, but Eannatum raised the stakes to a military level and attacked Umma, sacking that rival city.

Eagal Eannatum recorded his military victory in stone in the engraving of the Stele of Vultures. As the third ruler of the First Dynasty of Lagash, he extended the practice of military diplomacy with other cities over a thirty-year reign from 2455 to 2425 BCE.

Yet, it was Lagash that produced our first Peace Hero by name, Urukagina. See chapter 5 for details.

In the mid-24th century, Lugalzagesi came to power in Umma and started on a career of conquest. He subdued one city after another in Southern Mesopotamia and made Uruk, the largest city, his capital. He believed it was his mission to unite all the cities between the Euphrates and Tigris and thus issued a proclamation that Enlil, the chief god of the pantheon, had granted him suzerainty over all the lands "between the Upper and Lower Seas"(Mediterranean Sea to Persian Gulf). It was the beginning of serious war and the way to establish a legacy. But, he never completed his divine assignment. Sargon, cup-bearer to the King of Kish, had recently overthrown his sovereign and assumed that throne. The King of Kish was traditionally seen as the ruler of all Mesopotamia, the kingship having been lowered from Heaven to Kish after the Great Flood. Of course it was Sargon's divine duty to stop Lugalzagesi. The ensuing war was protracted and finally ended with a series of battles at Uruk, the last of which ended with the capture of Lugalzagesi. Sargon, it is told, led him ignominiously in a neck stock to the holy city of Nippur.

Akkadian Empire

The Dynasty of Akkad thus was founded in 2340 BCE in a newly built capital of Agade. Sargon the Great went on to establish the first empire, complete with a standing army of 5,400 soldiers. He controlled all the lands from the

Mediterranean to the Persian Gulf, from the silver mines of the Taurus Mountains of Anatolia to the cedar forests of Canaan. How ironic that Sargon's daughter, Enheduanna, a well-known poet, was also a Peace Hero with her poem, "Lament To the Spirit of War." (See p. 51.)

The empire did not include Elamite areas to the east or Hurrian areas to the north. But it was a start. Continuing the Akkadian Dynasty, two of Sargon's sons ruled briefly, and then his grandson, Naram Sin, expanded the empire further and, proclaiming himself divine, became the ruler "of the four quarters of the world." He was arrogant enough to challenge the god Enlil by invading Nippur and razing the temple at Ekur. It was the beginning of the end for the empire.

Soon after the death of Naram-Sin and the undistinguished rein of his son, Shar-kali-sharri, the empire went into decline. The Gutian tribes tested the Akkadian defenses, and finding them weak, swept down from the Zagros Mountains and destroyed the empire about 2200 BCE. Most of Mesopotamia fell into a dark period.

Just before the turn of the millennium, Utu-Hegal of the city of Uruk drove out the Gutians and reestablished Sumerian rule, culture, and language. Of course, he was only continuing the tradition of Lugalzagesi. Ur-Nammu, Utu-Hegal's brother, proclaimed the Third Dynasty of Ur and, while everyone was amenable, pronounced himself King. (Some controversy exists as to the chain of events and the relationship between Utu-Hegal and Ur-Nammu.) Ur-Nammu ruled for eighteen years and expanded his control of Mesopotamia to include Umma, Kish, and Adab. He also invaded Lagash and Uruk—both of which were less reasonable and needed persuasion.

Following Ur III, the First Dynasty of Babylon was established under Amorite rule. The Dynasty was happy to live as a city-state until Hammurabi came to the throne—he of the Law Code chiseled in stone. Naturally, he had a tradition to uphold—the Akkadians had been Semitic, too. Hammurabi set out on a patient era of conquest, one city after the next, until finally the cities of Eshnunna and then Mari were under Babylonian rule.

Babylon I lasted until about mid-2nd millennium. In the second half of the millennium, Babylon fell into decline and controlled little more than the city of Babylon itself. The rest of the Near East was divided into several spheres of sovereignty: Kassites, Mitanni, Assyrians, and Hittites. There were also Elamites in the East, Mycennaeans in Greece, Trojans on the coast of Turkey, and Egyptians who were interested in both the cedars of Lebanon and Sidonian glass in the Levant. Considering the potential for contention over territory and resources, violence was surprisingly limited. In one notable attack on Babylon, the Elamites took as spoils the Stele of Hammurabi's Law Code. Another exception was the war between the Hittites and the Egyptians, which culminated in the battle of Kadesh in northern Canaan in 1274 BCE. In that battle, both Ramses II and Muwatalli claimed victory, in that neither was defeated, but the casualties were so extensive that both sides agreed to a treaty of peace, the first ever recorded. We may note that both sides claiming victory may be a diplomatic way to settle disputes, even today.

Further west, the war between Greece and Troy, about 1200 BCE, is well known, courtesy of the writing of Homer a few centuries later. That war was, as we know, fought not for treasure but over personal pique and a beautiful woman—ten years worth of conflict.

China

The Xia Dynasty, which began with Yu, the third of the Sage Kings, was peaceful and benevolent in the tradition of Yao, Shun, and Yu, for over 400 years, through sixteen successive kings. The seventeenth, Jie, however, was corrupt, oppressive, and outright cruel. Stories of summary executions for the crime of not preparing a royal meal to his liking and of royal drunken orgies are told by historians. Armed insurrection finally occurred in the fifteenth year of his reign and continued for fifteen more years, but the revolution finally succeeded with the defeat of Jie at the Battle of Mingtiao.

The Shang Dynasty that followed (17th to 11th centuries BCE) produced several significant advances, including the development of writing, the alloying of copper with other metals to produce bronze, and the use of spoked wheels for chariots. With bronze-tipped weapons and the horse-drawn war chariots, the Shang were able to embark on a long military campaign of conquest. Warfare, along with royal hunts and banquets, became the principal occupation of the nobility.

Moreover, when a prince died, many servants were sacrificed to be with him in his grave. Cruelty and violence were a hallmark of the later kingdoms of the dynasty.

Finally, King Wen, from a neighboring province, stood against the corrupt and war-driven Shang, and he and his son Wu drove them from power. (See chapter 5 for more details.)

India-Pakistan

The first warfare we know of is the Mahabharata epic of the war at Kurukshatra between the friends and relations of the respective clans of the Pandava and Kaurava. The battle lasted only eighteen days but enormous numbers of casualties were sustained. The archaeological evidence of the war is weak, and the dating is questionable. The best estimate is that it occurred in the late 4th millennium or early 3rd millennium BCE. But the myth was strongly held and became tradition for many of the dynasties throughout Indian history.

In contrast, the city of Mehrgarh, which existed from 7000 BCE to about 2600 BCE, left a detailed archaeological record, as does the Indus Valley civilization of Mohenjo-daro and Harappa, dated from 2600 BCE to the early centuries of the 2nd millennium. In these early cultures, there is no evidence of warfare.

A short time later, in the mid-2nd millennium, the Aryans from Central Asia moved into the Ganges Valley in India, where they held power for several centuries. Aryan history tells of the Kshatriya warrior class that was developed to protect the rest of the people, but we know how easily order can be confused with law and aggression is thought necessary for protection.

Violence among humans was a matter of the culture of the group and their history and tradition, not the genome of *Homo sapiens*.

How wondrous an organ
the brain is — several wrapped up
in one. The basics — sensations

and movement — only told
of centuries to come, of
more centers and work to do. More

connections — neurons and
chemicals — next door and far,
always ask the question "Why Not?"

Chapter 4

War in the Near East and around the World: Neolithic Period until Today

By the late 2nd millennium BCE, the Assyrians began an ascendancy in Mesopotamia from their northern cities of Assur and Nineveh that eventually led to the fierce NeoAssyrian Empire. A succession of Assyrian kings, in an expansionist policy, attacked and defeated Urartu, Syria, Babylon, the Hurrians, Scythians, Cimmerians, Egyptians, and Elamites, among others. The empire reached its zenith between 900 and 630 BCE. Assurbanipal, who ruled from 668 to about 630 BCE, was a skilled warrior who led his troops in battles from Elam to Egypt, and sacked Susa and Thebes as the chance arose. Assurbanipal is also noteworthy as a scholar and for assembling a great library at Nineveh. While we may be thankful for the library, we cannot consider him a Peace Hero.

As the Assyrian Empire expanded, it became stretched for resources, in warriors, supplies, and treasure. It had also accumulated a wide assortment of enemies—Babylonians, Medes, Scythians, and Cimmerians in the lead—and in a series of decisive battles was finally brought down. Over just seven years, Nineveh, Harran, and Carchemesh all fell, and the Chaldeans established full Neo-Babylonian rule by 605 BCE.

The Neo-Babylonian focus on religion is seen in the change

in form and iconography of the seals. Neo-Assyrian seals were cylinders showing scenes of power and glorifying the king. Their propensity for violence is well illustrated in the Neo-Assyrian cylinders of the 10th to 7th centuries BCE: archers and stags, kings hunting lions, a king grasping two ostriches by their necks, and other motifs depicting the exercise of physical might. The Neo-Babylonian seals, in contrast, were all stamp seals usually depicting a priest praying before an altar, with the symbols of Nebo, the god of scribes, and Marduk, the patron god of Babylon. The Neo-Babylonians under Nebuchadnesser built many temples, completed the royal palace, erected the Ishtar Gate to the city, and developed a network of canals and aqueducts. They are also credited with the Hanging Gardens of Babylon and a great Ziggurat: plainly it was an era of building and culture. But Nebuchadnezzar was also a warrior who conquered Babylonia and Assyria, Phoenicia, Israel, and Arabia, though his NeoBabylon empire lasted a brief 66 years.

Cyrus The Great, the founder of the Achemenid (Persian) Empire that followed, conquered the Lydian Kingdom under Croesus and then, in a bloodless invasion, took control of Babylon, preserving the achievements of the NeoBabylonians. The last years of Cyrus's rule were a mixture of military campaigns and peaceful years, but Cyrus's legacy was remembered as one of generosity and benevolence.

These who followed Cyrus—Cambyses, Darius, and Xerxes—sought their own legacy through through military victories. The last half of the 1st millennium BCE was a time of endemic war around the Mediterranean and Western Asia. Historians, from that time to this, have recorded all the conflicts from the Greek-Persian wars of 490 and 479 BCE through all the other conflicts right up to today's 21st-century wars. History has since been written in milestones of battles, wars, and war heroes. The following timeline offers the highlights:

The Greek and Persian wars begin under Darius, continue with Xerxes, and have since become classic history, including the famous Battle of Marathon and the naval battle at Salamis. We unfortunately have the history only from Herodotus. The Persians left no historical records of these wars.

The Peloponnesian Wars between the Athenian League and the Spartan League start in 457 BCE, and are interrupted by the Thirty Years' Peace of 445.

Contention begins again in 431 BCE, and lasts until 405–404 with the defeat of the Athenian fleet.

The glory of conquest in the guise of bringing Greek high culture to the poor backward folks of Egypt and Asia continues under Alexander III ("the Great"), son of Philip of Macedon, who uses the powers of the army to back up his persuasive diplomatic charms from 336–323 BCE.

To the East in South Asia, the Aryans of the Ganges Valley live quietly under Khsatriya protection, but sixteen contentious kingdoms and republics arise after 800 BCE, and at about 600 BCE the stronger ones dominate. By the 5th century, the Nanda amass a huge war machine of over 200,000 troops, cavalry, chariots, and 4,000 war elephants. That military might is well applied, and Nanda becomes an empire that lasts for 100 years, principally around the Ganges Valley but extending from Bengal to Punjab.

In 323 BCE, Chandragupta Maurya, with a couple of allies, defeats the Nanda and others and unifies most of the subcontinent. The Mauryan Dynasty, through four kings, extends Mauryan rule quickly and widely, even challenging Seleucus I, the Macedonian ruler of western Asia following Alexander the Great. Seleucus, in a peace treaty with the Mauryans, cedes a large amount of territory and a Macedonian princess to Chandragupta in exchange for a battalion of war elephants.

A break in the continual violence in India in the 1st millennium BCE occurs during the reign of Ashoka, the third king of the Mauryan Dynasty. Ashoka was reputed to be cruel and ruthless in gaining the throne and during his first ten years as king. Indeed, he was known as Ashoka the Fierce. Then, after success in the Kalinga War of 261 BCE, as he surveyed the battlefield and saw the thousands and thousands lying dead, he was struck by the reality of all warfare and decided that he would like his regime to be remembered as one of peace and respect for life. A further description of the remaining twenty-nine years of his monarchy is discussed in chapter five. After his death, India returns to the business of war.

Further East, China in the 5th century BCE is divided into seven major contentious kingdoms beset by shifting alliances, constant intrigue, and frequent military adventurism. The Warring States period continues into the 3rd century, when the Qin Dynasty gains ascendancy. In 221 BCE, the Qin defeats the remaining kingdoms, and King Ying Zheng changes his name to Qin Shi Huangdi as he proclaims himself emperor.

The Three Punic Wars between Carthage and Rome take place, the second of the three featuring Hannibal and his war elephants. The wars continue from 264 to 146 BCE, interrupted only by short breaks for peace.

The conquests of Roman generals of the Republic and the expansion of the Empire under the Caesars take place throughout Europe and the Near East. Julius Caesar, as a general, fights a successful campaign against the ornery King Pharnaces of Pontus and sends his famous message back to Rome: "Veni, Vidi, Vici." ("I came, I saw, I conquered.")

The plunder of Rome by the Visigoths in 410 CE, the occupation by the Ostrogoths in 493 CE, and the defeat of the Goths by Emperor Justinian I in 554 CE are just three highlights of the empire's dislocations and relocation.

The Arab conquests of the 7th century CE (post-Jesus, the Prince of Peace) sweep across Arabia, Mesopotamia, Persia, Egypt, and all of North Africa.

Berber tribes (Moors) cross the Straits of Gibraltar to invade Spain and occupy Al-Andalus in the 8th century, establishing a great cultural and academic tradition amidst the military activity and theological fervor.

From the 8th to 10th centuries, Viking raids by Danes, Norwegians, and Swedes occur in England, Ireland, France, and across to Kiev in Russia. Charlemagne expands the territory of the Franks with many military campaigns across Europe, particularly thirty years of warfare against the Saxons. with only brief interruptions, between 772 and 804.

The Seljuk Turks capture Baghdad in 1055.

The Battle of Hastings in 1066 is the deciding event in the conquest of England by the Normans, wherupon William the Conqueror becomes king.

Count nine Crusades from 1096 to 1291: in 1098 the Crusaders capture Antioch and in 1099, Jerusalem. In 1187 Saladin retakes Jerusalem. In the Fourth Crusade in 1198, Crusaders defeat the Byzantine Christians and destroy Constantinople.

The Ottoman Turks occupy Constantinople in 1453 and rename it Istanbul. They go on to conquer the Balkans.

The Mongol Empire is established and expands from Yellow Sea to Black Sea under Genghis Khan in the 13th century. The modus operandi was, of course, primarily military, but also the taking of many wives and the birth of many sons to administer the many lands.

Tamerlane (Timur) conquers a large area of Central Asia in

the 14th century. His ongoing military campaigns include all of Persia, northern Mesopotamia, northern India, and Anatolia (Turkey). In the early 15th century he attempts the conquest of China but is repulsed by the Ming Dynasty, before succumbing to a fatal fever.

The Hundred Years War between Britain and France, actually lasting from 1336 to 1453, is remembered for its heroine, the 14-year-old warrior Joan of Arc.

The Wars of the Roses, setting factions of English kings and dukes and their allies against one another, continues from 1455 to 1485. The rivalry between the Dukes of Lancaster and York provides Shakespeare with material for several historical plays.

Queen Isabella and King Ferdinand drive out the Moors and reunite Spain (by force, of course) in 1492.

Cortes conquers the Aztecs in Mexico in 1521. Pizarro conquers the Incas in South America in 1533.

The Mughal emperor, Abkar, conquers central India in the mid-16th century.

Japan invades Korea, but a combined force of the Korean Navy and Chinese troops drive them out in 1592.

Philip II sends the Spanish Armada to dethrone Elizabeth, the "heretic" Queen, in 1588. The British Navy, with the help of a fierce storm, defeats the Spanish.

The Habsburgs and Ottomans fight for thirteen years, 1593–1606, alternating victories and defeats. Even after the war has been over for almost fifty years, another conflict, the Great Turkish War, breaks out in 1663.

King Gustavus Adolphus of Sweden, 1611–32, modernizes military tactics, establishes a well-trained standing army, and raises his nation to major powerhood in Europe. The 17th century is a time of perpetual war in Europe.

The (official) Thirty Years War, fought mainly in the

German States from 1618 to 1648, actually involves most of Europe, the Holy Roman Empire, and the Habsburg dynasty. It is essentially a war between Catholics and Lutherans, though politics plays a large role.

England and France fight a war in North America, now known as the French and Indian War (1754–63), in which the British and the Colonists are aligned against joint French and Indian forces for control of Canada and the present Midwest region of the United Sates.

The American Revolutionary War (1775–83) becomes the centerpiece of the 18th century. In France, the French Revolution is the main event of the 18th century. 1789 sees the storming of the Bastille; in 1793, King Louis XVI is guillotined, and Robespierre, later beheaded as well, justifies La Terreur.

The slave trade, largely between the 16th and 19th centuries, reaches a peak of activity during the 18th century. Violence is part of the capture and shipping of African slaves as cargo to the Western Hemisphere. Further violence often occurs in their treatment by their new owners if they don't perform as expected.

Russia and the Ottomans go to war, 1768–74. The Turks underestimate Tsarina Catherine II ("the Great"); the Russian Navy becomes a major force on the Black and Mediterranean Seas, destroying the Turkish navy; Turkey is forced to sign a treaty granting independence to the Crimea and giving up two ports on the Black Sea to Russia.

Portugal establishes rule over Brazil, politically and linguistically, in 1777.

The 18th century draws to an end with the beginning of the Napoleonic wars in 1799. Napoleon, a professional soldier, meets with success in many battles, is appointed 1st Consul and, in 1804, Emperor. Paris falls to a coalition of allies in

1814, and the following year Napoleon is defeated at Waterloo by the British Duke of Wellington. The French of the 21st century still refer to him as the Emperor. Others in Europe use less complimentary language.

The 19th century was no less riven by wars. Throughout the century, Native Americans are driven from their land, treaties are broken wantonly, and America's First Peoples are deceived, starved, or killed outright, all as part of the United States' Doctrine of "Manifest Destiny." They are still being manipulated and treated unjustly today.

The War of 1812 between the United States and Great Britain—mostly along the Canadian-US border but including one seaborne assault on Baltimore—ends with the prewar borders unchanged.

In the 1821–1832 Greek War of Independence against Turkey, the death of the British poet, Lord Byron, leads to support of the Greeks by other European nations.

A decade later, 1839–42, the First Opium war between England and China sets a precedent for chemical warfare. England, victorious, dictates the terms of the Treaty of Nanjing whereby the port of Shanghai is open to trade and Hong Kong is ceded to the British. The second Opium war, 1856–60, opens more ports to trade.

The British also are involved in a pair of Afghan wars, 1839–42 and 1878–81. In the First Afghan War, the British are forced to retreat into India. In the Second, they win the major battles but, weary, withdraw and leave the Afghans to fight it out among themselves.

The British are involved, about the same time, in colonizing New Zealand, much to the displeasure of the Maori natives. Two actual wars are fought, 1843–48 and 1860–72.

The United States annexes Texas in 1845, over the

objections of Mexico. The US sends troops to defend the new territory, and the US-Mexican war begins the next year, lasting into 1848. After the US capture and occupation of Mexico City, the war ends and Mexico is forced to "sell" southern California and New Mexico to the United States for $15 million.

The Ottomans and Russians go to war again in 1854 over the Crimea. This time Great Britain and France are allied with the Turks.

The US Civil War starts in 1861 over economic issues and slavery and lasts into 1865, with horrendous numbers of casualties on both sides. Some say it hasn't ended yet.

The Franco-Prussian war of 1870 lasts less than a year. Much like the Marx Brothers' film *Duck Soup*, it started over a purported personal insult. In this instance, the French ambassador is snubbed by the Prussian King.

In the 1880s the French establish French IndoChina. They occupy Hanoi and Hue and decree a "protectorate." The widespread uprising by the Vietnamese over the following years is put down by the French forces. Opium as a commercial commodity plays a major role.

The massacre of as many as 200,000 Armenians by Ottoman Turkey between 1894 and 1896 is still remembered, and denied, as a genocide today.

The Spanish-American War is set off with explosions and the sinking of the *USS Maine* in 1898. Although the exact cause is unclear (even a century later), the US declares war and blockades Cuba, then invades the Island at Guantanamo Bay, takes Santiago, and defeats the Spanish. As part of these military actions in the Caribbean, the US occupies Puerto Rico. Then, across the Pacific Ocean, US forces attack the Philippines, ostensibly to help the insurgents in their revolt against Spanish rule. The Spanish soon withdraw, the US annexes the Islands, and the Philippine revolutionary forces turn their attention to the Americans.

The Spanish American War quickly becomes the Philippine War of Independence, which continues until 1902, when the US establishes a Philippine Assembly, declares the war ended, but keeps the islands as a colony. Some want to declare the Philippines a Commonwealth territory of the US, but in 1946, the Philippines are granted full independence, with just a few reservations such as US control over major and minor naval bases—and a few favors for US corporations.

The Boer Wars, 1880–81 and 1899–1902, involve the Zulus, the Boers, and the British in the Transvaal, the Orange Free State, and the Cape Colony. The discovery of diamonds and then gold complicates the motivations of the combatants. South Africa becomes part of the British Empire.

The Sino-Japanese War of 1894–95 is fought over control of Manchuria and of Korea. Japan emerges as a major regional political power.

In the Russo-Japanese War of 1904–05, the Japanese unpredictably win and are ceded the Southern half of Sakhalin Island. The Russians give up their lease at Port Arthur. The war creates hard feelings between the two nations.

In the First Balkan War, 1912–13, the Serbs, Greeks, and Bulgarians are allayed against the Turks.

1914 begins the Great War (WW I) in which more than eight million soldiers die, including the poet Wilfred Owens. The casualties and disfigurements from tear gas and other chemical weapons led it to be called, at first optimistically but later sardonically, "the war to end all wars." The war eventually involves scores of nations, including the US starting in 1917, until its end on Armistice Day, November 11, 1918.

In the Russian Civil War, several different revolutionary groups and powerful individuals participate in the in-fighting, not just the Romanoff royal family versus the people. The war lasts from 1918 to 1922.

1918 marks the Finnish War of Independence from Russia.

In 1935–36 the Italian-Ethiopian War establishes a neo-Roman empire in North Africa.

In the Spanish Civil War, 1936–39, several foreign governments and volunteer groups take part on either the side, the Republicans vs. the Nationalists. Generalissimo Francisco Franco names himself dictator and rules until his death in 1975.

The Chinese Civil War, in the patient spirit of East Asians, extends from 1927 to 1949.

The Sino-Japan War, 1937–45, is engulfed by, and becomes part of, World War II.

The Finish-Soviet War of 1939–40 ends when the Finns grant the Soviet Union permission to establish military bases on their territory.

The Second World War (WWII) begins in 1939 in Europe with Germany's invasion of Poland. Though the war begins in Europe. it becomes global in 1941 with the attack by Japan—allied to Germany—against the US naval base at Pearl Harbor in the US Hawaiian Islands. The war ends in August 1945 with the US dropping atomic bombs on Hiroshima and Nagasaki, two southenr Japanese cities, and the Soviets entering the war at the same time. Japan surrenders unconditionally, but the US spares the life of the Emperor. Historians now note that the Japanese were willing to surrender some weeks before, the only condition being that the Emperor would not be executed.

After WW II is over, the dangers of peace are feared, and a few memorable conflicts are remembered by many folks today: Korea, Vietnam, Iraq twice, Panama, Granada, Afghanistan, and a number of proxy wars.

Civilization

East of the Black,
    the Caspian,
where compass stars led
    Sumer, Hatti

westward to the
    fertile valleys,
to highlands that would
    yield base riches —

ores to transform,
    fearsome weapons
of war and glory.
    Five millennia,

and we are at
    plutonium.
How long before we
    rise to chess and go?

Chapter 5

Peace Heroes, Peace Victories in Early History

Overall, for the past 5,000 years, life was rife with violence. But the human genome was formed long before, during the Upper Paleolithic period. Rather than being possessed of (or by?) a violent gene, we became a creature that survived because of the neural wiring that gave us the sense that we needed to cooperate, to share our cleverness and insight, and to nurture our children for several years after birth. If anything, we can be said to have an altruistic gene.

On all the continents where *Homo sapiens* roamed during the Upper Paleolithic period, mankind made a living by hunting and gathering, trying to keep the species from extinction. Our numbers had been tenuously small for the first 100,000 years after *Homo sapiens* first appeared in East Africa. We had no natural weapons such as horns or strength or speed, and we were not endowed with great speed or strength. Our weapons were our intelligence and a spirit of mutualism.

Violence and out-and-out warfare emerged after the many peaceful millennia of the Paleolithic Period and even after the agricultural and pastoral revolution, the ownership of goods, and the development of efficient weapons (at first, for hunting). The timeline for war varies a little among the civilizations in Egypt, Mesopotamia, India, and China, as a result of the geologic and geographical differences. Generally, however, organized warfare started in the 3rd millennium BCE in the various populated regions of the world.

Despite the seeming universality and general continuity of this violent form of human discourse since that time, there have always been individuals who promoted peace, and there were times and places during which peace was, in fact, maintained. Throughout history there have been Peace Heroes, sacred ground, and periods of armistice. The trend is accelerating. Let us begin at the beginning.

The Upper Paleolithic

In Paleolithic times, there is some fair evidence showing that mankind was largely peaceful by nature. The initial paragraphs of this thesis discuss a) the evidence from genetic and species population studies; b) the need for cooperation in hunting bands; c) the natural nurturing skills of the Paleolithic female; and d) the cave paintings and fertility carvings found in Europe and dated to the Upper Paleolithic period.

We have no names of individuals who stand out as peace advocates in this prehistoric period, but if peace is the general condition of the species, one need only be a proponent of the status quo to promote peace.

As our genetic code was being settled in the Upper Paleolithic (60,000–12,000 BP) our skills as hunters derived not from a genome of violence but from intelligence, foresight, cooperation, and mutual assistance. Nor must we forget the skills at gathering, mostly attributable to females, who identified wild edible grains and eventually led to the first Agricultural Revolution.

Neolithic

In the following period, the Neolithic, approximately

10,000 to 3200 BCE, when *Homo sapiens* learned how to herd goats and sheep and how to plant barley, wheat, and certain vegetables, the archaeological finds of stamp seals and evidence of trade among villages and early cities offers us no witness to warfare between communities.

Catal Huyuk, the largest city of the mid-Neolithic, has been extensively excavated and suggests a people interested in a) human fertility and b) trade, not warfare or even defense. The economy was prosperous, relying on obsidian (volcanic glass) as its major natural resource. The city had built many temples, but no defensive walls. Catal Huyuk was a going city in Turkey for about 2,500 years, but there is no evidence of destruction at any level of the excavations. The consensus of archaeologists familiar with the excavations is that the city-state was a matriarchy and entirely peaceful. We have no names of peace heroes or even the mother goddess whose statue is widely published.

The other large city of the early and mid-Neolithic was Jericho. The surrounding walls are legendary, but in the early history of the city they were likely built for flood protection, not as fortification. Nor was the 28-meter-high tower built for military purposes. The tower lines up with nearby Mt Qarantal and the setting sun on the longest day of the year—a construction of cosmological design. The people of early Jericho lived fairly simple lives, unchanging over many years with few innovations. For a city to withstand repeated attacks, the residents could not depend just on a fortification wall: they would have had to develop counter-measures against ever more sophisticated weapons such as siege engines and tunneling that would be used by aggressive neighbors. Nothing worthy of war has been uncovered in excavations. Indeed, agricultural tools, but few weapons, have been found. As in Catal Huyuk, we have no names of the Peace Heroes of the Neolithic Period.

The stamp seals of the early and mid-Neolithic—the Amuq and Halaf periods—are simple geometric patterns with an occasional circular design of a snake. A rare love seal is also known. The seals of the Uruk period, 4000 to 3200 BCE, show representations of animal forms—almost entirely hoofed quadrupeds, not carnivores. Neither are hunting scenes depicted, although an exceptional seal with a human stick figure and a bow has been found. Stamp seals representing the fecundity of nature are the rule. The humans of the Neolithic did not have violence in mind as they went about the activities of daily life, but we do not know of particular Peace Heroes from this time. They all may be fairly considered so.

The very late Neolithic in the Mesopotamian Valley overlaps with the beginning of the Sumerian or Early Dynastic period. The time from 3100 to 2900 BCE is called the Jemdet Nasr period. The seal-carving workshops of the time invented the cylinder seal, which an individual could roll on soft clay to produce a continuous pattern across the full width of a clay tablet, for example, along the length of the sealing of the door to a storage room, or on the clay wrapping of export goods.

The designs carved into these seals generally depicted fish, eyes, mountains, or working women ... but no violence.

The leaders of the early cities of the Jemdet Nasr period were called "ensi." The function of an ensi, in addition to administrative work, was to represent the people to the city god and other gods of the pantheon. The ensi did not have the political power to lead armies in invasion of neighboring cities.

Third Millennium BCE Sumeria

The beginning of the 29th century BCE, which we call the Early Dynastic, brought many changes and advances, including the alloying of copper with tin to produce bronze, the invention of a base-60 number system, and cuneiform writing. The cities grew in size and prosperity as a result of trade, but as first citizen, the ensi's duties were still only religious and administrative. In the workshops the cylinder seal carvers of the Early Dynastic preferred the artistic style of crossed animals standing on their hind legs, often lions attacking stags. It was a preview of politics to come a few centuries later.

Urukagina

The first Peace Hero of Sumerian times was Urukagina, the last of the nine rulers of the Lagash Dynasty. Under the previous rulers Lagash was ridden with corruption, conflict of interest in officials, and arbitrary violence. Urukagina was known as a social reformer who brought honesty to government by eliminating bribes among inspectors, tax collectors, and judges, and bringing equality and freedom to his people. The "Praise Poem of Urukagina" lists the various reforms of this ensi of Lagash and Girsu and represents the first written law code. The years of his leadership, 2380 to 2360 BCE, brought peace and justice to Lagash and set an example for other cities. We may count Urukagina as a true Peace Hero.

In the mid-23rd century, Lugalzagesi came to power in Umma and started on a career of conquest. He subdued one city after another in Southern Mesopotamia and made Uruk, the largest city, his capital. He believed it was his calling to unite all the cities between the Euphrates and Tigris Rivers and so issued a proclamation that Enlil, the chief god of the pantheon, had granted him suzerainty over all the lands "between the Upper and Lower Seas (Mediterranean Sea to Persian Gulf)." His declaration was the beginning of serious war and the way to establish a legacy. Lugalzagesi gained the fealty of a few of the city-states but never completed the divine assignment. Sargon, the cup-bearer to the King of Kish, had overthrown his sovereign and assumed the throne of that city. The King of Kish was traditionally seen as the ruler of all Mesopotamia, the kingship having been lowered from Heaven to Kish after the Flood. Sargon of course considered it his divine duty to stop Lugalzagesi. The ensuing war was protracted and finally ended with a series of battles at Uruk, in the last of which Sargon captured Lugalzagesi and, it is told, led him in a neck stock to the holy city of Nippur.

The Dynasty of Akkad, thus was founded in 2340 BCE in a capital at Agade. Sargon went on to establish an empire that extended from southwestern Persia to the forests of Lebanon to the silver mines of the mountains of Turkey.

<u>Enheduanna</u>

To preserve order in the troublesome Mesopotamian cities of Ur and Uraq, Sargon appointed his daughter, Enheduanna, as priestess at the temple of Nanna, the moon god. Enheduanna had previously attained some honor as a literary figure, and with her appointment as the representative of Nanna, the god who was in charge not only of the passage of time but also of fertility and abundance, she would ensure loyalty to the dynasty.

Enheduanna, despite being high priestess at the temple of the moon god, wrote three major psalms to Inanna, the goddess of love and queen of the heavens. The princess/priestess also wrote over forty hymns celebrating the temples at different cities in Mesopotamia. A short poem, "Lament to the Spirit of War," is also attributed to her. In the poem the horrors of war are compared to the rage of a hurricane, the scream of a tempest that impels evil winds, and the rushing of blood down a mountain in hate and anger. The last line asks of the Spirit of War, "Who can fathom you?" It is her only work that condemns war directly, but the poetic style is in keeping with the other work. A translucent white stone disk that preserves Sumerian cuneiform script and addressing Inanna on one side and the image of Enheduanna on the other is the only artifact that can be dated to the Akkadian period. The major portion of the literary work of the princess/priestess comes from tablets dated to the Old Babylonian period, hundreds of years later, and found at the holy city of Nippur. Considering the power of the Lament, below, we must call Enheduanna a Peace Hero.

Lament to the Spirit of War

You hack everything down in battle… God of War, with your fierce wings you slice away the land and charge disguised as a raging storm,

growl as a roaring hurricane, yell like a tempest yells, thunder, rage, roar, and drum, expel evil winds!

Your feet are filled with anxiety! On your lyre of moans

I hear your loud dirge scream.

Like a fiery monster you fill the land with poison. As thunder you growl over the earth,

trees and bushes collapse before you. You are blood rushing down a mountain, Spirit of hate, greed, and anger, dominator of heaven and earth!

Your fire wafts over our land, riding on a beast.

With indomitable commands, you decide all fate.

You triumph over all our rites. Who can explain why you go on so?

—Enheduanna, c. 2300 BCE, Sumerian poet and priestess
Translation by Daniela Gioseffi

Gudea

The Akkad dynasty lasted only four generations before going into severe decline. Around 2200 BCE, The Gutian tribes tested the defenses, and finding them weak, swept down from the Zagros Mountains and destroyed the empire.

It was during Gutian rule that the next Peace Hero appeared—Gudea of Lagash. Gudea, called the Prince of Lagash, deemed himself, not Lugal, as ensi. Despite the Gutian control of the other cities of Mesopotamia, he kept Lagash peaceful and productive with a series of projects to advance religion, the arts, and architecture. Many statues of Gudea have been found that were dedicated to the deities Ningirsu and Nanshe—each a finely executed work of art. Nothing less would have been sufficient for such a pious leader. During the twenty years of his leadership, Lagash enjoyed a reign of peace.

China – the Sage Kings

We know of the Sage Kings by way of legends passed down through the centuries. The Sage Kings were real people, not divine beings like the Culture Heroes of the Neolithic Era. The Sage Kings ruled between the 24th and 22nd centuries and rightly belong at the very beginning of the time-line of Chinese history.

Yao

In the 24th century BCE, according to Han Dynasty scholars, the early Chinese civilization in the Valley of the Yellow River was ruled by a sage king named Yao. He was intelligent, diligent, and benevolent. He lived not ostentatiously but simply and was mostly concerned with the welfare of the people. Yao promoted trade and friendly relations among various clans and communities, and his kingdom became prosperous. War was unknown.

When Yao was in his middle years, he selected a talented commoner with a streak of virtue—Shun—to become the next king. Shun then spent thirty years under Yao's tutelage learning the trade. Only then did Yao abdicate in his favor. Yao, it is told, lived to 119 years and held the position of Living Legend for close to five decades.

Shun

Shun was a man of the people and, throughout his reign, eschewed privilege. He appointed officials in accordance with their skills and integrity, not their connections. He himself often went among the people to intervene personally in any conflicts that arose. If a dispute developed between farming communities or between fishing villages he would go to live there and, by his own behavior, show how working together would benefit all sides in the disagreement.

A problem brought to him by Mother Nature, however, was beyond all the honest efforts of his public works department. The Yellow River periodically overflowed its banks and did great damage to the countryside. His engineers built levees, but they, too, would overflow with record floods. Finally, he appointed an innovative environmentalist who, rather than opposing the natural cycles with dams or dikes, planned out an extensive series of drainage channels to divert the overflow. This man, Yu, spent thirteen years of long days traveling from village to village along the river, persuading the people to dig drainage aqueducts that would allow the overflowage to pass benignly into the countryside. The strategy was successful, and Yu became known as Yu the Great. Naturally, Shun anointed Yu to succeed him as King.

Yu

As King, Yu continued a regime dedicated to public works and the improvement of the various industries: agriculture, pottery, silk, weaving of fabrics, stone carving, etc. But he also continued to promote fairness and equality and tempered justice with humanity. Under his example, innovation and integrity became so much a part of society that when he finally died after forty-five years of leadership, the people acclaimed his son as the next king. So, the Xia Dynasty began, and for fifteen successive generations kept true to the ways of the Sage Kings.

Yao, Shun, and Yu are universally recognized as true Peace Heroes.

South Asia – Indus River Civilization

Just as in the Nile Valley, Mesopotamia, and the Yellow River Valley, a civilization developed in the Indus River Valley during Neolithic Times. Villages gradually expanded to towns and small cities, starting at about 9000 BCE. By the 7th millennium, the settlement of Mehrgarh grew into a city and set the standard for commerce in South Asia. Meanwhile, in Mesopotamia a breakthrough point was reached by 3000 BCE: in bronze technology, cuneiform writing, a base-60 number system, and a wide-ranging trading network. The Indus Valley reached a similar sophisticated state about 200 years later. Two major cities, Harappa and Mohenjo-daro, and a number of smaller towns have now been well excavated, and we know a fair amount about the civilization. The cities were well planned with grid networks of streets and houses, baths with wells and sewer drains, but no grand temples with fire altars. Apparently the Indus folks did not engage in blood sacrifice. Some houses were larger than others, perhaps belonging to successful merchants, but no elaborate mansions or royalty-suggestive palaces were evident.

Many cylinder and stamp seals were found, generally depicting animals such as water buffalo, humped bulls, elephants, and antelopes. Some of the detail is particularly elegant. One artistically carved sculpture was found: a neatly bearded male who is now called a priest-king, but not wearing a crown or the helmet of a monarch.

There is no evidence of warfare or even a kingship that could provide the organization of an army or weapons of warfare. Rather, extensive trading networks with distant lands from the mountains to the seas and beyond can be deduced from the materials and artifacts found.

We cannot designate any individual from this civilization as a Peace Hero. The "script" on some of the seals—some 200 symbols—has not been deciphered as yet, but the culture that existed until 1900 BCE seems to be one of peace and prosperity through cooperation and exchange. Perhaps we should consider all the various merchants and crafts people of the Harappan civilization of the Indus Valley as Peace Heroes.

Malta

Malta, a small island in the Mediterranean just south of Sicily, was occupied by *Homo sapiens* by early Neolithic times. Between the mid-4th and mid-3rd millennia, a series of temple complexes, some with massive stone construction, was completed. Excavations have discovered a number of female figurines, including the famous "Sleeping Venus" sculpture. A few archaeologists have proposed that the ancient Maltese worshiped a mother goddess and were more concerned with creation and nurturing than violence and war. What is certain is that the construction of the temple complexes required great cooperative effort, and the time and attention of the inhabitants were devoted to life and death and stone cutting. Let us call the sculptor of the Sleeping Venus a Peace Hero.

The 2nd Millennium BCE Mesopotamia
Ur III

Just before the turn of the 2nd millennium, the Gutians were driven out of Southern Mesopotamia by Utu-Hegal of Uruk, and the Third Dynasty of Ur was established by his brother Ur-Nammu. Initially, Ur III controlled the cities of Isin, Larsa, and Eshnunnna, in addition to Ur. Ur-Nammu ruled for eighteen years and expanded his control of Mesopotamia to include, as well, Umma, Kish, and Adab.

He also invaded Lagash and Uruk—both of which were less reasonable and needed persuasion. Ur III might belong in the beginning of the Chapter on War after War, but his rule arguably could be placed here as an introduction to Codes of Law.

Although a warrior—he died on the battlefield—he is best known for his code of civil law known as the Code of Ur-Nammu. In its prologue he states its purpose: "to establish equity in the land." It explains by example: "The orphan is not to be delivered up to the rich. The widow is not to be delivered up to the rich man. The man of one shekel is not to be delivered up to the man of one mina." [one mina = 60 shekels] The Code addresses wrongs and punishments and restitution. The Code covered murder, rape, bodily injury, robbery, adultery, perjury, sorcery, abuse of agricultural land, insolence by a slave, and other behaviors. Ur-Nammu became known as the righteous shepherd who abolished violence and strife. In one respect, Ur-Nammu was a Peace Hero, but he still oversaw the exercise of violence as he deemed needed.

After Ur-Nammu's death, Shulgi ascended to the throne. He not only supported the arts, he participated, too. But he also became trained in handling weapons, and his early reign was punctuated by a series of punitive wars against the

Gutians and the Elamites. Having proclaimed himself a god, he needed to show his physical skills and power. He is best known for construction of the monumental Ziggurat of Ur, which he ordered built so he would be, or be seen as, closer to his fellow gods.

Toward the last years of his long rule he became less fierce and promoted peace and cooperation, initiating a period of peace that extended throughout the reigns of his successors Amar-Sin and Shu-Sin. Perhaps they should be the real Peace Heroes.

The Rules of Law

Many leaders of many dynasties in the Near East and the Far East felt a calling to establish a spirit of fairness and administer justice. One cannot help but speculate whether it was in their genetic heritage. Several law codes had been written on tablets found in excavations. The laws of the praise poem of Urukagina, written in cuneiform, preceded the Code of Ur-Nammu of Ur III by over 200 years.

Following Ur III, the Code of Lipit-Ishtar of Isin, the Ishnunna Laws, and the Laws of Larsa under Rim-Sin, all appeared. Then, contemporary with Rim-Sin, came Hammurabi of Babylon with an eight-foot-tall basalt stele inscribed with the Law Code given him by the sun god Shamash. A Law Code carved in stone!

Though the various laws of the several codes did not primarily establish peace, they put limits on human behavior. The rich or strong could not live an anything-goes life. By means of their law codes the rulers dealt primarily with trade and commercial transactions, the family as a social institution, agriculture, assault and bodily harm, offenses against property, and ownership of slaves. They may have established peace and order among their subjects, but in foreign affairs most of them still followed the doctrine of might makes right.

The letters of Hammurabi boast, "I promoted welfare in the land. I had the people reside in friendly habitation. I have governed them in peace and made an end to war." But Hammurabi went on to invade the surrounding countryside, bringing many cities under the control of Babylon, including Mari and Assur in the far north of Mesopotamia. All were subject to the Law Code inscribed in stone, and of course, to taxes.

In the second half of the 2nd millennium, The Hittites, who could make war as well as anyone, observed a law code and even established a peace treaty between Hattushilish and Ramses II. In Assur, the Assyrians, also warriors, also had a law code, though it was repressive for women.

The various law codes of the 2nd millennium notwithstanding, the kings of the Near East can be counted only as partial Peace Heroes. An accurate assessment would balance their military adventures abroad against the administration of justice at home.

Egypt
Hatshepsut

In Egypt, Hatshepsut declared herself Pharaoh, the divine ruler of Upper and Lower Egypt, in 1476 BCE. She was the daughter of Thutmosis I, married Thutmosis II (her half brother), and was regent for her stepson Thutmosis III.

Hatshepsut ruled from 1478 to 1458. She brought prosperity to Egypt by expanding trade, not by military conquest. She imported lapis lazuli from Afghanistan, turquoise from the Sinai, silver from Nubia, and gold from the Near East. She sent a trade delegation, led by Chancellor Nehsy (secretary of state), to Punt, and she opened trade with Phoenicia, Syria, and Crete. Her rule was marked by a major building campaign—obelisks, temples, sanctuaries, and amphitheaters. Her man Friday was an architect and teacher, not a military figure.

With a reign that was a twenty-year golden age of peace, notable for a wealth of culture, Hatshepsut was a Peace Hero.

Amenhotep III

Later in the 18th Dynasty, Amenhotep III came to the throne while still a child; he reigned for seven years from 1386 to 1349. With the exception of one small military expedition into Nubia early in his rule, it was a reign of peace and prosperity. He accomplished this by means of an extensive trade network, diplomacy including lavish gifts to other rulers, and marriage to the daughters of their royal houses. His first marriage was to Tiye, a commoner. Though he later could have as many wives as he wished, Tiye was always special. She bore him six children including a son who would become Pharaoh Akhnaten. Queen Tiye was given the title of "the King's Great Wife."

Amenhotep III engaged in a vast building program of temples, palaces, large statues, monuments, and galleries. He built irrigation canals and harbors, the Avenue of the Sphinxes, and major sections of the temples at Luxor and Karnak. The artistic style of the sculptural works set high technical and artistic standards which persisted into the Amarna period of Akhenaten and Nefertiti, a time that became known for artistic excellence.

Amenhotep demonstrated that peace was an integral part of the riches that a society could attain. He was a Peace Hero and was duly noted in the Amarna tablets, the historical documents of ancient Egypt.

The Levant

The coast of the Eastern Mediterranean in the late 2nd millennium was contested between the Hittite and Egyptian

Empires. After a battle of chariots between Ramses II (Egypt) and Muwatalli III (Hatti) at Kadesh in northern Canaan, losses were so great that both sides ceased fighting and called it victory. A few years later Ramses signed a peace treaty with the next Hittite king, Hattusili. It is said that the power behind the throne in Hatti was Queen Puduhepa. The Peace Treaty was inscribed on a large clay tablet, of which only fragments remain. One copy of the treaty, however, refers to the Queen's royal seal on the document.

Puduhepa was active in foreign policy with many letters exchanged with other rulers and their wives and arrangements for marriages between her own children and foreign royalty. She is the Peace Hero of the age.

The Sinai

Between Egypt and Caanan, in the 13th century BCE, the prophet Moses deseves a prominent place in the annals of law. As a law giver, he may claim some of the trappings of a Peace Hero by establishing rules of conduct among the Israelites: the five "do not" Commandments forbidding murder, adultery, theft, bearing false witness, and coveting a neighbor's wife.

Moses never led the Israelites into Canaan—Joshua was their military leader—but Moses, according to different sources, was not opposed to violence when he thought it necessary. Thus, he may be a great figure in the history of law, even a prophet espousing virtue and justice, but he cannot be counted as more than a partial Peace Hero.

Crete

Neolithic habitation occurred on the island of Crete in the Eastern Mediterranean Sea about 6,000 BCE. Millennia later, Crete had reached a notable level of civilization as evidenced by its architecture and art. Great temples (not palaces, as once thought) serving religious ritual and administrative functions were constructed at the major cities on the island and the Minoan civilization reached the height of culture in the first half of the 2nd millennium BCE. Based on extensive archaeological findings, especially at Knossos, Phaistos, Malia, and Festos, and at the nearby island of Thera (Santorini), the Minoans are believed to have been a peaceful nation built on trade, principally around the eastern Mediterranean. No fortifications or other defensive measures existed at any of the major cities, no large caches of weapons were found, and none of the many wall paintings are about the glory of battle and conquest. An exception is the small city of Gournia, where fortification walls were recently excavated which protected two of the four promontories of the coastline.

The Minoans had a large fleet of vessels for trade, which could have also been used for patrol, keeping Crete free of war. Minoan Crete had extensive trade contacts around the eastern Mediterranean, especially with the Cycladic Islands. It is even thought that the Cycladic islanders supplied many of the sailors and perhaps ships for the Minoans. Between them they ruled the seas, not by military might but by their thalassic presence. The prosperity of both provides evidence that cooperation was the norm. Further, frescoes of ships with long prows that curve upward show no battering rams such as appear on the later Greek triremes designed as warships. One fresco at Thera, however, does show the prow of a ship with a figure standing holding a long spear or lance near three drowning seamen in the water. A terrestrial scene above depicts marching soldiers holding long spears, and at the very top of the same wall painting there is a pastoral landscape of animals and herders. The other frescoes at the excavation are more celebratory of life and nature.

Trade with Egypt under Hatshepsut, listed above as a Peace

Hero, was also well established in the late Minoan period.

Some bronze artifacts have been excavated, including some knives and daggers and even almost-three-foot-long swords. But the former were more likely to have been used for preparing food and the latter, showing little wear, might well have been for ritual and ceremonial use. Plentiful bronze-tipped spears, bronze swords, and thick leather shields found at Mycenaean excavations, in contrast, were obviously of a military nature.

There was also equality between the sexes — in government, the priesthood, crafts, and sports, even those with great risk such as bull jumping. The Minoans worshipped a mother goddess who represented the plants and creatures of nature in celebration of life and regeneration. We see dolphins, ducks, bulls, lions, butterflies, snakes, and griffins—none portrayed aggressively. It is all consonant with a culture of peace. We do not know the names of the Peace Heroes—their language in linear A has never been deciphered—but for over 500 years the culture enjoyed the rewards of peace.

At a recent conference discussing the veracity of Arthur Evans's "Pax Minoica," one of the speakers noted that the Hittites and expansionist Egyptian dynasties proudly and frequently expressed their military successes carved in stone. Any Minoan militarism can only be inferred from very occasional archaeological finds among the many to the contrary. We can feel confident in designating the people of Crete as Peace Heroes.

The Middle East
Zoroaster

In ancient Persia, about 1200 BCE, there lived a prophet-philosopher-theologian who brought a new religion to that part of the world. His name was Zoroaster, whom we may know as Zarathustra.

Some heard his teaching as a highlight of the pervasiveness of the dark side of humanity and the evil and chaos thereof. Others, however, perceived that he balanced the darkness with a quest for the good and preachment that we must be good in our thoughts, words, and deeds—an active goodness. He said mercy must be accompanied by friendship to become compassion, and that we were created free to decide so.

Zoroaster was arguably a monotheist, though a few centuries after Abraham, and the first to preach the doctrine widely. He saw man in a subservient position and said only God can be the master, not otherwise. The prime purpose of man's existence was what is now called Creation Care—reverence for the forces of the natural world. Further he saw the oneness of all humans as universal brotherhood. He sought to protect the weak, the poor, and the vulnerable.

Though his life is misted in myth (or perhaps because of that), Zoroaster had a profound influence on civilization, from the ancient Greek philosophers to the Sasanian empire in Persia, to the Renaissance painters, to today's Central Asian republics.

He was a true Peace Hero, and despite his dark visions, saw that we must work actively to achieve peace in the world.

China

The 2nd millennium in China ends with the beginning of the Zhou dynasty. In the 11th century, King Wen (a regional king) and his son Wu fought against the corrupt Shang Dynasty who, they said, had offended the mandate of heaven. On the defeat of the Shang at the battle of Mu-Ye, near the Yellow River, Wu became king ... but he lived only three years. On his death his son Cheng, though still a young teenager, assumed the crown. Wu's uncle, Zhou Gong Dan (known as the Duke of Zhou), became regent to guide the young king. During the seven-year regency of the Duke of Zhou, the kingdom was peaceful and stable: virtue and justice were paramount, not hunting, feasting, or occasional warfare as with the Shang. During his lifetime the Duke wrote *The Book of Dreams* and many of the poems in the *Book of Songs*.

Although King Cheng ruled for over 20 years, he is remembered throughout history as the "King of Exemplary Culture." He was a true Peace Hero.

First Millennium BCE

During the first half of the first millennium BCE, while the NeoAssyrians, NeoBabylonians, and others were warring, the Phoenicians became a seafaring people and pursued commerce around the Mediterranean coast. The sailors from the cities of Sidon and Tyre ranged far from home among the Greek Islands and along the north African coastline, peacefully trading their goods. The Tyreans, after a time of sailing for a living, established a major trading colony at Carthage (Tunis) in the 9th century BCE. It was purely a trading colony, not a military base. The Punic wars were still to come, and Hannibal was not yet born.

Archaic Greece – The Olympiad

In 8th century BCE Greece, sports began to set the standards for society, just as basic principles in literature, philosophy, art, architecture, and medicine did three centuries later in the era of Classical Greece.

The first Olympic Games were held in Olympia in the city-state of Elis in 776 BCE. The only event that initial year was the *stade*, a 192-meter sprint. The Games, thereafter held every four years, gradually added a two-stade foot race, boxing, wrestling, *pankration*, javelin, discus, and chariot racing.

The Olympic traditions were modeled on previous cultures. The Mycenaean Games and the Minoan Contests are two that are known from frescoes, bronze urns, and stone carvings, but such sporting events must have gone back even further into prehistoric times. Sports seem to be part of our genome. Just watch kids today, from young to old, skateboarding, skiing hot-dog style, or surfboarding at a big-wave beach. Such activities for most of them are done just for the fun of the physical effort—the activity is its own reward. The first Olympic champions, similarly, received no prizes of gold or silver—just a crown of interwoven wild olive branches.

In ancient Greece, the Olympic Games were held in honor of the ruler of the heavens, Zeus who, it was believed, would exact retribution upon anyone who disrespected him by cheating or otherwise not adhering to the strict traditions of the Games. The Sacred Truce that the Heralds announced in all the major regions of Greece took precedence over all business-as-usual such as war, executions of prisoners, or carrying swords on the road to Olympia. At first, the Truce was for one month, then two, then three, as the Games grew to include more events. The Heralds came to be known as the Peace Bearers. Elis soon became the City of Peace. The enduring Olympiad is surely a Peace Victory.

Ephesus

In the Aegean, the islands of Lesbos and Samos and the cities of Miletus and Ephesus on the coast of Anatolia were colonized by Homeric Greeks in the early centuries of the 1st millennium. About 650 BCE, Ephesus was attacked by Cimmerians who razed the city, including the temple of Artemis. It proved unwise to tangle with the goddess of hunting—the Cimmerians were promptly driven out. However, the warfare brought a series of tyrants to political power, with all the bribery and corruption anyone could imagine. After the people at last revolted and deposed the contemporary tyrant, they established democratic rule through a citizen's council. The city prospered and became a magnet for important cultural figures, the poet Callinus and the philosopher Hericlidus among them. Both deserve the designation of Peace Hero.

The Greeks also established prosperous colonies in Sicily at Naxos and Syracuse as early as the mid-8th century. The age of Greek colonization in the first half of the 1st millennium BCE was largely peaceful. Triremes for naval warfare, according to Herotodus, date to 525 BCE.

Isaiah

From the years 740 to 700 BCE, Isaiah held his ministry in Jerusalem. He was well spoken, even poetic many times, and was regarded as the Prince of Prophets. With his verbal skills, he was granted access to the royal courts of Judea. Isaiah felt a calling to warn King Ahaz (whose reign he had prophesied) and the people of Judea who were becoming less faithful to Yahweh, not to depend on alliances with Egypt or any other nation but to trust in the Lord. Yet, we remember not so much his loyalty to the Lord, but his words that tell of peace: "And He shall judge many people and shall rebuke strong nations—they shall beat their swords into plowshares and their spears into pruning hooks; nation shall not lift up sword against nation; neither shall they learn war anymore." Further, he specifically intoned strong nations in metaphor that "the wolf shall dwell with the lamb, and the leopard shall lie down with the kid, and the calf with the lion, together." As well, he is quoted in every Christian Bible: "Cease to do evil; learn to do good; seek justice; relieve the oppressed; advocate for the orphan; plead for the widow."

Regarding war or peace, his words, more than prophesy, condemn war as an evil pursuit. He exhorts mankind to "come and let us reason together." Isaiah was, and is, a Peace Hero of peace heroes.

Rabbi Hillel

Long after Isaiah, a Jewish sage and scholar whom we know as Rabbi Hillel, lived in Jerusalem at the time of King Herod and the Roman Emperor Augustus. As a young man born in Babylon, he traveled to the Holy City and worked as a woodcutter to support himself while he studied the Torah. A kind and gentle man, Hillel eventually gained the knowledge and great insight to be recognized as a spiritual authority among the Pharisees. He taught, "What is hateful to you, do not do to your fellow—that is the Torah; the rest is commentary. Go and learn." He urged upon his followers the love of mankind, a spirit of benevolence, and a love of peace. He is a Peace Hero three times over.

The Essenes

In the Levant in the 2nd and 1st centuries BCE, the Jewish people were divided into three principal sects: the Dadduces, the Pharisees, and the Essenes. The Essenes were scattered in many cities in Judea, and in their own neighborhoods within the cities. They lived simply and their lifestyle was righteous, refraining from all activity considered immoral. But, it was the treatment of their fellows and fellow creatures that is especially noteworthy. They would not offer animal sacrifices, nor eat meat. They condemned slavery. And, of course they were absolute pacifists—Peace Heroes all.

Cyrus the Great

On the Western Asiatic mainland, the Persians under Cyrus

took over the Median Empire at Ecbatana, next conquered the Lydian Kingdom and its ruler Croesus, and finally in 539 BCE, marched into Babylon, ostensibly unopposed, to occupy the seat of the NeoBabylonian Empire. Cyrus then turned generous and benevolent and did not destroy Babylon. He allowed the Jews, deported by Nebuchadnezzar, to return to their homeland. He was tolerant of the religious beliefs of others, and established the first charter of human rights, inscribed in Akkadian cuneiform on a ten-inch clay cylinder. On the cylinder, Cyrus is not shy about calling himself the King of Sumer, Akkad, and Babylon, king of the four quarters of the world, but he also specifies the repatriation of prisoners and deportees and tolerance of other religions. The cylinder states, too, that Cyrus would have the people of Babylon and other cities live in peace, and he would rebuild their temples. He was later acknowledged by Isaiah as a compassionate ruler.

Some historians regard the Cyrus Cylinder as only a foundation stone and its text as nice words. Others point to Herodotus's story that Cyrus died in battle against the Scythian Queen, Tomyris. Let us split the difference and give Cyrus a few points as a Peace Hero. A copy of his famous cylinder is on display at the United Nations to remind its members of the ideals that are inscribed on the Cylinder.

<u>Classical Greece</u>
Plato and Aristophanes

Not far from Western Asia, the people of the Greek city-states gradually evolved a civilization that became the model for the philosophy, politics, science, medical ethics, art, and drama of today. In the 5th century BCE, Greece reached its height—the Classical Age. One might have expected that in the birthplace of democracy. One of its great philosophers—

Socrates, Plato, or Aristotle—might have included a course in peace studies along with deductive logic. No such luck.

The best Plato could do was a couple of pages from *The Republic* in which he proposes to remove the incentive of becoming a soldier or a ruler by prohibiting either from owning property or silver and gold. Thus, rulers would not go to war expecting to become rich, and soldiers would not fight to acquire the spoils of war. Only the highest expression of patriotism would prevail, and wars would be fought only for defense. Plato's ideal citizen soldiers, *hoplites*, would "behave like watchdogs and not like wolves." But it was only a short chapter in all of his writing.

It was left to a playwright to wage peace. Aristophanes, with all the force of a first-rate satirist, wrote *Peace*, which was staged in 421 BCE. In the play, Aristophanes took aim at a principal pro-war activist, Cleon. In addition, he makes fun of his fellow playwrights Sophocles and Euripides, as if to say, "Why don't you write anti-war tragedies?"

A few years later, Aristophanes wrote another anti-war parody, *Lysistrata*, that has retained its popularity across the ages. In the play, the protagonist, Lysistrata, organizes the women of Greece to go on strike by withholding sex until their men stop warring. In addition to their individual actions, the women take over the Acropolis, where the treasury of Athens was held, and so deny the generals the financial means of pursuing warfare. At the end of the play, Lysistrata meets with delegates from Athens and Sparta. She is accompanied by her handmaiden, Peace, who appears in full undress. The men, well distracted, agree to a peace treaty and map out a settlement of boundaries.

One of the lessons of *Lysistrata*—the women's occupation of the Acropolis—is being played out in most cities across the US in the 21st-century CE. Aristophanes is a Peace Hero immortal.

Hegetorides of Thasos

During the Peloponnesian War between Athens and the cities of the Peloponnesian League, there lived on the island-state of Thasos one Hegetorides. When Thasos broke away from the Athens-dominated Delian League, the Athenian fleet reacted with a naval blockade, and the population of the island suffered deprivation and hunger. Hegetorides foresaw that the naval might of Athens, once having defeated the Persians at Salamis, would bring starvation and death to many Thasians, but the council ruled that anyone who spoke of peace would be accused of treason and subject to execution. Hegetorides went to the town square with a rope around his neck and preached peace. He was a spark that ignited a demand for a truce with Athens. Thasos soon sued for peace.

Hegetorides set an example as a Peace Hero for all times by waging peace.

India
Dravidian Culture

Not Dravidian dynasty, or empire, but Culture and Language. Though the history of the Dravidians is shrouded in myth, it is generally accepted that they were an ancient civilization, non-Aryan, and indigenous to South India. Some research archaeologists have them originating with the Harappan culture of the Indus Valley at the beginning of the 3rd millennium BCE.

The language of the Dravidians—non-Indo European—has ties to ancient South India, the Elamites of southwestern Persia, and the Brahui tribe in Baluchistan. It has come down from Old Tamil literature, as well. As it has evolved, the language now resides in South India—Tamil, Telugu, Kannada, and Malayalam—and is spoken by some 200 million people.

The history of the culture may be somewhat obscure, but is thought to have been matrilineal and, perhaps, matriarchal. The Dravidians revered a mother goddess, the blue sky god Vinnu (Varuna), holy rivers, and sacred pools. We also know of their majestic architecture with ornate carvings, their preference for fine silk clothing, hair coiffed in top-knots, communal meals, love of Carnatic classical music, and equality between men and women. We find in their Sangam literature the concept of love and the freedom to decide on their own love companions.

As well, the Dravidian culture contributed to the pacifist ethic of Jainism. They also had a tradition of Ahimsa (non-violence). For these qualities alone, the Dravidians, from ancient times onward, deserve to be called Peace Heroes.

Jainism

Sometime in the 9th century BCE an ascetic humanism arose in India. The Jains insist that the principles by which they live are timeless and that their "religion" had no one founder. Yet their historical texts designate as spiritual leaders twenty-four successive Tirthankaras who attained full enlightenment in their lifetimes. Jains adhere to three basic principles: right thinking, right knowledge, and right conduct. Parshva, the 23rd Tirthankara, taught followers to be guided by four rules of living: *ahimsa* (non-violence), *satya* (truthfulness), *asteya* (prohibition of stealing), and *aparigraha* (non-materialism). Mahavira (Great Hero), the 24th and last Tirthankara, added *bramacharya* (chastity). In addition, they must resist anger, pride, deceit, and greed. They are vegetarians, as well.

Mahavira lived at the time of Gautama Buddha and the two may well have met. The Jains have a tradition of scholarship beyond their high ethical standards and have always had a strong influence on Indian society, far out of proportion to their numbers. A prime example was Chandragupta Mauryan, the founder of the Mauryan dynasty, who had established the first great empire in India. In 298 BCE, after twenty-two years in power, he abdicated the throne and gave up all the luxuries of the palace to live an ascetic life with a group of Jain monks.

We should count the Tirthankaras, from Rishabha (the first) to Mahavira (the 24th), as Peace Heroes.

Gautama Buddha

In the 6th century BCE in northern India, there lived a prince who at age 29 left the palace, his wife and child, and renounced all material goods and comforts to seek personal peace and enlightenment. His name was Siddhartha Gautama. On the road he met others who were also searching. He came to learn the practice of trance, to experience extreme deprivation, and gradually to realize that such emotions as anger, hatred, desire, and yearning were the source of grief, suffering and despair among humans.

By renouncing five conducts—violence, stealing, lying, intoxication, and sex—he could begin on the "Middle Path." With yogic exercises, the practice of mindfulness, the renouncing of possessions, and the withdrawal from desire, greed, lust—the very self—he could become enlightened and achieve an inner peace and harmony. Gautama had achieved this state of being after about five years since starting his journey.

Gautama, having given up all worldly goods and becoming a true renunciate, experienced enlightenment and realized that a true Buddha could not just withdraw into his own state of peace. He must bring good will toward all and free mankind of every enmity. He must become a teacher. Indeed, King Pasenadi of the Kosala region of northern India became one of his followers. Today, Buddhism has spread widely to all parts of the world. Gautama Buddha, for his philosophy of non-violence and his advocacy of peace beyond personal tranquility, richly deserves to be a Peace Hero.

Ashoka

Three centuries after Gautama Buddha reached enlightenment, his teachings found a following far greater than during his own lifetime. It was a time of the Mauryan Dynasty of India, and the third king, Ashoka, was on the throne. He maintained order and obeisance through the use of force, both in far off provinces and in his home district, even in the royal harem. Tales of his cruelty became legend.

In 261 BCE, he sent the army into the feudal republic of Kalinga to instruct the people in proper respect. His troops met with resistance, and full war broke out. The final battle for Kalinga became a massacre. Ashoka won the war, but when he surveyed the battlefield afterward and saw the blood and bodies of over 100,000 dead, the sight and smell unnerved him and he became distraught. From that moment, he became a convert to peace. He adopted Buddhism, became merciful and magnanimous, tolerant of all sects, and showed respect for all life, even animals. He renounced war for the 30-year remainder of his reign. The Edicts of Ashoka were carved in rock near the final battlefield and on pillars erected throughout Northern India and as far as Greece and Egypt. The edicts expressed his own remorse for his earlier barbarous behavior and proclaimed that he would lead his empire in the principles of righteousness and tolerance.

How do we judge Ashoka? His early life was heartless, even vicious, but thirty years of peace is worth something in balance. A Peace Hero? Perhaps the answer is a pre-war "never" and a post-war "absolutely."

The Pyu in Burma

Sometime during the late to mid-1st millennium BCE, the Pyu people migrated from northern India and Tibet to the Irrawadi River Valley in northern Burma. They built settlements and a few cities, indicative of a large population movement. Three cities—Beikthano, Halin, and Sri Ksetra—have now been excavated to a good extent, and their architecture is well delineated. Sri Ksetra, the largest, had an extensive system of irrigation canals and ponds, which provided for a prosperous farming community.

The Pyu in Burma, according to records of the Tang Dynasty (618-907 CE), were a peaceful culture in a holy land of 1,000 temples. In the early centuries of the 1st millennium CE, the Pyu converted to Buddhism. But, already living as a peaceful people, they must have had a natural affinity for a Buddhist philosophy. Indeed, they went beyond simplistic Buddhist tenets to develop a multifaceted yoga system. They also prohibited torture and executions. Those traditions lasted close to a millennium.

Although their cities were walled, there were never any enlargements of their perimeter walls or evidence of military adventures. Nor were there any destructive attacks on their cities. But by the 10th century CE, about 1,000 years after settling in Burma, the Pyu culture began to decline and their people were gradually absorbed into the larger Pagan Empire.

The different Pyu cities and settlements were independent and administered their own affairs. Thus, there could not be a king of the Pyu nation—ipso facto, little likelihood of war. We can't identify any individual leader of the Pyu. So, let us award a designation of Peace Culture to the Pyu nation.

China

The last half of the 1st millennium BCE saw a blossoming

of philosophers in China: Lao Tzu, Confucius, Motse, Mencius, Xunzi, and others. They all spoke of The Way of Heaven, and each offered his views on the proper role of mankind in the natural order of the universe.

Lao Tzu

Lao Tzu, consensus has it, lived during the 6th century BCE, the time of the Zhou dynasty. The "Old Master" had many followers but never wrote down the principles of his teaching, despite his position as the Keeper of the Archives in the royal court of Zhou. Over many years Lao Tzu became more and more disillusioned by the corruption in society and the government, and set out for the countryside. As he left the city he was persuaded by the keeper of the western gate to write his thoughts. He thereupon put down a series of aphorisms and poems we call the Tao Te Ching, which has since become the foundation of Taoism (Daoism). Lao Tzu then traveled into the mountains and was never seen again.

Among the eighty-one insightful epigrams, the following will give the reader a sense of the whole:

> *Contentiousness is opposed by the Tao (the Way). Achieve Tao by acting in accord with the Way of Nature.*
>
> *The order of the universe is perceived by reason and intuition.*
>
> *Be chary of war.*
>
> *When the Way prevails, horses plow the fields; when the Way does not prevail, horses are bred for war.*
>
> *Weapons are instruments of ill omen, hateful to all creatures. Therefore, he who has Tao will have nothing to do with them.*

Lao Tzu became a legend, and Taoism gained millions of adherents. A thousand years after his vanishing, the rulers of the Tang dynasty accorded him the highest reverence by tracing their lineage to him. Lao Tzu is a Peace Hero for all millennia.

Confucius

The second great Chinese philosopher of the 1st millennium BCE was K'ung Fu Tzu, known in the West as Confucius. He lived between 551 and 479 BCE, during the long and legendary lifetime of Lao Tzu. It is told that the two met in colloquy and that Confucius was much influenced by the Old Master.

Confucius is known for advocating a personal system of ethical thought and conduct. The many qualities included in the "Good" or what is "Right" are part of Confucius's philosophy: righteousness, humaneness, honesty, courtesy, kindness, gentleness, modesty, forgiveness, altruism and generosity, diligence, sincerity.

Confucius was little concerned with a deity or an afterlife; he focused instead on human affairs in the here and now. He was a Humanist in all his teachings. Although he was not primarily known to condemn war or speak of nonviolence, he propounded the Silver Rule (the obverse form of the Golden Rule): What you do not wish for yourself, do not do to others. Someone who taught that the Way of Heaven demands a personal ethic of highest virtue must necessarily be opposed to war and violence. A close reading of the nineteen chapters of the Confucian Analects, written after his death by students and historians of subsequent generations, sets out specific expressions of peace and opposition to war.

Music, art, and poetry are the Arts of Peace.

Let happiness, good, and peace replace misery and war.

Government should not be in the business of killing.

Confucius held different government positions during his middle years, and in his early fifties became Minister of Justice in the state of Lu. Stories tell of his ordering violent punishment for an offender on at least one occasion. But the strength of his philosophy weighs heavily toward counting him a Peace Hero.

Mo-Tzu

Mo-Tzu was born about 469 or 470 BCE, in the same decade that Confucius died. He was born into an artisan class and learned carpentry from his father. As a thinker, he translated wood-working skills into principles of mechanics and physics, then mathematics.

It was the beginning of the Warring States period in China, and Mo-Tzu was called on to develop effective fortifications—he expounded only defensive strategies. He condemned military aggression and war for glory and spoils, but saw a need for defensive war or war to overthrow wicked tyrants. He called war and violence a threat to social stability. Although Mo-Tzu proposed universal love as the ultimate basis for avoiding war, he also addressed war in practical terms:

If it is winter, it will be too cold. If it is summer, it will be too hot.

If it is spring, it will take people from sowing and planting.

If it is autumn, it will take people from reaping and harvesting.

One wonders if war could perhaps be waged in a mythical fifth season—though Mo-Tzu also often commented on war in terms of ethics and virtue:

To attack another state is a great unrighteousness.

When the lords of the world attack others, it is a thousand times worse than killing one innocent individual, a thousand times worse than maltreating his children, a thousand times worse than stealing his oxen and horses.

Yet, they claim to be righteous.

Beyond words, Mo-Tzu traveled about the countryside and preached pacifism in terms of pragmatism to the rulers of different states to dissuade them from attacking any of the others. He traveled to Chu, Qin, Lu, Wei, Song, and elsewhere. According to historians, he was successful in preventing Chu from attacking Song, Qin from invading Lu, and perhaps slowing down the developing free-for-all war in China.

Despite his position on "just" wars, Mo-Tzu deserves designation as a Peace Hero.

Mencius

The fourth major Chinese philosopher in the parade led by Lao Tzu was Mencius (Meng KE, Meng Zi). He was an ardent Confucian and systematized the thought of the great sage into four cardinal virtues—benevolence, justice, humanity, and righteousness.

Mencius lived from 372 to 289 BCE, during the Warring States period. He traveled from court to court, using his skills as a philosopher and logician to try to convince each ruler to renounce war. He reasoned that the role of a monarch was to promote peace and that a benevolent government would bring harmony among his subjects. Once, he met a man who was on his way to the court of Chu hoping to convince the king that war against an adjacent state would be unprofitable. Mencius agreed with the man's goal of peace but not the argument. He said that the rationale of morality, rather than profit-or-not, would lead to a longer, firmer peace.

Further, Mencius stated that self-proclaimed military experts are "grave criminals." In broader terms, he said it is contrary to kill even one person.

Although Mencius believed that unjust rulers should be

overthrown and righteousness established as state policy, he deserves designation as a Peace Hero.

Xunzi

Born toward the end of the Warring States period, when the more powerful Chinese states had absorbed the smaller ones, Xunzi (310 to 220 BCE) had a rich history to draw upon—the Sage Kings, the Duke of Zhou, Lao Tzu, Confucius, Mo-Tzu, and Mencius—in the development of his own philosophy.

Xunzi, seeing the destruction of incessant war, evolved a view of mankind that was realistic in context of the time. He proposed that the nature of man was selfish, irresponsible, and violent. Yet, Xunzi was optimistic that it was possible for the state to teach humanity, generosity, truthfulness, and respect by setting an example of justice and beneficence and guiding the people in proper ritual and conduct. His goal was a strong, united, benevolent China. For Xunzi, militarism and war was inimical to that goal.

These are a few of Xunzi's pronouncements:

> *The lowest of all rulers is the one who relies on military power and taxes his people heavily. The highest type of king is one who rules through proper ritual and benevolence and follows the Way.*
>
> *Virtue before violence.*
>
> *In the war dance, flash weapons. In the peace dance brandish feathers, and belligerence will turn to harmony.*

Xunzi was a Peace Hero in times of war and the beginning of the militaristic Qin Dynasty.

Emperor Wen – Han Dynasty

The Western Han dynasty was established in China at the

end of the 3rd millennium BCE by Liu Bang (Gaozu). His son, Wen (Liu Heng) ascended the throne as a young man aged 22 in 180 BCE and steered a course for the Han dynasty away from the repression and militarism of the previous Qin Dynasty. He set a personal example of thrift and virtue. Harsh laws were relaxed, and taxes on peasants were lowered to provide incentive for increasing food production.

His court encouraged literature, art, and technology, and he established a system of civil service exams and appointment based on merit.

Wen's rule was known for social stability, peace, and prosperity. Very early in his reign he joined in a peace treaty with King Zhao Tuo of the Nanyue territory. Wen deserves the title of Peace Hero.

Matrifocal Cultures

Three widely separated cultures existed during the 1st millennium BCE that were female centered: the Etruscans of Italy north of Rome; the Basques of northern Spain and adjacent France; and the Picts of Scotland. Although little if any contact existed among them, all three were matrifocal. The languages they spoke were all non-IndoEuropean.

In Etruria, women were the equal of men had an equal legal and social status. They owned property and benefitted from a matrilineal succession. They attended banquets and public events along with their husbands and were not ashamed to drink with them. Women were proud of their bodies and not ashamed to exercise in public or in the nude. They served roles as diverse as seers, priestesses, and politicians.

Etruria was a major maritime nation with extensive trading ties with the eastern Mediterranean, often exchanging goldsmiths and ceramicists with the Phoenicians and adapting the Greek alphabet to their own language. Etruscan artwork was renowned in painting, pottery, bronze work, and stone and terra cotta sculpture.

The Etruscan religion was polytheistic with dozens of gods and goddesses; some archaeologists and anthropologists have called Etruria a theocracy. Two of the principal goddesses were Uni, the principal goddess of the pantheon, and the mother-earth goddess Cel. A third deity, Turan, was the goddess of love, important in the daily lives of Etruscans. Peace was the default state of life in Etruria, and had equal status with art, trade, religion and love (not always in that order).

The Basque culture, language, and religion have developed and persisted over many millennia, going back to Neolithic and possibly Paleolithic times. In the 1st millennium BCE, the Basques practiced a goddess-centered religion, used a lunar calendar, and were legally bound by matrilineal inheritance. Women were the heads of households on a hereditary basis and were responsible for agricultural work, but women also served in significant social positions as arbitrators and even judges.

Basque religion was more than pagan and polytheistic, it was full of magic, genies (*lamies*), and witches. Orzi was the sun god, Ilargia the moon goddess, and Mari (Lady) the goddess who inhabits the deep caves and subterranean realms of the earth. She is also a storm goddess and rides the heavens on a ram. Mari is not only a goddess but an oracle and prophet. She demands high moral conduct and, as an alchemist, she can transform gold stolen from her cave sanctuaries into coal or wood. Mari also disapproves of lying, breaking promises, and showing disrespect. She lives on in the beliefs of many Basques today.

The early Pictish culture of Scotland, which goes back at least to 1200 BCE, was based on an agricultural, pastoral economy. As they became skilled mariners, fishing and trading with distant lands became a source of livelihood. The folklore of Roman Britain suggests that the Pict sailor-merchants were pirates when opportunity arose; Pict folklore has it otherwise. What is more certain is that matrilineal laws of inheritance held sway. Pict princesses would select a well-bred, noble male, often from foreign lands, and suggest a visit for a week of revelry. The offer was likely to be accepted. With good timing, she might well become the mother of a future leader, perhaps a future king of one of the seven Pict clans.

As to Pict religion, it was likely polytheistic, and stone carvings of female figures with arms and legs of intertwined snakes have been interpreted as goddess representations. Druid belief with reverence for fountains and rivers has also been proposed. Later, in the 1st millennium CE, the Picts organized cults of saints, and practiced solemn rites to celebrate their favorite deity.

Here were three separate cultures of Europe in the 1st millennium BCE, each of which was matrilineal and accorded women equal rights. Would the influence of a more pacific nature of women lessen the likelihood and incidence of war in their societies?

The Etruscans, although they expanded the territory under their control, depended on mining, craftsmanship, and commerce for their prosperity. Etruria was organized into three confederacies of city-states, not a political structure conducive to waging wars. However, Etruscan cities were sited on hills and built with high protective walls. With a long coastline on the Tyrrhenian Sea, the Etruscans became skilled mariners and established an extensive maritime trading network ranging across Magna Graecia, Carthage, Greece, Anatolia, and the Levant. They were fine potters, sculptors, metalsmiths, and jewelers, and their wares were in demand all around the Mediterranean. They possessed a fleet of two-masted sailing ships that could carry many amphorae filled with commercial goods. Still, they did build warships, as evidenced by their swift ships, each fitted with a bronze rostrum or battering ram.

Etruria was a land that celebrated the joys of life and the prosperity of commerce, and did not exhibit a warrior culture. The Etruscans certainly were not as warful as the Romans or Carthaginians, but they did engage in various military activities on land and on the sea. Were they Peace Heroes? Perhaps not quite always.

The Basques, the longest-surviving culture of the three, had a long history of women's equality. In addition to matrilineal inheritance, women had special roles as witches, midwives, herbalists, and practitioners of traditional medicine. In post-Roman times, they could also officiate in church services and were custodians of village funds as keeper of the keys.

Did the Basque women who had equal civil rights with men and, as followers of the goddess Mari, magical powers as well, influence the Basque men to be peaceable? A history of the Basque culture tells of their relative autonomy through Roman, Visigoth, Moor, and Frank occupations. During the many centuries of such domination and attempts at converting them, the Basques were resistant to all other religious entreaties. They were known as magi or pagan wizards. In 1,000 CE, the Basques were independent again under the leadership of Sancho the Great. Sancho then ruled the Kingdom of Pamplona for 35 years.

Over the many generations from pre-Roman times into the 21st century, there have been occasional battles, revolts, and internal squabbles using force of arms. The Basques have not always been pacifists. But, they survive to this day in their homelands in Spain and France and as a diaspora around the world with their language and culture intact. They usually find ways of persuasion or noncooperation to keep their own identity despite other governments and amidst other cultures. Their goddess Mari, who is known to be immortal, must be faithful to her followers. When they use nonviolent means to keep their culture alive, we can consider them as Peace Heroes.

The Picts of Scotland also were governed by matrilineal laws. They, too, were guided by a polytheistic and, possibly, goddess-centered religion. In Pictland, women could follow any line of endeavor of their own choosing. Equality of the sexes even extended to the military. A Roman general, astonished at the sight of Pict women fighting alongside their men, remarked what fierce warriors the women were. Some British historians today believe that the Antonine Wall was built as much to keep the Romans out of contact with the unruly Picts as to keep Pict raiders out of Roman Britain.

Did the Pict women keep the men peaceful? It seems not—the women, who could select an advantageous male contribution for the Pict royal lines, could be physically aggressive in other pursuits. The relationship between the Picts and Celts, though not clearly defined, may have been another influence on the behavior of Pict women. Gaulish women were noted to be equal in stature and strength to men. Legends of the Celtic queen, Boudicca, describe a huge and terrifying woman whose thick red hair reached to her knees. Boudicca was known to have led a rebellion against the Romans to reclaim her inheritance and status.

The Celts, renowned for their horsemanship and a horse-centered culture, were often warlike. The Picts, although their horses were of smaller size, developed a two-pony chariot that was remarkably agile and effective in battle.

The Pict population may have been fifty percent female and matrilineal, but that was not enough for a Nobel Peace prize for the culture, nor individual Peace Heroes.

First Millennium CE
Augustus and the Pax Romana

The term "Pax Romana" pertains to the beginning of the Roman Imperial period with the reign of Augustus as emperor. Some historians place the "Roman Peace" across the broad time frame from the ascension of Augustus until the death of Marcus Aurelius (27 BCE to 180 CE); others include only the four-decade rule of Augustus (27 BCE to 14 CE) and sometimes call it Pax Augusta.

Certainly, the longer interpretation, until 180 CE, can be dismissed when we consider the emperors immediately following Augustus: Tiberius, Caligula, Claudius, and Nero.

The reign of Augustus did promote order, reduce crime, establish a postal system, provide for the welfare of the people, stabilize the finances of the empire, and promote art and literature. Augustus was a skilled administrator and a good diplomat, and although he liked to be known as First Citizen, he was also Imperator, the commander of twenty-five Roman Legions relegated to the provinces and the 9,000-strong Praetorian Guard that kept order in Rome. The empire was extensive—western Europe to the Atlantic, southern Europe including the Balkans to the Danube, western Asia including Anatolia and the Levant, and coastal north Africa including Egypt, Cyrenaica, and Numidia. Augustus controlled the lands to the west of the Rhine and the Alpine region of central Europe, but he had covetous eyes for the territory of the Germans. It looked to be a routine matter for the Roman Legions. After initial successes, the Germans under the command of Arminius made a stand at the Teutoberg Forest, killing the Roman General Varus and decimating three Roman Legions.

Augustus was an able administrator, a reformer, and a

consummate politician, but not a Peace Hero. Pax Romana should be translated Roman Order.

Seneca

Lucius Annaeus Seneca was born in 4 BCE in Cordoba, Spain. He was but 18 years old when Augustus died and was destined to live his adult life through the tumultuous times of the four Julian emperors who followed.

Seneca was educated in Rome, where he took a keen interest in philosophy. Although wealthy by both birth and marriage, and despite societal connections, he followed much of the Stoic philosophy. Seneca the Younger, as he was known, was a natural orator but also became a prolific writer of philosophy, natural sciences, essays on morality, and several plays. In addition to his belief that individuals should live in accord with a philosophy of Middle Stoicism, Seneca addressed societal and imperial issues, as well. A few quotations are illustrative.

> *Of war, men ask the outcome, not the cause.*
>
> *Worse than war is the fear of war.*
>
> *We are mad, not only individually but nationally. We stop individual murder, but what of war and slaughtering whole people?*
>
> *Philosophy does not fashion arms for war, but is a voice for peace.*
>
> *Philosophy avers that people ought to live in harmony.*
>
> *He who you call "slave" is also of the same species, lives under the same skies, and like you breathes, lives, and dies.*
>
> *Mercy is the great sovereign quality of an emperor.*

Seneca sought to exert a humane influence on the empire. Living amidst the most tyrannical, insane, and violent of

Roman emperors, as well as the cruelty of the gladiator shows, Seneca was an extraordinary Peace Hero.

After Augustus

Nero was the last of the Julian-Augustan Emperors. Contention for the succession followed in 68 to 69 CE. Indeed, 69 is known as the Year of the Four Emperors: Galba, Otho, Vitellius, and the first Flavian emperor, Vespasian (69 – 79 CE).

Vespasian eliminated the excesses of the court, replenished the treasury, began a program of public building, and encouraged the literary arts. Titus (79 – 81 CE) ruled with benevolence and kindness, and relieved the suffering of the people of Pompeii and Herculaneum following the eruption of Mt. Vesuvius. Domitian (81 – 96 CE), the younger brother of Titus, was generous only to the military. He persecuted Jews and Christians alike, treated the Senate with disdain, confiscated properties, and acted the part of a despot. He did, however, balance the budget and re-evaluate the denarius to 98% silver content.

Despite various good works, the Flavian emperors brought about the destruction of Jerusalem, the suppression of the Gauls, the expansion of the Roman province in Britain, and military actions in Dacia to the east—all quite enough to deny any of the three the role of Peace Hero.

The Good Emperors – Nerva

The era of the Five Good Emperors started with the brief rule of Nerva (96–98 CE). He was the antithesis of Domitian, banning extortion or confiscation of property and abolishing the secret informer trade. He granted amnesty for exiles of Domitian's rule and welcomed them home. He ended trials based on the accusation of treason. Previously, royal properties were allocated to the needy, and he renamed the Flavian Palace the "House of the People."

Nerva was elected by the Senate rather than the Praetorian Guard or the Roman Legions, as was the case with some of the other emperors; thus he was not indebted to the military. Nerva had been in civil service for many years and never pursued a career as a Legion commander. In ancient Rome, military and civilian affairs were often conflated. During his fifteen months as emperor, he undertook civilian projects—aqueducts, roads, and granaries—but no new conquests.

Nerva, despite the title of emperor, can be counted as a Peace Hero.

Hadrian

Hadrian was the adopted son of Trajan and, with a little help from Trajan's wife, heir to the throne. When Trajan died in 117 CE, Hadrian was proclaimed by the Praetorian Guard, but he requested formal election by the Senate as well. In contrast to Trajan, Hadrian sought to bring glory to Rome with a major program of public building, elimination of poverty, and promotion of art and literature. He did not believe the glory of Rome lay in extension of the empire by military conquest, but in furthering prosperity and civility of her subjects. He not only talked the talk, but he actually gave up the conquests of Trajan in the Near East: Mesopotamia, Assyria, and Armenia. In central Europe, he built long palisades reinforced with lookout towers between the headwaters of the Rhine and Danube, and in Britain an actual wall to keep the unruly Picts separate from the civilized Romans and Brits. There would be no raids by Barbarians on Roman territory and none by ambitious Roman generals who wanted to ever enlarge the empire (and one day perhaps become emperor themselves).

Hadrian traveled widely throughout the provinces, listening

to the concerns of the people and addressing them when he returned to Rome. Corruption throughout the empire was thus eliminated. He humanized the law code and forbade torture, though he didn't abolish slavery.

In rebuilding the Second Temple of Jerusalem, he dedicated it to Jupiter instead of allowing the Jews to consecrate the Temple in honor of Yahweh. Simon bar Kokhba organized a revolt which took on serious proportions when it initially isolated the Roman garrison in Jerusalem, inflicting significant losses on the Roman troops. Hadrian could not allow such disloyalty to Rome and brought in additional Legions commanded by General Julius Sevrus. The war lasted three years with the razing of 1,000 villages and towns and Jewish losses of more than half a million. The repression of Jews continued even after the last battle with a ceremonial burning of the Testament scroll.

Were it not for this brutal suppression of the Jews in the Holy Land toward the end of his reign, Hadrian might have been a Peace Hero.

Antoninus Pius

Despite the 23-year reign of Antoninus Pius, he was little noted by historians, for there were no conflicts, no conquests, no war heroes. He was an uneventful emperor, which is how he would have it. His adopted son and successor, Marcus Aurelius, described him best: "I saw mildness of manner, firmness of resolution, contempt of vainglory. He taught me how to conduct myself as an equal among equals … to bear myself calmly and serenely … to worship the gods without superstition, and to serve mankind without ambition. Such was the character of his life and manners—nothing harsh, nor rude, no roughness and no violence."

There is no record of cruelty, extortion, revolution, or territorial expansion under Antoninus. How could anyone named Antoininus Pius ever be a conqueror. In fact, he never commanded a Legion, even in peacetime. The Senate called him the Father of the country, and indeed he looked after the welfare of his subjects. Doubtless, his wife Annia Galeria Faustina, was a compelling influence. She was reputed to be wise and beautiful, and she showed her character by caring for the poor and disadvantaged.

Antoninus was a radical in one area, though: the law. Not only ruling with compassion, not just granting clemency in deserving cases, and not merely favoring the spirit over the letter of the law—Antoninus changed some of the basic tenets of Roman law, showing foresight that was centuries ahead of its time. He established the principle of innocence until proven guilty. He insisted on trials being held in the locale where the alleged crime was committed. Not least, he mitigated the abuses of slavery, declaring that a slave owner has neither the right to torture or kill his own slave nor the slave of another man.

A 23-year reign of peace and prosperity certainly entitles Antoninus Pius to be a Peace Hero.

Jesus

Jesus lived at the time of the beginning of the Roman Empire. The dates of his birth, his brief ministry, and his death have been studied by historians, theologians, and even astrophysicists, but many questions remain. The date of his birth is generally agreed to be 4 to 5 BCE, the date of his crucifixion 33 or 34 CE, with his ministry beginning at about age thirty.

Throughout the few years that Jesus preached, he urged people to live in kindness, forbearance, mercy, righteousness, love and, most important, peace. Most of his principles and personal counsel are known through his disciples.

Peace was always a prominent theme of the many sermons and parables that were written down by scribes many years later.

- The Gospel of John tells of Jesus confronting a crowd of Pharisees about to stone an accused adulteress to death: "Let the one who is without sin cast the first stone."
- John quotes Jesus asking grace, mercy, and peace from the Almighty for His true son Timothy.
- Titus enjoins the followers of Jesus to "be peaceable and considerate, and always be gentle toward everyone."
- James says "Those who sow in peace reap a harvest of righteousness."
- Jude blesses the followers: "Peace and love be yours in abundance."
- Matthew describes the Sermon on the Mount and quotes the Beatitudes in which Jesus says "Blessed are the Peacemakers for they shall be called the children of God."

Jesus certainly deserves a prominent place among the many Peace Heroes throughout all of history.

Tertullian

Tertullian, 155–220 CE, was an early Church writer from Carthage who defended a Christian soldier who defied the authorities in Rome by refusing to wear a laurel crown at a military ceremony. Indeed, Tertullian justified the refusal of any Christian to bear arms at all. He wrote: "Shall it be lawful to make an occupation of the sword when the Lord proclaims that he who uses the sword shall perish by the sword? And shall the son of peace take part in the battle when it does not become him even to sue at law?"

Tertullian deserves notation as a Peace Hero.

Maximilian Tebessa

Born in 274 CE, Maximilian was a Roman citizen, and therefore was required to join the army at age 21. He refused military service and was brought before the proconsul of Numidia, Cassius Dion. Even then, Maximilian was insistent: "I am a Christian and cannot serve." Even as his father, Fabius Victor had been a soldier, and even when threatened with death, Maximilian stood firm in the teachings of the Prince of Peace. And so, at age 21 Maximilian was beheaded and became a martyr.

In that Maximilian Tebessa would not be a soldier and would refuse to kill designated enemies, he is a worthy Peace Hero, and perhaps the first recorded conscientious objector.

Cordoba, Spain

In the 7th century CE, the followers of the Prophet Mohammed militarily moved west from Palestine and conquered Egypt. To protect their newly acquired territory, Islamic forces pushed further east along the north African coast into Byzantine Cyrene and thence toward the major economic center of Carthage.

Finally, despite almost three decades of combined resistance by the Byzantines and Berbers, Carthage was captured in 698 CE. The indigenous Berbers accepted Muslim rule and religion but maintained their culture and a good amount of autonomy.

Once Carthage was under Islamic control, it was on across the Straits to the Iberian peninsula.

The Berber-led invasion of 711 CE occupied most of today's Spain and Portugal. In the ensuing years factional squabbles among Arabs, Syrians, Persians, Turks, and Berbers were frequent. Back in Damascus, the Umayyad royal family was treacherously murdered in 750 CE, and the Abbasid caliphate was established. One prince, Abd-al-Rahman I, escaped and, in a series of adventures, reached Spain in 755. He was a charismatic figure who the following year led an army of Umayyad loyalists, first securing Seville without bloodshed, then winning a decisive battle on the plains near Cordoba. With southern Spain secure, he was named the Emir of Cordoba. His successors established a center of culture and learning at Cordoba that rivaled Constantinople. Palaces and mosques were built, as were public baths, hospitals and asylums, colleges, and markets. The University of Cordoba attracted poets, artists, and scholars from all over Europe and the Near East. The last two centuries of the first millennium in Muslim Spain were devoid of major conflict. It was an exemplary period of cooperation in which all faiths and cultures were welcomed in the spirit of amity and cooperation. A Peace Victory for history.

England
Alfred the Great

From 871 to 899 CE, Alfred ruled Wessex and fashioned himself king of the Anglo-Saxons. He began his career in government as the principal aide de camp of his brother Ethelred. During those campaigns, Alfred scored a decisive victory over the Danish Vikings at Ashdown. When his brother died the following year, Alfred, at age 21, became King of Wessex.

The Danes continued their raids and established permanent settlements in East Anglia and eastern Mencia, while Alfred continued to defend disputed territories. In 879 he won a decisive victory at Ethandun and agreed to a treaty of

Wedmore with Guthrum whereby each side would respect the boundary set along the Thames and the Lea. Alfred, although the victor in battle, asked only that Guthrum be baptized and become his godson. Guthrum kept his promise to withdraw from Wessex, and life was fairly peaceful for a few years. Then in 885 the Danes attempted a siege of the city of Rochester in Kent. Alfred, upset that the peace of Wedmore was violated, personally led a strong force against the Danes and intimidated them into withdrawal. Sources are ambiguous as to whether or not there was an actual battle; Alfred's show of force might well have been sufficient to force the Danes to leave.

Alfred also consolidated peace through marriage. His daughter, Ethelfleda was given in matrimony to the ealdorman of Mencia, assuring allegiance to Wessex. Alfred himself had married Elhswitha, a Mencian noblewoman.

Also a scholar, Alfred encouraged education among his subjects and has been quoted "… as we have peace, let all the youth be devoted to learning." He was especially interested in history and in philosophy. Alfred also established a firm legal code and showed himself to be merciful and wise. He was considered the protector of the poor and provided alms to both his own people and to foreigners in the land. He was painstaking in his deliberations and required judges to be faithful "to the pursuit of wisdom."

Although Alfred was known for his military prowess and his innovative military strategies, the Treaty of Wedmore, his emphasis on education and on the law, and his rebuilding of London, make him a Peace Hero of his own time.

Aethelstan

In 924 CE Aethelstan was the King of the West Saxons. In 927, with the death of King Siihtric of the Danish Kingdom of York, to whom his sister was married, Aethelstan occupied that territory. Under political rather than military pressure, his authority was accepted additionally by Northumbria, Wales, and Cornwall.

Aethelstan thus became the King of the Anglo-Saxons, the first King of England, reigning from 927 to 939.

In 936 he granted Sanctuary to the Church in Padstow, Cornwall that was first founded by St. Petroc in the 6th century CE. That church, rebuilt in its present structure in the early 15th century, has continued its tradition of Sanctuary and extended that protection the full length of Church Street. Sanctuary there is worthy of designation as a continuing Peace Victory.

Armenia – Ashot III

Armenia, a land located in the Chorokhi Valley, south of the Black Sea and west of the Caspian, traces its history as far back as the 13th century BCE, the Middle Assyrian period. Known as Urartu, the kingdom was looked on as a great prize by the NeoAssyrians and, thereafter, by the NeoBabylonians.

In the following centuries, empires rose and fell, and by the 4th century CE the Bagratuni dynasty was founded. In 953 CE, Ashot III came to the throne and, once settled, moved his capital to Ani, a city with good natural defenses that was centered on important trade routes. He was a skilled diplomat and had earned the loyalty of the various cities and regions. With such backing he was able to maintain neutrality between contentious Byzantium and the Abbasid Caliphate of Islam.

Ashot III, known as a great philanthropist, embarked on a major building program of not only monasteries and churches and schools, but also hospitals and almshouses. He justly became known as Ashot the Merciful. Under his rule, Armenia prospered, not as a result of conquest but by becoming a center of learning, of art, literature, philosophy, and medicine. It was a golden age of Peace, and Ashot III must be recognized as a Peace Hero.

South Asia – Asvaghosa

In the 2nd century CE in northern India, a young Asvaghosa lost a debate with an elderly Buddhist scholar. The argument that "The world should be made peaceable, with plentiful harvests and joy throughout the land" won the day. Asvaghosa became a disciple of the older man and, in a short time, converted to Buddhism with a vengeance. He thereafter grew into a scholar, philosopher, and poet. His principal work was the 28-canto (translated into Tibetan) epic life of the Buddha, in classical Sanskrit. Asvaghosa was a great proponent, some say the founder, of the Mahayana philosophy of Buddhism.

It was the time of the powerful Kushan empire under Kaniska who, with good reason, was reputed to be a great conqueror. When Kaniska attacked an adjacent kingdom, he demanded a large amount of gold as tribute. The ruler of the besieged kingdom, under Asvaghosa's counsel, agreed to offer a token amount of gold and the alms bowl reputed by legend to belong to the Buddha himself. In addition, Asvaghosa agreed to attend the court of Kaniska and must have been the counselor who convinced him to convert to Buddhism. Kaniska thereafter became a wiser ruler who promoted the arts, architecture, literature, and learning.

Asvaghosa spread the doctrine of Mahayana Buddhism, teaching a religion of Essence, Deep Reality, and the Way of Enlightenment. Prominent in Mahayana Buddhism are its ten great principles, including: 1) do not kill, 9) do not deceive or insult, and 10) shun anger. For his great zealous advocacy of Buddhism as well as his peacemaking skills, Asvaghosa earns the title of Peace Hero.

The Gupta Empire

The time of the Gupta empire that spanned the 4th and 5th centuries CE is called the Golden Age of India. The empire was prosperous and maintained strong trade ties. The rulers were tolerant of the different religions in the subcontinent, particularly Buddhism and Jainism, and they established a law code that was gentle with no capital punishment.

The Gupta kings, especially Chandra Gupta II, encouraged: mathematics and science, medicine and surgery, poetry and literature, painting and sculpture, and philosophy. The many intellectual giants of the time produced astounding discoveries in astronomy, inventions of theoretical mathematics, and new and enduring literary forms.

Of course, the expansion of the Gupta empire until it extended across three-fourths of South Asia was not achieved by negotiation. Rather, military conquest was the rule, especially during the reign of Samudra Gupta. But, there were enough periods of peace and domestic tranquility that the Gupta empire became a center of culture and intellectual exchange for the entire region of South and East Asia.

Let us count Chandra Gupta II, the most enlightened and humane of the Gupta monarchs, as a Peace Hero for the greater part of his 33-year rule.

Harsha Vardhana

Harsha Vardhana came to power in 606 CE, after the Gupta Empire had disintegrated in the mid-6th century and the region became divided among many small republics and kingdoms. Harsha Vardana was a great warrior even in his teens—he was crowned king at age 16—and between conquest and alliances, he expanded his realm across the north of India for the first fourteen years of his rule. When he tried to extend his realm to the south, however, he was unsuccessful when he came against Pulakesin II of the Chalukya kingdom. The two established a truce and set the boundary between the two kingdoms as the Narmanda River in a peace treaty.

Harsha Vardhana then looked more to religious and cultural pursuits and to the well-being of the people. He himself was a convert to Buddhism, but he welcomed Jainism and Vedism. He established great theologic debates and a grand Buddhist convocation that attracted thousands of pilgrims, including more than a few kings who traveled great distances. He toured the country to determine the needs of the people and funded programs of tree planting and road building. He was a champion of education, opening many schools and supporting the University of Nalunda where 10,000 students were enrolled. He also welcomed poets, playwrights, painters, and philosophers. The great Indian mathematician Brahmagupta lived peacefully in the western part of the empire under his rule and pursued astounding advances in his discipline.

Harsha Vardhana was not only popular with his own subjects, he also was skilled in foreign statecraft. He sent a mission to China and established the first diplomatic relations between India and China.

Although he became king and expanded his empire largely through military means, Harsha Vardhana matured to serve the needs of his people, especially in education and the arts. He may fairly be called a Peace Hero. Could a Buddhist convert do less?

<u>China</u>
The Tang Dynasty

The period of the Tang Dynasty, 821–903 CE, is called the age of prosperity, if not always of peace. The dynasty was founded by Li Yuan, the Duke of Tang. His son, Taizong (T'ai

Tsung), took power in 627, starting his career with fraticide and, in 630, a military campaign against Tujue in central Asia.

On his return to the capital at Chang-an, Taizong undertook a study of Confucianism, which influenced his reign thereafter. He refused extravagances and elaborate entertainments and allowed the palace ladies-in-waiting to return home and be productive. Throughout the nation the emperor eliminated the harsh repression that had been in place in the name of law and order. He allowed convicts out of the prisons to till the fields productively. He largely eliminated poverty and thereby reduced crime. He was an able and humane administrator and chose his advisors well.

Although prosperity and domestic tranquility were hallmarks of his reign, intrigue still turned up at the royal court as one individual or another sought to gain influence. In foreign matters, emperor Taizong engaged in military actions both early and late. We may consider him a military hero, a fine calligrapher, perhaps a great emperor, but not a Peace Hero.

Xuanzong

The Tang dynasty reached the pinnacle of glory under the brilliant administration of emperor Xuanzong who, upon ascending to the throne in 712 CE, instituted sweeping reforms. He reduced the number of palace advisors to two or three trustworthy individuals who emphasized honesty, the rule of law, and administrative efficiency. The emperor himself dissolved the secret police and exiled them and their families to the far reaches of the empire. He replaced the conscription system that was used for maintaining a large standing army with a recruitment approach and a smaller professional army whose soldiers were paid. He eased the tax burden on the peasants to encourage the production of rice, spices, silk, and crafts.

He built a system of granaries and restored the decaying canal system to transport grain harvests and other goods.

Xuanzong was also eager to establish the capital of Chang-an as a cultural center of the world. To that end he brought distinguished poets and painters to the royal court. A talented musician and composer himself, he established an imperial conservatory, and he welcomed diplomats, scholars, monks, and merchants from all over the world to Chang-an. The people meanwhile, were prosperous, content, and lived and worked in peace. It is said that doors were left unlocked at night.

In 742, the emperor increasingly came under the influence of a favorite consort, Yang Guifei, and he increasingly withdrew from public affairs. Lady Yang sought to promote her own relatives in the royal court, much to the displeasure of the chief minister, Li Linfu, who was assuming more and more political power. As Xuanzong retired further into the pleasures of feminine beauty, matters of state became worse. Much intrigue developed within the ministry and among the commanders of the army during the late 740s. By 750 different divisions of the army engaged in various military adventures and lost many thousands of troops. In 751, the Abbasid Caliphate attacked on the western front and, at the Battle of Talas, soundly trounced the Tang forces. In 755, the An Lushan rebellion took shape and lasted eight years. By 756, Xuanzong gathered Lady Yang and a small group of relatives and courtiers and fled the capital. A great power struggle ensued and Xuanzong's son, crown prince Li Heng, was proclaimed Emperor Suzong. Xuanzong recognized Suzong as emperor and took the title of Taishang Huang (retired emperor) for himself.

Xuanzong certainly must be given all credit for the peace and prosperity of the Kaiyuan era (713–741 CE) of his long reign. It is only during the shorter Tianbao period (742–756) when he neglected matters of state, that he may be faulted. I think we may honor him with the title of Peace Hero.

Tibetan-Chinese Peace Treaty

In the time of the Tang dynasty in China, there were occasional raids from the Tubo kingdom in Tibet into China—and sometimes the other way. During the time of emperor Taizong, princess Wen Cheng of China was wed to Songtsan Gambo, king of Tibet. The relationship between the two nations became one of exchange and trade instead of rivalry. By 821-822 CE, they were ready for a formal treaty. The "Great King of China and the Miraculous Lord and Great King of Tibet," uncle and nephew, agreed to respect each other's territory. The text of the treaty states that even the word "enemy" shall not be spoken, and all shall live in peace and share the blessings of peace, and is carved on stone pillars which still stand in Lhasa, a Peace Victory to set a standard for all time.

2nd Millennium CE – Moses Maimonides

Maimonides was born in Cordoba in Moorish–Muslim Spain in 1135 CE. He was recognized in his own time for his intellect and his wisdom. Maimonides was a polymath: a physician, Torah scholar, and philosopher.

As a physician he not only treated patients for physical and mental illness, he sought to guide the profession with his writing. He saw as medicine's responsibility: a) the prevention of illness, b) the diagnosis & treatment of illness, and c) the care of the disabled and chronically ill. His medical papers were many, including an extensive pharmacopoeia.

Maimonides studied the Torah extensively and is known to this day as having established the codification of Jewish Law and Ethics and the development of Torah scholarship.

His knowledge of philosophy, based on the Greek philosophers of the Golden Age of Pericles and subsequent schools of philosophy in both ancient Greece and Rome, gradually led him to his own individual set of beliefs and principles. He was a rationalist and a humanist, stressing the importance of honesty and humility.

Like Kant centuries later, Maimonides opposed the use of force and war to attain individual and state aims. He opined that King David was denied the building of the Temple in Jerusalem with God admonishing him, "Your hands have spilled much blood." [Many were the wars of King David.] In his advocacy of justice and peace, Maimonides shared a philosophy of generosity, humility, and restraint.

> *There are eight levels of charity—at the highest, neither the giver nor the recipient knows the other.*
>
> *It is better to acquit a thousand guilty persons than to put a single innocent one to death.*
>
> *Whoever strikes his fellow transgresses a negative Commandment.*
>
> *Humans must pursue reason to bring a reign of peace and prosperity on earth as envisioned by the biblical prophets.*

Maimonides often intertwined biblical quotations with philosophical pronouncements. A few examples will be illustrative:

> *Great is peace to those who love your Torah.* —Psalms 119:165
>
> *God is good to all, and his mercies extend to all his creatures.* —Psalms 145:9
>
> *Peace be upon Israel.* —Psalms 125:5
>
> *Turn from evil and do good. Seek peace and pursue it.* —Psalms 34:14

Peace, peace — to the distant and the close. –Isaiah 57:19

Behold, I give him my covenant of peace. –Numbers 25:12

And I shall place peace upon the land. –Leviticus 26:6

Maimonides was unequivocal in his linkage of religious ethics and peace: "God's seal is Peace; Peace is his Name." Let us know Moses Maimonides as a Peace Hero and add it to his fame as a physician, Torah scholar, and philosopher.

First branch of the family tree
   of apes, the question is not
why orangs are solitudinous,

but why bonobos and chimps
   and Homo sapiens are
so social. Of all, only human

mothers let trusted others
   hold their infants — a certain
sign of cooperation. Just that,

and possibly a little
   cleverness, not strength or speed,
is why we're around today at all.

MAY FIRST

A birch, bent to horizontal
in a winter storm. has survived
   the winds and ice of January.

Now, in May, it wears a dress of
new green leaves, its network of roots
   assures it water and nutrients.

The earth, the worms, the weeds and bees,
even other trees, long ago
   learned common kindness — now it's the Law.

Chapter 6

Peace Heroes, Peace Victories: The Renaissance to the Modern Era

England
The Hundred Years War and The Peace Movement

In England, the Hundred Years war began in 1337 to contest the French throne and establish the British claim of Edward III to French lands. The claim had originated almost three centuries earlier when William, the Duke of Normandy, conquered English forces and was proclaimed King of England in 1066.

As the war between England and France dragged on with less and less respect for the Law of Arms (*jus in bello*), the currency of Just War (*jus ad bellum*) became ever more debased among poets and clerics. Taxes were raised to pay for the war and commerce became disrupted, and opposition among the common people increased. By around 1375 CE, a genuine anti-war movement had developed and, over the ensuing twenty-five years, grew to an anti-all-wars movement. The leading lights were John Gower, John Wyclif, and Geoffrey Chaucer—poet, theologian and poet-story teller, respectively.

John Gower, the poet, was only a child when Edward III first staked his claim to the French throne with sword and lance. Gower, early on, wrote of man's personal sinfulness and the general corruption of society. He revered honesty, integrity and all manner of morality, but he also had a say on war and peace. In *Confessio Amantis*, he condemned soldiers and lords who make war. "As for courage, they are likely to make war and pillage for lucre and for no other skill," he wrote. Nor did he excuse the clergy: "Peter preached, but today's pope fights. The one sought souls; the other greedily seeks riches." In later years as the war went on, Gower strengthened his position further.

He wrote that war perverts or destroys love, whereas "love for others will prevent wars." At the time of the accession of Henry IV, he advised the king in a public address, "The best rule is that which leads to peace," and concluded, "Peace is the chief of all the world's wealth." In one of his short works, the 385-line poem "In Praise of Peace," Gower set forth all the reasons for peace and against war:

- *War benefits the few who loot and pillage at the expense of the people*
- *War brings destruction of life and property*
- *War brings corruption*
- *Peace is, as it were, a sacrament of God.*

John Wyclif, the philosopher and heretic theologian, concentrated his writing on war and peace. He recognized that all wars—both "just" wars and those for gain through plunder and spoils—were for personal gain. He gave voice for the truth that even "just" wars were accompanied by terrible abuse. (Similarly, 21st-century writer Gadfly Zeeks commented "A just war is just war.")

Wyclif declared that fighting for the church brings no salvation. He stated "Christ taught not His apostles to fight with a sword of iron but with a sword of God's word." He railed against clergy who incited war and senseless bloodshed, and was especially vehement against the papacy that prevented the peaceful Gospel of Christ by justifying war. Nor did knights, the ostensible protectors of the weak and the innocent, escape the sharp quill of Wyclif's pen. He saw them imbued with vice, not virtue. Slaying in service of chivalry based on selfishness was not honorable even in a "just" war, as declared by the pope. Indeed, he painted clerics of all office who supported the unholy practice of war in any way as "enemies of peace whose prayers are cursed."

In his treatise *On The Seven Deadly Sins*, Wyclif attributed the cause of war to the sin of anger, and "Ire is full contrary to fellowship and charity that should be in all people." He went on, "By God's law we should love our enemies and so, make them friends by the strength of charity."

Geoffrey Chaucer, the poet and author of *The Canterbury Tales*, was the narrator himself of "The Tale of Melibee." In that satire, war is condemned in its every aspect. Melibee's wife, Prudence, is a principal character who argues, "Vengeance is not conquered by another vengeance, but wickedness shall be conquered by goodness, discord by accord, war by peace." She noted that compassion precludes just causes and cautioned, "There is great peril in war and a man should eschew battle." She even commented on accepting advice from a woman, pointing out that such advice may be more valuable than that of "flatterers and strange folks who show you reverence when the thing itself is changed," an obvious reference to King Richard II's court and the changing events of the time. Richard ruled from 1377 to 1399, and by the 1380s, when Chaucer wrote *The Canterbury Tales*, the war had gone on for over forty years. Chaucer was saying through the words of Prudence that it was time "to give peace a chance."

The Hundred Years War began in the reign of Edward III and proceeded through the monarchies of Richard II, Henry

IV, Henry V, and most of Henry VI's long tenure. Other pacifists joined the increasing opposition:

- William Langland, who wrote *The Vision of Piers Plowman*
- The Lollards who, under Nicolas Hereford and William Swynderby, presented the "Ten Conclusions to Parliament"
- Michael de la Pole, the Earl of Suffolk who worked tirelessly to convince both Richard II and Parliament to make peace with France
- Several administrators of the Church including bishop Thomas Brinton, archbishop Richard Fitzralph, and Dominican John Bromyard who wrote *Summa Proedicantium* (*Notes for Preachers*)
- Thomas Hoccleve who wrote *Regiment of Princes*, advising Prince Henry (soon to be Henry V) that a way to peace and unity would be through marriage to French princess Katherine
- John Lydgate, author of *Troy Book*, *The Siege of Thebes*, and "A Praise of Peace" that pleads for peace between England and France and the end to all war
- On the continent, just a few French critics of the war added their voices: Philippe de Mezieres was prominent with his *Epistre Au Roi Richart*

The Hundred Years War finally ended in 1453, with the loss of English claim to French territory, without an immediate peace treaty, with the perception that the social and political order had fallen apart, and with widespread economic hardship. Yet, it was a chance for a new beginning, which was to come within a decade with the reign of Henry VII.

The various figures of the Peace Movement during the Hundred Years War should include all the religious and literary figures of the time—John Gower, John Wycliff, Geoffrey Chaucer, William Langland, John Bromyard, Thomas Hoccleve, and John Lydgate among them. They all deserve to be Peace Heroes."

Henry Tudor (Henry VII)

Britain emerged from the Hundred Years War shaken politically and economically. The nobility in York and in Lancaster each found conditions to their liking and waged civil war, the War of the Roses, to establish claim to the throne. The Hundred Years War ended during the reign of Henry VI. Edward IV (1461–83) and Richard III (1483–85) followed after. Then Henry Tudor defeated Richard at the Battle of Bosworth to take the throne as Henry VII. He immediately embarked on a new policy to establish prosperity through peace and commerce. He set unity as his goal for the English nation rather than empire through conquest.

In 1486 Henry married Elizabeth of York to consummate his peace efforts by uniting Lancaster and York under the House of Tudor. In 1492, he concluded a formal peace treaty with France: "… a sure, firm peace and unity." He strengthened his friendship with Scotland's James IV in 1502 with the Anglo-Scottish Treaty of Perpetual Peace and gave his daughter Margaret in marriage to James.

Henry's peace-making efforts had the support of the commercial sector, especially British merchants in Calais and Bruges who saw the benefits of peace in trade. Henry also had the sanction of the clergy in the person of John Colet, the dean of St. James Cathedral. But, it was Henry Tudor as king who moved the nation into a period of peace.

Whether his primary motivation was amity, unity, or prosperity, Henry VII is a bona fide Peace Hero.

Nicholas de Cusa (Cusanus)

Nicholas de Cusa lived from 1401 to 1464, a little over half a century before the Renaissance. He was a scholar, philosopher, theologian, and diplomat. He also studied mathematics and astronomy/cosmology and proposed a heliocentric model of the solar system, with the earth revolving on its axis in an elliptical orbit around the sun.

Nicholas was educated in the liberal arts and philosophy at Heidelberg University. Then he enrolled in the University of Padua and in 1423 received a doctorate in canon law.

As a young German theologian, Nicholas de Cusa attended the 1431 Council of Basel to contest the appointment of a successor to Otto, Archbishop-elector of Tier. At the Council discussions, Nicholas became known as a conciliator, writing *De Concordantia Catholica*, which balanced the primacy of the Vatican with consent of the jurisdictions of the regional cathedrals. He wrote: "Since by nature all men are free, all government arises solely from agreement and consent of the subjects."

In 1437 Nicholas was part of the three-man delegation to the Eastern Orthodox Church in Constantinople to seek reunification of the Eastern and Western Churches in defense against the Ottoman Turks. Nicholas won over many of the major and minor lay and religious leaders of Byzantium, but he did not achieve the full set of goals of the delegation. By 1453 the Turks achieved military success in taking Constantinople. Later that year, Nicholas wrote *De Pace Fidei (Peace of Faith)*, in which he expressed the view that all religions were inspired by God and therefore see their relationship with the deity in their own way, employing different means of prayer and praise.

Unhappy that religion was used to back war, he questioned the reluctance of all peoples to to know those of other faiths—and actively advocated dialog between Christianity and Islam.

Despite his work as a reformist theologian, his reputation as a humanist, and his cosmologist theories which denied the earth as the center of the universe, Nicholas was nominated to be a Cardinal by Pope Eugene IV and was elevated to that high position by Eugene's successor, Pope Nicholas V.

Nicholas de Cusa (Cusanus) was a man ahead of his time. He fully deserves designation as a Peace Hero.

The Renaissance: John Colete, Sir Thomas More, and Desiderius Erasmus—the Oxford Reformers

The years on either side of 1500 CE saw the advancement of painting and sculpture to the high standards of the Classical Age of Greece. The three major figures—Leonardo, Michelangelo, and Raphael—are the first to come to mind when we speak of the High Renaissance.

Science, however, made advances far beyond the science of the Classical Age. Copernicus, Brahe, and Kepler revolutionized the knowledge of astronomy by correctly depicting our heliocentric solar system. Vesalius established an accurate knowledge of human anatomy, in particular the circulation of the blood. A less appreciated facet of human life that made important strides in the Renaissance concerned society itself, its political make up, and the issue of war versus peace.

John Colet

John Colet (1467–1519) lived through this time of transition and helped bring England out of the Medieval period. In 1497, he preached from the pulpit: "For it is not by war that war is conquered but by peace, forbearance, and reliance on God." He continued "We ought to aim for goodness in order to conquer evil, and at forbearance to overcome war and unjust actions."

His words found common cause with the king, Henry VII, who was interested more in unity and pragmatism than morality and religion, but for whom peace as a means was next best to peace as an end in itself. Henry died in 1509, however, and was succeeded by his son, who became Henry VIII. The new king soon set about on a quest for glory by means of military victory. In 1513 he sent troops into France, captured the towns of Therouanne and Tournai, and defeated the French forces in the Battle of the Spurs. He also supported the Earl of Surrey, who invaded Scotland, and was victorious at the Battle of Flodden.

The martial euphoria brought by these military successes was dampened by Colet, who was by then was Dean of St. Paul's Cathedral. In a Good Friday sermon he preached that the soldiers "were warring under the banner not of Christ but of the devil." He noted that each might "have the brotherly love without which no one would see God, yet bury his sword in his brother's heart."

Henry VIII may have been the King of England, but he didn't want to cross swords with the Dean of St. Paul's and even toasted him publicly. Colet, of course, continued to oppose war. He, Sir Thomas More, and Desiderius Erasmus were known as the Oxford Reformers. They influenced the culture of Europe away from seeing glory in the success of war to a movement to oppose war for the reasons of common sense and following the example of Jesus. They spoke of peace, not just as the absence of war, but as a value in itself.

John Colet earned a prominent place in the annals of Peace Heroes.

Desiderius Erasmus

For Erasmus (1466–1536 CE), peace was central to his life's work. Yet he is little known as a pacifist, but rather as a humanist, philosopher, educator, and theologian. The omission of any reference to his many writings as severe critic of war and adherent of peace by many of his biographers speaks more to their deficiency. than his Indeed, even in the Maison d'Erasme at Anderlecht, near Brussels, Erasmus's works on peace are not to be found. He is described there as a humanist, a theologian, a philologist, and intellectual. Why should peace be so controversial?

Erasmus's most notable pacifist writings were:

- *Dulce Bellum Inexpertis* (*War is sweet to those who know it not*)
- *Querela Pacis* (*Complaint of Peace*)
- *Institutio Principis Christiani* (*Education of a Christian Prince*)
- "Letter to Anthony A Bergis"
- *Antipolemus—The Plea of Reason, Religion and Humanity Against War*

The many aphorisms that can be gleaned therefrom show Erasmus to be a vehement, unapologetic pacifist, both intellectually and emotionally.

- Erasmus declared that "war wasn't a natural prerogative of rule."
- To those who said, "The rights of kings must be pursued at all costs," Erasmus countered, "The strictest right is often the greatest wrong. What good can there be of spilling of human blood?"
- To those who spoke of the glory of military victory, Erasmus replied, "It is infinitely more glorious to

build and establish your own kingdom than to lay waste to the flourishing community of a foe."

- To allay anyone's doubts about his convictions, Erasmus said of war, "There is nothing more wicked, more disastrous, more loathsome, in a word, more unworthy of man, not to say of a Christian."
- Erasmus spoke of the monarchs of Europe: "Christian kings raging against each other with all the madness of so many devils let loose. Raging for what? For power, for empire, and dominion."
- Erasmus also opined that Mars was "the most stupid of gods."

Erasmus's *Institutio Principis Christiani* was printed in 1516, three years after Niccoló Machiavelli circulated correspondence copies of *The Prince*. To this day, *Institutio* serves as a powerful counterweight to Machiavelli. Erasmus fully deserves to be the father of pacifism and, for us, a Peace Hero.

Thomas More

Thomas More (1478–1535) was a major figure in English political and religious life. He early followed the disciplines of prayer and penance learned at a Carthusian monastery, even while he pursued the study of law in London.

The law, and then public service, were early callings. He became a barrister in 1501 and a member of Parliament in 1504. He continued in politics and, known for his sense of fairness and advocacy for the poor, was elected to the Privy Council in 1518. He was knighted by Henry VIII (1521), became Speaker of the House of Commons (1523), and went on to replace Thomas Cardinal Wolsey as Lord Chancellor to the king (1529).

Beyond his immersion in politics and religion, Thomas

More was a statesman, philosopher, and writer. He became a friend to both Erasmus and Colet. Erasmus dedicated his *In Praise of Folly* (*Encomium Morias*) to More, knowing he would agree with the satire, which stands as a classic depredation of human foibles and failings to this day.

Thomas More was a prolific writer in his own right. Although he often wrote of the ecclesiastic hierarchy in his mature years, while still in his thirties he authored *Utopia*, which has remained his best-known work through the centuries. *Utopia* describes the social and economic affairs of an imaginary island nation where the land is owned in common, where men and women are equally educated, where there is tolerance for all religions, and where people are learned, civil, and happy. When the main character, Raphael Hythlodaeus, describes the worthy republic to contemporaries, they regard him as a fool, but the insightful reader sees him as a prophet.

There is no question that Thomas More was a humanist, but it is also true that in his position as Lord Chancellor, he ordered six Lutherans, a former Benedictine monk, and a writer & priest to be burned at the stake. Were it not for these executions between 1529 and 1533, Thomas More would be a Peace Hero.

Perhaps, the author of *Utopia* and friend of Erasmus should be so considered, anyway.

Bartolome de Las Casas

This Spanish scholar, historian, humanist, and theologian lived in the time of the conquistadors of the 16th century. Born in 1484, he left for the New World in 1502 at the age of 18. He returned to Spain four years later and studied for the priesthood. As an ordained priest he continued his studies in canon law and, by 1510, returned to the Indies.

He was a chaplain in the Spanish expedition of 1513 that

conquered Cuba, disturbed by the many atrocities he witnessed. He said, "I saw here cruelty no one has ever seen or expects to see." Within the next year, he learned of the earlier preaching of the Dominican Antonio de Montesinos: "By what right or justice do you keep the Indians in such horrible servitude? Are they not men? Have they not rational souls? Are you not obligated to love them as you love yourselves?"

Las Casas also engaged in much introspection and self-confession. By 1514 he freed his own slaves and publicly challenged the serf-like system of *encomienda*. He said, "I affirm that all that has been done in the Indies by the Spaniards is without legal standing." At first, he opposed the slavery of Indians, though not of Africans, but not long after found all slavery reprehensible.

Las Casas found much opposition to his preaching in the New World and realized he would have to plead his case in Spain. He sailed to Spain in 1515 and was able to arrange an audience with King Ferdinand, who seemed open to his cause. Unfortunately, the ailing king died within a few weeks of his arrival. Thereafter, Las Casas spent the rest of his life between Spain and the New World pursuing freedom and justice for the native Indians, stopping the conquest of their lands, and converting the Indians to Christianity by peaceful individual persuasion. A listing of his activities and achievements will give an overall picture of this Peace hero of the Spanish Empire during the Renaissance.

- Las Casas was named "Protector of the Indians by Cardinal de Cisternos of Spain.
- In 1522 he joined the Dominican order, which advocated conversion of Indians only by peaceful means, eschewing mass conversions and conversions by force.

- He traveled widely through Central and South America, preaching opposition to conquest and enslavement of Indians.
- He presented both the moral-humanist position against slavery of the Indians and the legal argument to "affirm that all that has been done in the Indies by the Spanish is without any legal standing."
- In 1537 Pope Paul III issued a Papal Bull protecting the right of Indians in the Americas after receiving a letter from Las Casas and two other prominent missionaries.
- In 1540 he returned to Spain to plead before Charles V, then both Holy Roman Emperor and King of Spain. As a result, the New Laws of 1542 were enacted, prohibiting enslavement of any Indians and declaring the system of *encomienda* ended.
- Again in Spain in 1550, Las Casas participated in the Valladolid debates concerning the justice and lawfulness of the Spanish occupation of the Americas, bringing to bear arguments drawn from theology, philosophy, and the law. He said, "All men have understanding and will and free choice, and all are made in the image of God. The entire human race is one." He left no doubt that "Indians are our brothers."
- He spent the remaining years of his life in Spain, writing, lecturing, and arguing for the rights of the Indians. He also completed his three-volume *History of the Indies*.

Bartolome de Las Casas and his mentor, the Dominican Antonio de Montesinos, may be regarded as pioneers in advancing the concept of Universal Human rights and, as such, are true Peace Heroes.

James I

James became King James VI of the Kingdom of Scotland in 1567 at the age of one, when his mother, Mary Queen of Scots, was forced to abdicate. In England, when the childless and unmarried Queen Elizabeth died in 1603, James became King James I of England as well. Although he was greeted with great enthusiasm as he traveled from Edinburgh to London for his coronation, his popularity waned thereafter and he never received good press—until recently. He often squabbled with Parliament, having previously proclaimed the divine right of kings in his essay, "The True Law of Free Monarchies," in which he set out a theological basis for divine monarchy.

Moreover, as James I, the counsellors of his court were often incompetent and his policies inconsistent, though previously, as king of Scotland, he had established effective royal government and peace among the quarrelsome lords. As James I, he held different favorites amid much scandal, bestowed lavish gifts, and was given to personal extravagance. Much of his time was spent in the pursuit of leisure, especially the hunt, instead of the executive duties of government.

Yet he presided over a time of great literature: William Shakespeare, Ben Jonson, and John Donne were all active during what came to be called the Jacobean era. James himself, was a scholar and author of several books.

In a semblance of balance between literature on one hand and self indulgence and playing favorites on the other, James's avowed pacifism was the determinant of his place in history.

In 1588 he published *Basilikon Doro*, modeled after Erasmus's *The Education of A Christian Prince*. The frontispiece of James's book featured a picture of Pax (Peace) carrying an olive branch and treading on the figure of Vanity. At his 1603 coronation as king of England and Scotland, the image of Peace standing with Mars at her feet in submission was prominently displayed. James proclaimed that "Peace alone was better and more to be coveted than innumerable triumphs … for it is a triumph in itself."

In his first speech before Parliament he offered, "The first of these blessings which God hath with my person sent unto you is peace and amity where war was before." James was unconditional in that he sought "Peace abroad with all foreign neighbors." James would always identify himself as a peace bringer and peacemaker, his personal motto being "Beati Pacifici" (Blessed are Peacemakers). Early in his time on the throne of the two kingdoms, James concluded a peace treaty between Spain and England and arranged a great celebration to commemorate the event. He simultaneously maintained good relations with France, despite the difficulties inherent in being friendly with two Catholic rivals.

In his twenty-two years on the throne of England, James's rule over a peaceable kingdom was challenged on many fronts: Guy Fawkes and the gunpowder plot; the adventurer Sir Walter Raleigh, who endangered the peace treaty with Spain by burning a Spanish settlement in South America; and the various members of Parliament who pressed for war against Spain at one time and against the Habsburg monarchy at another. Even amidst the Thirty Years War, which tore apart Central Europe and saw the interventions of many nations and municipalities of Europe, England would not engage in hostilities.

James I would be a Peace Hero despite his ongoing disputes with Parliament and his assertion of divine right, except for three matters of personal violence. First, as a young King James VI, he entertained a fascination with demonology and witchcraft: he is said to have personally supervised the torture of suspected witches in the wild and unruly Scotland of the time. Once on the throne of England, though, he was more intent on gaining the reputation of an intellectual and so gave up interest in the belief. Second, James saw Sir Walter Raleigh as disloyal and ready to hatch a plot against him. He imprisoned the adventurer in the Tower of London for a dozen years, but released him to lead an expedition to the New World to search for gold, with the warning not to make trouble with the Spanish colonies there. Raleigh found no gold, and instead sacked a Spanish settlement. On his return to England, he was arrested and charged with treason and thereafter executed. Third, in response to finding Guy Falkes tending a large quantity of gunpowder in the undercroft of the House of Lords, he imprisoned Falkes and had him tortured until he revealed the names of the conspirators, all of whom were executed and their bodies cut in pieces. Falkes, too, was executed, although he may have been set up as a fall guy.

James I unquestionably acted as a peacemaker, keeping England out of war in the early 17th century, but he was an imperfect Peace Hero.

Hugo Grotius (Hugo de Groot)

In the Dutch humanist tradition of the 16th century, Grotius (1583–1645) was a jurist, philosopher, and scholar of political theory and law. He had the large shoes of Erasmus to fill as he strove to continue the tradition of peace that Erasmus had established at the beginning of that century.

Of the sixty book-length works Grotius wrote and/or edited, primary were *De jure belli ac pacis* (*On the Law of War and Peace*) and *De jure preadae commentarius* (*Commentary on the law of prize and booty*). He was a staunch opponent of war his entire life. His works on the theory of politics and law were ahead of his time, and today, he is known as he father of modern international law. Hugo Grotius is an unquestionable Peace Hero.

Emeric Cruce

The 17th-century French writer and scholar Emeric Cruce (1590–1646)—some historians say he was also a monk, others a college instructor—became the first to propose that conflict between nations be brought to peaceful resolution by decision of an International Court of Arbitration.

In *The New Cyneas (Le Nouveau Cynee)*, Cruce recalls the peace efforts of the diplomat Cyneas of ancient Greece. He also follows the compelling arguments for peace expressed by Erasmus and the other Renaissance pacifists before him.

Then he reaches out to new political territory: an internationalist mechanism for peacefully resolving conflicts. Cruce was centuries ahead of the international institutions established in the 20th century: the League of Nations, the United Nations, and the International Court of Justice. In *The New Cyneas*, Cruce presents his philosophy:

- War, by interrupting trade, destroys the wealth of both conquerors and the conquered.
- Hostilities are merely political and cannot take away the ties that exist and must exist between men. These affinities are the foundation of friendship and human society.
- If arrogance and cruelty were to be abandoned, wars would cease.
- Alexander's conquests, Caesar's triumphs, and Hannibal's strategies were all founded on vanity, and their glory based on murder and plunder. Instead, it should have resulted in perpetual regret and shame.

- Whatever the controversy, it will be of greater advantage for the parties to the dispute to submit to the award of a Court of Arbitration rather than to the chances of war with its uncertain results and its heavy cost in blood and treasure.

Cruce further suggested free trade, a single currency, and standard weights and measures to cement peace and cooperation.

Emeric Cruce was a Peace Hero not only for advocating the end of war but also for offering the concept of an international court of arbitration to settle disputes. Imagine, an International Court in the 17th century.

Hans Jakob Christoffel von Grimmelshausen

As a child of about 10 years, HJC von Grimmelshausen (1625–1676) was carried off by Hessian and Croat soldiers who had raided his home. His great novel, *The Adventuresome Simplicissimus*, was drawn from the horrors of the Thirty Years War, the multifaceted conflict that involved many of the nations of Europe on one side or another. The hero is a boy who describes the attack of the soldiers who not only destroyed his home, stealing, smashing, or burning the household goods, but also torturing the men and raping the women. He describes the tortures in some detail: stuffing one of the men into the oven with burning sticks of wood, force feeding another with liquid manure, and using the flintlocks of pistols as thumbscrews on still others. As to the raping of the women, he could give no eyewitness accounts except for their screams and their being exceptionally disheveled and barely able to speak afterward. The writing style is often satirical, and no doubt is left that the tale is a polemic against war. Von Grimmelshausen also wrote other works of fiction including a few that were spin-offs from *Simplicissimus*.

The title of *The Adventuresome Simplicissimus* today is better known than the name of the author; let us redress this inequity as we celebrate HJC von Grimmelshausen as a Peace Hero.

George Fox

Born in England in 1624, George Fox as a young man heard ghostly voices and felt a divine spirit. He was certain that "Jesus might be the pre-eminence who enlightens and gives grace and faith and power." Believing that people should follow their own "inner light," he turned away from the hierarchy of establishment religion, away from all the rights and rituals of the Church.

In his early twenties, Fox became an itinerant preacher. Attracting many to his spiritual ideas, including a few notable figures among them, he formed Friends of the Truth, which became the Society of Friends. As Fox's following increased, so did the body of his beliefs. From an early focus on the philosophy of religion, on not needing the church as the venue of religious practice, and on a personal relation with God through Jesus Christ, he expanded his vision and preaching to embrace personal morality and mutual respect, and to oppose: injustice, violence, and all war.

At the age of 27 Fox was imprisoned for blasphemy. He wrote afterward, "The time of my commitment to the house of correction being nearly ended, and there being many new soldiers raised ... so the keeper of the house of corrections was commanded to bring me before the commissioners and soldiers, and they offered me preferment, asking me if I would not take up arms for the Commonwealth against Charles Stuart [Charles II]. ... I told them I lived in the virtue of that life that took away the occasion of all wars. Yet they courted me to accept their offer. But I told them I was come into the covenant of peace, which was before all that took away the occasion of all wars. They said they offered it in love and kindness to me and because of my virtue. But I told them if that was their love and kindness, I trampled it under my feet. Then their rage got up, and they said, 'Take him away jailer and put him into the dungeon amongst the rogues and felons,' where I was kept almost half a year."

Fox also wrote, "... His [Christ's] kingdom starts in peace and righteousness. ... His kingdom is not of this world; it is peaceable, and the Gospel of Peace was before fighting was. They who would be wrestlers with flesh and blood throw away the spiritual weapons."

In 1655 Fox was arrested in Leicestershire and taken under armed guard to London. He was asked to declare that he would not take up a sword against Oliver Cromwell or the government. He wrote in declaration, "I, George ffox, refuse to carry or draw a carnall sword against any, or against thee Oliver Cromwell, or any men in the presence of the lord God. ... I am moved to stand witnesse against all violence and against all the workes of darkenesse, and to turn people to the light and bring them from the occasion of the warre ... My weapons are not carnall but spiritual." He thereupon was granted a short audience with Cromwell. On their taking leave, Cromwell asked Fox back in the future, having found some common ground with him.

George Fox lived until 1691, and to this day in the Society of Friends he founded four and a half centuries ago. He is certainly a Peace Hero.

William Penn

William Penn, a British subject, lived from 1644 to 1718 in the times of the Commonwealth under Oliver Cromwell and of the Restoration under Charles II. At the age of 22 he converted to Quakerism and came to know George Fox.

Penn was outspoken in the Quaker cause and was imprisoned six times. In 1667 he was at a Quaker meeting that the police raided. Everyone was arrested. Based on his bearing and aristocratic dress, the police released him, but he protested that he, too, was a Quaker and insisted he be treated the same as the others. While in prison, he wrote many pamphlets, creating a literature for the Quakers, including his well known "No Cross, No Crown." During his imprisonment in the cruel Newgate prison, he brought his legal training to bear and convinced the Court of Common Pleas to order the release of all eleven Quakers, establishing the right of habeas corpus.

In 1681, Penn requested a charter from Charles II for territory in the New World. The King granted him a charter to the territory west of the Delaware River and north of Maryland, and in deference to William's father, Admiral William Penn of the Royal Navy, suggested the name Pennsylvania, the Forests of Penn. There Penn established a Frame of Government, which guaranteed freedom of the press, trial by jury, religious freedom, a ban on military conscription, and the flexibility to change this document of government through amendments.

The very next year, in 1682, Penn sailed from England and arrived at Newcastle, Delaware (then part of Pennsylvania) and traveled on to the site he named Philadelphia, meaning City of Brotherly Love. He purchased the land from the Indians in a treaty that would establish peace between the colonists and the indigenous Indians. Having learned a few different Indian dialects, he met with clans of the Lenni Lenapi nation. The Indians headed by Chief Tamanend met Penn and his Friends under a great elm tree known as the Treaty Tree, at Shackamoxan. There, a Treaty of Amity and Friendship was wrought. Penn later wrote, "When the purchase was agreed, great promises passed between us of kindness and good neighborhood, and that the Indians and English must live in love as long as the sun gave light."

At the Treaty meeting, Penn offered:

"The Great Spirit who made me and you ... who knows the innermost thought of men, knows that I and my friends have a hearty desire to live in peace and friendship with you.... It is not our custom to use hostile weapons against our fellow creatures, for which reason we come unarmed. Our object is not to do injury and provoke the Great Spirit, but to do good.

We are met on the broad pathway of good faith and good will ... to openness, brotherhood, and love.... I will consider you as the same flesh and blood with the Christians."

Chief Tamanend replied:

"We will live in love with William Penn and his children as long as the creeks and rivers run, and while the sun, moon, and stars endure.... We will be brethren, my people and your people, as the children of one father.... The doors of the Christian shall be open to the Indian, and the wigwam shall be open to the Christian."

The only records of the Great Treaty are: a) a wampum belt of eighteen leather strands strung with shell beads which depicts, in deep purple beads, a colonist hand in hand with an Indian, and b) a large oil painting of the treaty meeting under the Elm Tree by Benjamin West. The Treaty was recognized some years later by Voltaire who wrote, "It was the only Treaty made by the settlers with the Indians that was never sworn to, and the only one that was never broken."

In the newly founded city of Philadelphia, Penn established an office of peacemaker in every county to represent the people to the courts, a sort of ombudsman. In the 1684 Council records, the Peacemaker, in one instance, advised the disputants to shake hands and forgive each other.

In 1693, William Penn brought his views of humanity beyond Pennsylvania when he advised all people, "Let us then try what love can do to mend a broken world."

Some have questioned Penn's full commitment to the spirit of humanity because he owned slaves. But we must remember his time and that he did advocate for the humane treatment of slaves. Perhaps if he had lived longer in the New World, he would have become an abolitionist.

We may count Penn as a Peace Hero for the work he had accomplished, but who, at the age of 74, had not yet reached his full potential.

Charles Irénée Castel de Saint Pierre

In the days of absolute monarchies throughout Europe, Charles Castel, Abbé de Saint Pierre (1658–1743), was so far ahead of his time that for 200 years he was seen as a hopeless Utopian. Few remember him today. He was a French political theorist and writer who proposed radical political, social, and judicial reform in France and internationally (among the various sovereignties of Europe).

Born to nobility, he was elected to the French Academy in 1695, though he had produced no significant publications. In 1818, he published "Discours sur la Polysynodie," which proposed the end of divine monarchy by the replacement of the court of appointed ministers by elected councils. He punctuated his proposal in an opinion denying the posthumous title "the Great" to Louis XVI. The French Academy expelled him within a year.

Saint Pierre's enduring legacy, however, rests on an earlier publication, *Projet pour Render la Paix Perpetual en Europe*. In this *Project for Creating Perpetual Peace in Europe*, he foresaw not only perpetual peace, but also the mechanism to achieve it. He wrote of a Concert of Europe and a Permanent Arbitration Council to be formed by all the sovereignties of Europe. He published an early version of the Project in 1712. That year, he had an opportunity to begin a series of peace processes when he was appointed Secretary to the French Representative, Melchior de Polignac at the Congress of Utrecht, which brought about The Treaty of Utrecht to end the fourteen-year War of the Spanish Succession.

In other writing, Saint Pierre made a case for a) an equitable tax system, including a graduated income tax, and b) free public education for all, including both men and women.

Saint Pierre, although dismissed as an impractical Don Quixote by such luminaries of the 18th century as Rousseau and Voltaire, was taken as a visionary by Kant, who refined Saint Pierre's ideas into his own *Perpetual Peace: A Philosophical Sketch*, complete with corollaries and details.

Abbé de Saint Pierre definitely deserves to be a Peace Hero for all time.

John Woolman

John Woolman (1720–1772) grew up in a Quaker household in New Jersey near the Delaware River. As a young man in his twenties, he became a successful tradesman, but he soon gave up the retail trade to act on his increasing opposition to slavery. In 1746 he and a friend, John Andrews, went on a three-month journey through Virginia, Maryland, and North Carolina, observing the slave-based society, visiting families of slaveowners, and preaching against the practice on religious and humanitarian grounds.

Thereafter, Woolman, a well spoken but gentle man, became an itinerant preacher in a lifelong campaign to convince slave owners from New England to the Carolinas to free their slaves. Many did so. He was especially effective in his quest in Pennsylvania among fellow Quakers. He urged slave owners to legally free their slaves (manumission), or at minimum, to treat them humanely, even to the point of working alongside them.

By 1753, his discourse "Some Considerations on the Keeping of Negroes" was published by the Society of Friends in Philadelphia. It proved highly influential at the 1754 Yearly Meeting, which issued a lengthy epistle admonishing against the importing or otherwise purchasing slaves.

Woolman was unceasing in his efforts as an abolitionist throughout his life, but other matters called him as well. He was a staunch pacifist and sought the amity of the Indians of the frontier in Pennsylvania so he could "feel and understand the spirit they live in" and promote peaceful relations with them. During the French and Indian War (1754–1763), he opposed military conscription and urged tax resistance among his fellow Quakers. In 1759 he authored "A Pacifist Epistle" which stated the principles for opposing all war. In 1763, his "A Plea For The Poor" examined the causes of wars, chief among them the seeking after material goods and wealth. In 1779 he followed with "Considerations on the True Harmony of Mankind and How It Is to Be Maintained."

John Woolman fully deserves the honor of designation as Peace Hero.

Immanuel Kant

In the latter half of the 18th century, Immanuel Kant (1724–1804) added the voice of philosophy to those pacifists who came before him. In his extensive essay *Perpetual Peace*, he used philosophical arguments to show that peace is not just the absence of war but a relationship between nations that is positive, natural, and valuable.

He called out those colleagues who found justification for war, deriding them as "philosophers who praise war as ennobling mankind are forgetting the Greek who said, 'War is bad in that it begets more evil than it kills.'"

Kant spoke against the conquest of indigenous people, although he lived in the age of exploration and discovery. He labeled alliances as illegitimate. He also opposed the use of mercenary forces, which he said were "used and abused at will as personal property." He described "standing armies as themselves the cause of wars of aggression."

"A mere truce, a mere cessation of hostility," he said, "was not a valid peace." He was suspicious that peace treaties were easily made with "the secret reservation of material for a future war."

Kant, as a student of Natural Law, wrote that "Nature guarantees the coming of perpetual peace. She separates nations by means of language and religion, She unites nations through their mutual interests. The commercial spirit cannot co-exist with war." Thus, states find themselves compelled, not entirely from motives of morality, "to further the noble end of peace and to avert war."

For those who would say that the goal of peace could justify preventive war, Kant said, "We cannot devise a happy medium between right and expediency. All politics must bend a knee to the principle of right and may, in that way, hope to reach a level where it may shine on men for all time."

Immanuel Kant was as distinguished a Peace Hero as he was a philosopher.

Francisco Goya

Francisco Goya (1746–1828) was a classically trained painter whose work was recognized in the community of artists, and indeed, in the royal court. Many portraits were commissioned by nobles, even Charles IV, King of Naples. He was especially noted for the clarity of the detail in his work.

In 1799 in France, Napoleon Bonaparte became First Consul of the French Republic and, five years later, Emperor. After another three years, in 1807, he arranged to oust the weak and ineffectual Charles and replace him first with Charles's son Ferdinand VII, and then with his own elder brother, Joseph, as king of Naples and then of Spain. The following year, despite a few Spaniards who welcomed the French, the people of Madrid began to protest and were brutally repressed. Thus, began the active opposition to the new "King" Joseph in many of the cities. Soon enough, the British and Portuguese intervened on the side of the majority of Spanish people. These foreign powers sent troops who were aided by local militias [at first it was the other way around]. After many fierce battles, and the call for additional French troops, fighting was still indecisive. Napoleon originally boasted that he could conquer Spain with just 12,000 men.

Napoleon decided to send a force of crack troops, leading them himself. Even with some tactical successes, he could not turn the tide. Added to significant losses on the eastern front where the main body of France's Grande Armée had invaded Russia, the French retreated from the Peninsula and signed the 2nd Treaty of Paris. A constitution was drafted, and the Spanish Monarchy was restored.

In the art world, Goya celebrated the success of the Spanish people with a painting he called *The Second of May*, depicting the mounted French Imperial Guard charging the actively protesting citizens of Madrid.

Following that work, Goya painted a companion canvas called *The Third of May*, which broke new ground stylistically and in depiction of an emotionally moving scene of violence. The painting was of a firing squad, mostly in the shadows, executing a group of civilians centered around a highlighted figure clad in a white shirt with his arms raised as in the crucifixion of Jesus. Goya also started on a series of etchings enhanced with aquatint and drypoint he called *Disasters of War*—over eighty in all. The etchings depicted the death and suffering of individuals and families. They are dark in spirit and give image to the cruelty and brutality that is part of all war. In preparation for the etching series, he made many study drawings in sanguine-colored chalk. As well, he titled many of them to evince further emotion from the viewer. A list of a few titles are indicative of the disasters of war: "Escape among the Flames," "Bury Them and Be Quiet," "The Beds of Death," "The Flesh-Eating Vulture," "They Are Like Beasts," "Ravages of War…"

Many artists were influenced by Goya and his anti-war work, perhaps most notably Picasso in his painting, *Guernica*. For the present thesis, he is a Peace Hero in addition to being a great artist.

William Godwin

William Godwin (1756–1836) was a major figure among English political radicals of the 18th century. He believed that man was inherently, or potentially, good and that evil, crime, and war were caused by society. War, particularly, originated with monarchy and aristocracy. He advocated a philosophy of anarchism and personal freedom, and denounced everything associated with government, from taxation to laws to the concept of private property.

Historians have largely focused on Godwin's anarchism, but his pacifism deserves equal weight. He said of war: "One part of the nation pays another part to murder and be murdered in their stead [for] the most trivial causes – a supposed insult or sally of youthful ambition." He noted the great destruction and many atrocities that are the hallmark of every field of battle:

Men deliberately destroy each other by the thousands without any resentment against or even knowledge of each other...

The plain is strewed with death in all its various forms.

Anguish and wounds display the diversified modes to which they can torment the human frame.

Towns are burned, ships are blown up in the air, while the mangled limbs ...

... children are driven forth to hunger and nakedness.

...these scenes of horror and the total subversion of all ideas of moral justice they must occasion ...

Godwin did not stop at enumerating the horrors of war; he even passed judgment on revolutions that might have justification in our eyes. He said, "Revolution is engendered by an indignation with tyranny, yet is itself pregnant with tyranny." He went further, "God, himself, has no right to be a tyrant." Commenting on the honor given to military leaders, he said, "To rove with two or three ships makes you a pirate. With fifty ships you are an admiral."

Godwin believed in the perfectibility of man" and was called the Apostle of Universal Benevolence. Certainly, he ought to be listed as a Peace Hero, too.

Noah Worcester

Noah Worcester (1758–1837) was a Unitarian clergyman and a principal peace advocate in New England society. Before he found his true calling he served in the Revolutionary

War, but as a fife player, not bearing arms. He founded the Massachusetts Peace Society in 1815, the year after writing *A Solemn Review of the Custom of War* under the pen name of Philo Pacificus. The small volume had an addendum to the title: "showing that war was in the effect of popular delusion, and proposing a remedy." The book was widely circulated in the US and Europe and has been reprinted to this day.

Worcester set an admirable example as a Peace Hero for us to follow today.

David L. Dodge

David L. Dodge (1774–1852) was, and still is, known for two works on pacifism and religion: "The Mediator's Kingdom Not of This World" and "War Inconsistent with the Religion of Jesus Christ," both written in his thirties. His autobiography, written late in life at his family's suggestion, describes his childhood and early adulthood, and provides us with context for his well-known books.

In the section "By Gospel Authority," he tells of his early life when military fever ran high in many towns in New England. As a youth just shy of 18 years of age, he obtained his parents' reluctant permission to join a company of Volunteers. It was a time when Militias, Governor's Guards, Grenadier Guards, and Artillery Companies sprang up everywhere.

In subsequent years, Dodge, having established himself as a successful merchant, experienced an event that can only be described as an epiphany. In 1804 or so, a daring series of robberies in and around Boston made the news. Having occasion to travel to Boston on business the following year, he discussed his safety concerns with some Christian friends. All agreed it would be his duty to protect himself by carrying firearms. He obtained two large double-barreled pistols, and as he traveled with the guns always at the ready, he looked upon all those he came across with suspicion. Despite, or because of, the guns he carried, he traveled in a state of fear. On one occasion while staying at an inn, he almost mistook the innkeeper for a burglar and leveled his pistols at the figure in the dim light. But, as he described it, "by providence I so far awoke as to recognize him by the light of his candle by which means I just escaped taking his life."

Dodge spent the next couple of years in self-examination and in "conversing with many esteemed, pious and well educated persons." They discussed not only personal defense with deadly weapons but the larger issue of "defensive war ... especially the heroes of the American Revolution, whose example seemed to be paramount to all other considerations." So disturbed was he that he might have taken an innocent man's life, or indeed any man's life, he "laid aside my pistols, exchanging them for the protection of the Lord of Hosts, and then was no more tormented with the fear of robbers."

Not long afterward, a near death experience confirmed his pacifist resolve. In 1808, he was stricken with "spotted fever" and given less than 24 hours to live by two respectable physicians. In Dodge's own words, "time appeared to be receding, and eternity opening with all its infinite importance, my mind being serene as the rising morning, this subject passing before me when I had no more doubt, from the spirit and example of Christ and the precepts of the Gospel, that all kinds of carnal warfare were unlawful ... From this period, my war spirit appeared to be crucified and slain; and I felt regret that I had not borne some more public testimony against it."

Dodge recovered from the spotted fever and went on to publish his first peace thesis, "The Mediator's Kingdom Not of

This World." Four years later he wrote "War Inconsistent with the Religion of Jesus Christ," in which he proclaimed "that no man can, on Gospel principles, draw a line of distinction between offensive and defensive wars … for in irony and truth all wars must be just and necessary on both sides."

Dodge, toward the end of his autobiography, advised his descendants "that whatever indulgence you may grant your grandchildren, I entreat you not to give them military toys, not to take them to visit military reviews. The sounds of the music and the brilliant parade of troops … were designed to foster the spirit and teach the art of war" which Dodge described as "this evil."

The influence of Dodge's books and other writings was considerable, and in 1815 he was instrumental in the founding of the New York Peace Society, a first for the young nation.

David Dodge was not a minister or a monk, but a businessman and a Presbyterian. He thus brought the influence of society as a whole to bear in condemning all war. David L. Dodge was worthy of designation as a Peace Hero.

Jean-Jacques de Sellon

Jean-Jacques de Sellon, a wealthy Genevan philanthropist, founded the Société de la Paix in 1830. He also was opposed to slavery and supported the abolition of the death penalty. On his country estate, he constructed a Peace Temple with the inscription "Blessed are the Peace Makers."

These public and private initiatives make de Sellon worthy of being called a Peace Hero.

Ralph Waldo Emerson

Ralph Waldo Emerson (1803–1882) did not need the epiphany or miracle that made David Dodge a pacifist. Emerson, as a lecturer, essayist, and poet, was a member of the intellectual community. In 1837, he delivered before the Phi Beta Kappa Society an address, "The American Scholar,", for which he became noted as a transcendentalist. Less well known was his address, "War," given in Boston the following year. A few lines from that discourse will establish his credentials as a Peace Hero.

At the beginning he states the problem: "All history is the decline of war, though a slow decline. All that society has gained is mitigation; the doctrine of the right of war still remains." He goes on to place peacemakers on the highest plane: "The cause of peace is not the cause of cowardice. If peace is to be maintained, it must be by brave men who have come up to the height of the hero ... but who have gone one step beyond the hero and will not seek another man's life." He then concludes: "The manhood that has been in war must be transferred to the cause of peace, and peace be venerable to men."

At other times he said: "Peace cannot be achieved through violence; it can only be attained through understanding ... tolerance, cooperation, ... diplomacy, and cultural exchange." His other insights include: "Peace has its victories, but it takes brave men and women to win them," and "The real and lasting victories are those of peace and not of war."

His poem, "Peace" is story-like and places peace in our culture in the most fundamental way. The last stanza reads:

Take of this grain which in my garden grows, and grows for you.

Make bread of it and in that repose and peace, which everywhere

with so much earnestness you do pursue is only there.

Ralph Waldo Emerson was one of the major poets of the 19th century. He also brought his intellect to bear as an abolitionist and must be counted, as well, as a Peace Hero.

Elihu Burritt

Elihu Burritt lived in the 19th century (1810–1879) but preceded some of the giants whose major work for universal peace developed only after the Civil War was officially settled and the women's rights movement blossomed. Now, in the 21st century, few Americans have heard of him. Yet he was as fervent a worker for universal peace as his better known brethren who followed in his footsteps from the late 19th to the 21st centuries.

He began with an intensity matched by few. In 1846 he was loud and clear in opposing slavery and advocating world peace. He edited the journal of the American Peace Society, *Advocate of Peace and Universal Brotherhood*. In 1848 he founded the League of Universal Brotherhood which organized the First International Congress of the Friends of Peace that same year, attracting luminaries to Brussels from around the world. That set the stage for the Second Peace Congress, held in Paris the following year, with Victor Hugo as chair. All through his career, he found common cause between the rights of the laboring man and the devotees of peace.

In 1844, Burritt founded the weekly newspaper *The Christian Citizen*, in 1846 published *Sparks from the Anvil*, and in 1855–56 *Citizen of the World*. The intensity of his missionary work can be seen from a couple of quotes.

He described war as the "sin of sins," and urged that Christianity abolish its "unnatural, ungodly wedlock with ... the fiendish spirit of war."

Trained in his younger years as a blacksmith, he devoted the rest of his life to being an activist in pursuit of peace and brotherhood. During those many years as a pacifist he became known as the "learned blacksmith." The "harmonious blacksmith" would be equally apt. Certainly, Peace Hero is most fitting.

William Lloyd Garrison

In the nineteenth century, many peace movements evolved. A leading figure was William Lloyd Garrison (1805–79), whose work on behalf of universal peace was less well known than his work as an abolitionist. In 1838, he and Adin Ballou, Edmund Quincy, and Maria Quincy formed the New England Non-Resistance Society.

In a Declaration of Principles it stated "We are bound by the laws of a kingdom which is not of this world, in which Mercy and Truth are met together, as are Righteousness and Peace … in which there is no distinction of rank or inequality of sex, the officers are Peace…

"We register our testimony against all wars, offensive and defensive, all preparation of war, against the militia system, against standing armies … against all celebrations in honor of military or naval exploits…

"We shall submit to every ordinance of man, obey all the requirements of government, except such as we deem contrary to the commands of the Gospel, and in no case resist the operation of the law except by submitting to the penalty of disobedience.

"It will be our leading object to devise ways and means for effecting a radical change in the views, feelings, and practices of society, respecting the sinfulness of war.

"We purpose to assail iniquity in high places and low, to apply our principles to all existing civil, political, legal, and ecclesiastical institutions. We shall employ lecturers, circulate tracts and publications, form societies, and petition our state and national governments in relation to the subject of Universal Peace."

It may be noted that twenty of the forty-four signers of the Declaration were women. The term "non-resistance" was more akin to nonviolence as used by Gandhi and Martin Luther

King, Jr., and did not imply being passive. Further, Garrison did not limit his views to the United States: "Our country is the world, our countrymen all mankind."

Garrison met with opposition from both the American Anti-Slavery Society and the American Peace Society for including women and for the term "non-resistance." Garrison stood up and spoke out women's rights (including suffrage), the abolition of slavery, and for perpetual peace. He was every bit a Peace Hero.

Adin Ballou

It remained for Adin Ballou (1803–90), a Universalist minister, to define "non-resistance" in his essay "Christian Non-Resistance": "Non-resistance announces the impossibility of overcoming evil with evil," he wrote, and the "principle of non-injury must be held inviolable."

Ballou, like Garrison, held non-resistance to be limited to the infliction of personal physical injury—the "sacrifice of life, breaking of bones, or mangling of the flesh." He certainly condoned and practiced moral resistance, considering it a duty to resist injustice and iniquity. But, what about ill-mannered children, the morally or intellectually deficient, the intoxicated, and the violently passionate? He said they should be kindly and noninjuriously prevented from inflicting injury to others. An evil man who is up to violent behavior or one who becomes passionate and dangerous thereby must be reproved, coerced, and restrained by noninjurious moral and physical force.

In the case of military threat, active moral non-resistance is to be employed, which then becomes the highest kind of resistance to evil. He is emphatic that a non-resistant "cannot be an officer or [even] a chaplain in the army, navy, militia of any nation, state, or chieftain."

Ballou was a cofounder of the New England Non-Resistant Society and was the force behind the Hopewell utopian community in Massachusetts. Through his sermons and writing he was also a significant influence on Leo Tolstoy.

He certainly was not passive in his life of non-resistance. Perhaps, if he called it nonviolent resistance less explication would have been needed. We acknowledge him as a Peace Hero.

Henry Richard

Henry Richard (1812–1888) was a Welsh minister, elected to the British Parliament, who was one of the first to advocate peace and international arbitration of disputes between and among nations. In Parliament, he became known as the "Apostle of Peace" long before there was a Nobel Peace Prize. He was also the secretary of the Peace Society in Great Britain for thirty-five years.

He also opposed slavery both in Britain and the US, though as a pacifist he could not support the American Civil War. He founded the Anti-Slavery Society.

Henry Richard was a worthy Peace Hero.

Henry David Thoreau

Henry David Thoreau (1817–1862) was a man of the 19th century. His judgements were shaped by the events of the time: slavery and the Civil War, the Mexican-American War, and Darwin's treatise on evolution. Thoreau is best remembered as a naturalist and for his living simply at Walden Pond, but he was a far more complex individual: he was a passionate abolitionist and advocate for justice in many domains.

His lecture, "Civil Disobedience (sometimes titled "On the Duty of Civil Disobedience"), delivered in 1848 and published the following year, had a profound effect on such figures as

Tolstoy, Gandhi, and Martin Luther King, Jr..

In "Civil Disobedience," he uses the Mexican-American War as a prime example of "the work of a few individuals using the standing government [and standing army] as their tool; for in the outset, the people would not have consented to this measure." He holds in contempt "the merchants and farmers here who are more interested in commerce and agriculture than they are in humanity, and are not prepared to do justice to the slave and to Mexico, cost what it may." He is absolute in his view that "the people must cease to hold slaves and to make war on Mexico, though it cost them their exigence …"

Alluding to his own imprisonment for failure to pay any tax to a government that follows unjust policies, he states, "Under a government which imprisons any unjustly, the true place for a just man is also in prison," and notes the unjust plight of the "fugitive slave, the Mexican prisoner, and the Indian."

Thoreau was a dedicated abolitionist: he participated in the Underground Railway and found legitimacy in John Brown's attack on the Arsenal at Harpers Ferry in his published essay, "The Last Days of John Brown."

He had already set down his principles eloquently in "Civil Disobedience": "Is there not a sort of blood shed when the conscience is wounded? Through this wound a man's real manhood and immortality flow out, and he bleeds to an everlasting death. I see this blood flowing now."

To the list of Thoreau's achievements as a pencil maker, a naturalist, an essayist and writer, philosopher, poet, fervent abolitionist, ethicist, and civil disobedient, we should add Peace Hero.

> Is your question Love?
> Daisies may say yes ... or no.
> Kindness is sure-fire!

Chapter 7

PEACE HEROES: 20TH CENTURY TO TODAY

Leo Tolstoy (1828–1910)

In 1885, well after *War and Peace* and *Anna Karenina* were completed, Tolstoy was taken by a spiritual epiphany which compelled him to oppose all violence, regardless of the reason, on a fundamental religious basis. He renounced establishment Christianity for a simpler Gospel based more directly on the words of Christ, particularly the Sermon on the Mount. In 1893 he published *The Kingdom of God Is Within You*, expressing the belief that "He is in me, and I in Him."

A few years later, in his little known "Letter to a Non-commissioned Officer," he attacks organized society as well as the Church: "...[S]oldiers are taught that it is right to kill people in certain cases and in war, while in the books admitted to be holy by those who teach, there is nothing like such a permission, but on the contrary, not only is all murder forbidden ... we are told not to do unto others what we do not wish done to us." He condemns governments directly: "The German government frightens its subjects about the Russians and French; the French government frightens its people about the Germans; the Russian government frightens its people about the French and the Germans; and that is the way with all governments. But neither the Germans, nor the Russians, nor the French desire to fight their neighbors and other people; but living in peace, they dread war more than anything else in the world ... war is an inevitable result of the existence of armies; and armies are only needed by governments in order to dominate their own working classes."

Tolstoy appeals to the noncommissioned officer as one of the "same peasants who are deprived of the land, the same strikers who want better wages, the same taxpayers who want to be rid of the taxes." He asks, "And why do these people shoot at their brothers?" He then answers the question at length: "Because it has been instilled in them that the oath they were obliged to take on entering the service is binding, and that, though it is generally wrong to murder people, it is right to do so at the command of their superiors.... However little education a man may have, he cannot but know that Christ did not sanction murder, but taught kindness, meekness, forgiveness of injuries, love of one's enemies—and therefore he cannot pledge himself in advance to kill all whom he may be ordered to kill."

Tolstoy then asks: "How can sensible people believe, as all now serving in the army have believed and still believe, such an evident fraud? The answer is that it is not this one fraud by itself that takes people in, but they have from childhood been deprived of the proper use of their reason by a whole series of frauds called the Orthodox Faith, which is nothing but the grossest idolatry. ... they are called on to enter the military service, where they are humbugged to any extent, being made to swear on the Gospels (in which swearing is prohibited), that they will do just what is forbidden in those Gospels, and then taught that to kill people at the word of those in command is not a sin, but that to refuse to submit to those in command is a sin."

Tolstoy ends with "And the will of God is not that we should fight and oppress the weak, but that we should acknowledge all men our brothers and should serve one another."

Tolstoy worked for universal peace and was a great influence on Mohandas Gandhi with his "Letter to a Hindu" in which he asks for "recognition of the truth that the law of human life is the law of love" as opposed to "the system of life built on the law of violence" that "has in our time reached an unbearable intensity."

Tolstoy is not only one of the greatest novelists of all time, he is unquestionably a Peace Hero.

William Randal Cremer (1828–1908)

Cremer was a trade unionist, an MP in the House of Commons, a pacifist, and a passionate advocate for the arbitration of international disputes.

Using his organizational skills, he co-founded the Interparliamentary Union and, with Frederic Passy, the International Arbitration League. He helped resolve several disputes between nations. He also promoted the Hague Conferences at the turn of the century. Cremer passionately believed that the only proper political structure for mankind was peace, and that arbitration was the way it could be achieved. In 1903, he was chosen the Nobel Peace Laureate. William Randal Cremer deserves to be remembered as a Peace Hero.

Mark Twain

Mark Twain (né Samuel Clemens, 1835–1910) is a major figure in American Literature. Who does not know of *The Adventures of Tom Sawyer*, *The Adventures of Huckleberry Finn*, *Life on the Mississippi*, and *A Connecticut Yankee in King Arthur's Court*?

As a young man, Twain worked as a newspaper correspondent, and traveled widely across the country and around the world. Later he was a sought-after speaker, storyteller, and humorist/satirist, often all three at a time. Around the turn of the century, after his return from a European tour, he became immersed in politics. He had entirely supported the American side in the brief Spanish-American War, but the Philippine-American War was another story. He wrote, "I have read carefully the Treaty of Paris, and I have seen that we do not intend to free, but to subjugate the people of the Philippines. We have gone there to conquer, not to redeem."

He became an ardent anti-imperialist, joining the American Anti-Imperialist League and writing many political essays and pamphlets for the organization. One of the pieces, "Incident in the Philippines," was his response to the Moro Crater massacre, a shameful part of US history. Twain was an equal opportunity anti-imperialist. In "Following the Equator," he turned his satire on England's Cecil Rhodes and Belgium's Leopold II. In "King Leopold's Soliloquy" he quotes Leopold that bringing Christianity to the country outweighs a little starvation. [Leopold was not trying to be a satirist.]

In 1905 he submitted a story entitled "The War Prayer" to *Harper's Bazaar*, but it was rejected as unsuitable for a woman's magazine. Twain predicted that it would remain unpublished in his lifetime because "None but the dead are permitted to tell the truth." It finally was published posthumously in an anthology in 1923, and then republished in support of protests against the Vietnam-American War. Several of the lines will give some idea of the power of the writing.

> "The War Prayer"
>
> It was a time of great and exalting excitement. The country was up in arms, the war was on, in every breast burned the holy fire of patriotism…in the churches

the pastors preached devotion to flag and country, and invoked the God of Battles beseeching His aid in our good cause in outpourings of fervid eloquence which moved every listener. ...

Sunday morning came—next day the battalions would leave for the front; the church was filled; the volunteers were there, their young faces alight with martial dreams... The service proceeded; a war chapter from the Old Testament was read; the first prayer was said; it was followed by an organ burst that shook the building... Then came the "long" prayer. None could remember the like of it for passionate pleading and moving and beautiful language....

An aged stranger entered with slow and noiseless step up the main aisle, his eyes fixed on the minister, his long body clothed in a robe that reached to his feet, his head bare, his white hair descending in a frothy cataract to his shoulders, his seamy face pale, pale even to ghastliness. With all eyes following him and wondering, he made his silent way; without pausing, he ascended to the preacher's side and stood there waiting.... The stranger touched his arm, motioned him to step aside—which the startled minister did—and took his place. During some moments he surveyed the spellbound audience with solemn eyes, in which burned an uncanny light; then in a deep voice he said: "I come from the Throne—bearing a message from Almighty God!"

The words smote the house with a shock; if the stranger perceived it he gave no attention. "He has heard the prayer of His servant, your shepherd, and will grant it if such be your desire after I, His messenger, shall have explained to you its import, its full import....

God's servant and yours has prayed his prayer. Is it one prayer? No, it is two—one uttered, the other not. Both have reached the ear of Him Who heareth all supplications, the spoken and the unspoken....

You have heard your servant's prayer—the uttered part of it. I am commissioned of God to put into words the other part of it—that part which the pastor and also you in your hearts fervently prayed silently.... Upon the listening, the spirit of God fell upon the unspoken part of the prayer. He commandeth me to put it into words. Listen!

"O Lord, our Father, our young patriots, idols of our hearts, go forth to battle—be Thou near them We also go forth from the sweet peace of our firesides to smite the foe. O Lord our God, help us to tear their soldiers to bloody shreds with our shells; help us to cover their smiling fields with the pale forms of their patriot dead; help us to drown the thunder of the guns with the shrieks of their wounded, writhing in pain; help us lay waste their humble homes with a hurricane of fire; help us wring the hearts of their unoffending widows with unavailing grief; help us to turn them out roofless with little children to wander unfriended the wastes of their desolated land, in rags and hunger and thirst, in the sun flames of summer and the icy winds of winter, broken in spirit, worn with travail, imploring Thee for the refuge of the grave and denied it.For our sakes who adore Thee, Lord, blast their hopes, blight their lives, protract their bitter pilgrimage, make heavy their steps, water their way with their tears, stain the white snow with the blood of their wounded feet! We ask it, in the spirit of love of Him who is the Source of Love, and who is the ever faithful refuge and friend of all that are sore beset and seek His aid with humble and contrite hearts. Amen.

(After a pause) Ye have prayed it; if ye still desire it, speak! The messenger of the Most High waits!"

In the last ten years of his life Mark Twin became a Peace Hero. His satirical essay, "The War Prayer," remains a brilliant and powerful argument for Peace, for all time.

William James

William James (1842–1910) was an American philosopher and psychologist who is often considered part of the peace movement of the late 1800s and early 1900s. He himself wrote that he was a pacifist, and in 1898 he joined the Anti-Imperialist League which opposed the annexation of the Philippines. But his books and papers are almost entirely on philosophical and psychological subject matter.

His status as a Peace Hero is founded upon his essay "The Moral Equivalent of War," first given as a speech at Stanford University in 1906 and published as an essay in 1910 by the Association of International Conciliation. However, at the very beginning he states his belief that "military feelings are too deeply grounded to abdicate their place among our ideals"; a bit further on he continues, "Our ancestors have bred pugnacity into our bone and marrow, and thousands of years of peace won't breed it out of us. ... [I]nordinate ambitions are the soul of every patriotism, and the possibility of violent death the soul of all romance." He avers that "Militarism is the great preserver of our ideals of hardihood, and human life with no use for hardihood would be contemptible."

Then James offers us a substitute for war: a conscription of young men into activities such as in "coal and iron mines, freight trains, fishing fleets in December, dishwashing, clothes washing, road building, tunnel making foundries, and the frames of skyscrapers—according to their choice—to get the childishness knocked out of them and to come back to society with healthier sympathies and soberer ideas. They would be better fathers and teachers of the following generations. The martial character would be bred without war."

Was William James a Peace Hero? "The Moral Equivalent of War," the only piece of his entire writing oeuvre that speaks to war and peace, is somewhat flawed in its underlying tenets. Yet it did energize the peace movement. We may fairly say he was a small case peace hero.

Bertha von Suttner

Bertha von Suttner (1843–1914) was an Austrian journalist, novelist, and pacifist, and above all a peace organizer. As a young woman, titled Countess Bertha Kinsky, she briefly became a secretary to Alfred Nobel but left to marry Baron Arthur von Suttner. The two left Austria to live in the Russian Caucasus, and together were voracious readers on serious subjects. Bertha was particularly impressed by Charles Darwin, the social evolutionist Herbert Spencer, philosopher Ernest Renan, and Hodgson Pratt, who founded the International Arbitration and Peace Association. The couple came to see that society could produce great progress by achieving peace.

In their first decade together, Arthur began to establish himself as a journalist, and Bertha, following his success, began writing as well. With the publication of her *Inventory of a Soul* (*Inventarium einer Seele*) she became noticed in literary circles. The couple returned to Austria, and she became a recognized and acclaimed author with the publication of *Daniela Dormes* and *The Machine Age* (*Das Maschinenzeitalter*).

The von Suttners then moved to Paris, where Bertha was reintroduced to Alfred Nobel, with whom she carried on a correspondence and maintained a friendship until his death in 1896. She is credited with convincing him to establish the Peace Prize in his will.

While in Paris, von Suttner became aware of the work of the International Arbitration and Peace Association and was inspired to use her literary talents to advance the cause of peace. She soon began work on what was to become her best-known novel, *Die Waffen Nieder* (*Lay Down Your Arms*). Despite many requests for revisions to make the controversial anti-war subject more acceptable, the book was finally released under the original title. It created a sensation, receiving praise from Leo Tolstoy and other luminaries, and became a best-seller. She became the editor of the new pacifist journal, titled, like the book, *Die Waffen Nieder.*

Bertha von Suttner became an internationally known leader of the worldwide peace movement. She founded the Austrian Peace Society, then the German Peace Society. She urged Emperor Franz Joseph of Austria to establish an International Court of Justice. She attended the 1899 Hague Peace Conference as a one-woman nonstate actor (NGO), and lobbied for such an International Court. The Conference established a Convention on the Pacific Settlement of Disputes which resulted in the Permanent Court of Arbitration.

For many years she also worked at the local level before audiences in many cities in both Europe and America. In 1905 she was awarded the Nobel Peace Prize for her unceasing work to bring peace to the world. At the Second Hague Peace Conference in 1907, she presented the Austrian Resolution supporting the pacific resolution of disagreements. Her young German-American protégée, Anna B. Eckstein, had collected two million signatures for "The World Petition to Prevent War between Nations," which was presented to the Conference. In 1911, at the age of 68, von Suttner was appointed to the Carnegie Endowment's Advisory Council.

Bertha von Suttner was a Peace Hero in her own time and an exemplar for all ages until world peace is achieved.

Peter (Pyotr) Kropotkin

Born into a family of nobility and privilege—as a child, he was called Prince Pyotr—during the reign of Tsar Alexander II, Pytor Kropotkin (1842–1921) was an unlikely radical and revolutionary. In his early teenage years, he refused the title of "Prince," yet, he served in the Tsar's Corp of Pages. At 18, he was chosen to enter the Army and selected as Attaché for Cossack Affairs to the governor of a province in Siberia.

Within two years, he was asked to direct a geographic survey expedition in Manchuria up to the Amur River. Along with his geographical work, he made many observations of the people who lived in Siberia. Those extensive observations became integral to his thesis on the cooperative and social nature of mankind.

After much observation of many villages, towns, and central governments throughout Europe, plus the study of ancient history, Kropotkin came to the belief that cooperation—mutual aid—was a large part of the Law of Nature, as it applies to mankind as well as most animal species.

In his writings, he puts forward the case for anarchism—not bomb throwing, but the social structure of society without need for the authority of state government. In his book, *Mutual Aid: A Factor of Evolution*, he writes of harmony among people, not by law but by free agreements between groups for the infinite needs of civilized beings. He asks what relevance is found in such vague formulas as "the right to work" or "to each the whole result of his labor," and proclaims, instead, "the Right to Well Being for All."

Throughout the book, he speaks occasionally of war, laying war at the feet of (in a loose paraphrase) quarreling kings, robbers, and tyrannical oppressors who leave the people with only blood and fire. Yet the nucleus of mutual aid institutions, habits, and customs grown up in the tribe and village keeps men united in societies, open to receive civilization, instead of bullets and a war of each against all. Many medieval cities and towns in Italy and in Germany formed leagues to maintain peace and protect their citizens against the wanton plunder of knights and nobles who lived high on the goods and riches thus obtained. Some leagues, further, formed peace districts.

It was all in illustration of mutual aid as a factor in evolution of mankind. Over a century ago, Pyotr Kropotkin presented a strong case that cooperation & peace was as much a part of our genetic heritage as is ego and individuality. It is a more than sufficient reason to include Pyotr Kropotkin as a Peace Hero.

Randolph Bourne

Randolph Bourne lived a mere 32 years (1886–1918), but he made good use of his short life with relentless, scathing criticism of the war-based state and the intellectuals who supported the US entry into the Great War (WW I).

In his essay, "The War and the Intellectuals," he disturbed the self-contentedness of John Dewey, his former mentor at Columbia University, and the other intellectuals who supported Woodrow Wilson's crusade to enter the war. He wrote that within his own lifetime "neutrality was a proud thing" and that the intellectuals could have been "endeavoring to clear the public mind of the great cant of war … they scarcely tried."

He continued: "It is not so much what they thought as

how they felt that explains our intellectual class. ... It reduced to rubbish most of the humanitarian internationalism and democratic nationalism which had been the emotional thread of our intellectuals' life." He exclaimed, "Of all the socialists, the college professors, and the practitioners of literature, their mental conflicts have been resolved much more simply. War in the interests of democracy!" He further accuses them of "primitive ways of thinking" and "easy rationalization."

Bourne concludes that the real enemy is "War rather than imperial Germany." He expresses a slight hope withal: "There must be some to call unceasingly for peace, and some to insist that the terms of settlement shall be not only liberal but democratic.... There must be some intellectuals who are not willing ... to support a peace which would leave all the old inflammable materials of armament lying about in the world."

In Bourne's long essay, "The State," not yet fully complete at the time of his death in 1918, he put into writing the differences between and among state, nation and country, government, and administration: "In our quieter moments, the Nation or Country forms the basic idea of society... Our idea of Country concerns itself with the nonpolitical aspects of a people, its ways of living, its personal traits, its literature and art, its characteristic attitudes toward life. We are Americans because we live in certain bounded territory, because our ancestors carried on a great enterprise of pioneering and colonization, because we live in certain kinds of communities which have a certain look and express their aspirations in certain ways. We can see that our civilization is different from contiguous civilizations like the Indian or the Mexican.

"The feeling for Country would be an uninflatable maximum were it not for the ideas of State and Government which are associated with it. Country is a concept of peace and tolerance, of live and let live. But State is a concept of power, of competition; it signifies a group in its aggressive aspects. And we have the misfortune of being born not only into a country but into a State, and as we grow up we learn to mingle the two feelings into hopeless confusion.

"Government on the other hand is synonymous with neither State nor Nation... Government is a frame work of the administration of laws, and the carrying out of the public force. Government is the idea of the State put into practical operation in the hands of definite, concrete, fallible men.

"Wartime brings the idea of the State out into very clear relief, and reveals attitudes and tendencies that were hidden. In times of peace the sense of the State flags in a republic that is not militarized. For war is essentially the health of the State.

"The triumphant orthodoxy of the State is shown at its apex perhaps when Christian preachers lose their pulpits for taking in more or less literal terms the Sermon on the Mount, and Christian zealots are sent to prison for distributing tracts which argue that war is unscriptural.

"War is the health of the State. It automatically sets in motion throughout society those irresistible forces for uniformity, for passionate cooperation with the Government in coercing into obedience the minority groups and individuals which lack the herd instinct... Minorities are rendered sullen, and some intellectual

> Basic Bombs
> Weapons less
> than elegant —
> but ably
> tearing limbs and
> trunks as if
> bricks and mortar.
> Long whistles
> then crashes near
> and far, to
> strike when and where
> as tokens
> of chance. These wars
> of no rules
>
> but precedents.

opinion becomes bitter and satirical. ... Loyalty—or mystical devotion to the State—becomes the major imagined human value. Other values such as artistic creation, knowledge, reason, beauty, the enhancement of life, are instantly and almost unanimously sacrificed.

Thus arises conflict within the State... The pursuit of enemies within outweighs in psychic attractiveness the assault on the enemy without... A white terrorism is carried out by the government against pacifists, socialists, enemy aliens, and a milder persecution against all persons or movements that can be imagined as connected with the enemy... The punishment for opinion has been more ferocious and unintermittent than the punishment of pragmatic crime.

"It cannot be too firmly realized that war is a function of States and not of Nations, indeed that it is the chief function of States. War is a very artificial thing... War cannot exist without a military establishment, and a military establishment cannot exist without a State organization... The State is not the Nation and the State can be modified or even abolished in its present form without harming the Nation. On the contrary, with the passing of the dominance of the State, the genuine life-enhancing forces of the Nation will be liberated.

"The American President himself, the liberal hope of the World, has demanded, in the eyes of the world, open diplomacy, agreements freely and openly arrived at. Did this mean a genuine transference of power in this most crucial of State functions from government to people? Not at all... For the last stronghold of State power is foreign policy... Certain of the Administration measures were devised directly to increase the health of the State, such as the Conscription and Espionage laws.

"A distinction is made between the Administration and the Government. It is quite accurately suggested by this attitude that the Administration is a temporary band of partisan politicians in charge of the machinery of the mystical policy of State... The inextricable union of militarism and the State is beautifully shown by those laws which emphasize interference with the Army and Navy as the most culpable of seditious crimes... Fifteen or twenty years in prison is not deemed too much for such sacrilege.

"There is no natural sanctity in the State any more than there is in the weather... not because there is anything reverential in the institution worshipped... The sanctity of the State becomes identified with the sanctity of the ruling class, and the latter are permitted to remain in power under the impression that in obeying and serving them, we are obeying and serving society, the nation, the great collectivity of all of us."

Randolph Bourne lived a short but white-hot life of commentary on the political social scene of the time. But, it may be applied to all wars of the United States throughout the 20th century to the present. Bourne lived as a Peace Hero during his own time and into the future.

Jane Addams

Jane Addams (1860–1935) was born to privilege and could work in any discipline she chose, or none at all. In the time she lived, three different ones chose her.

In the late 19th and early 20th centuries, women started agitating seriously for women's rights in every area of society. Addams was an ardent feminist and supported women's rights as she took part in strong advocacy positions on different political and social issues.

During a trip to England she visited Toynbee Hall, a new concept for socially conscious America. She was so impressed that on her return to the US, she looked into copying the

British model in a needful neighborhood in Chicago. In 1889, she established Hull House, the first Settlement House in the New World. Hull House grew in size and services, and by her example, the profession of Social Work was established.

With the success of Hull House, Addams turned her energies to opposing war. In 1898, the brief war with Spain resulted in Spanish withdrawal from Cuba, Puerto Rico, Guam, and the Philippines. Cuba became independent as a result of the many-faceted revolutionary efforts of José Martí and a strong Cuba Libre movement. The US annexed Puerto Rico and Guam but, in attempting to exert political control over the Philippines, met with a deep-rooted revolutionary movement against Spain that had started years before. Jane Addams opposed the US attempt at annexation, expressing her belief that women had a special duty to preserve peace.

That was just the beginning of her peace work worldwide. She gave many speeches on ending war, and in 1907 her book, *Newer Ideals of Peace*, was published. She opposed US entry into World War I, and from 1919 to 1929 was president of the Women's International League for Peace and Freedom. For her opposition to US involvement in WW I, she was considered not only unpatriotic but a dangerous radical, and was expelled from the Daughters of the American Revolution. Along with expulsion, DAR issued an extensive dossier on Addams as a radical pacifist. A few other matters of peace in Jane Addams's portfolio were: membership in the National Women's Peace Party; membership in the notorious ACLU in the company of Scott Nearing, Norman Thomas, A. J. Muste, and Eugene Debs; membership in the Fellowship of Reconciliation; participation in the American Neutral Conference; author of *Peace and Bread in Time of War*. She also worked with President Calvin Coolidge to prohibit the use of poison gas and exploding bullets, and to outlaw war.

Finally in 1931, she received an overdue Nobel Peace Prize. There can be no argument that Jane Addams should be prominently listed as a Peace Hero.

Emily Greene Balch

Emily Greene Balch (1867–1961) was a well-educated young woman who grew up in circumstances of affluence, but she did not rest easy. She started her career in education and by 1913 rose to the position of Professor of Sociology and economics at Wellesley. Along the way, she earned a fellowship to study economics in France. As a result of those studies, she assembled ideas and solutions to alleviate poverty and suffering in her book *Public Assistance of the Poor in France*, published in 1893. She went on to become an advocate for workers, women, children, and immigrants.

In 1903 she cofounded the Women's Trade Union League of Boston. In 1910, she wrote *Our Slavic Fellow Citizens*, based on her own original work with immigrants from Austria and Hungary.

Then, beginning in 1914, came the Great War (WW I). The following year she traveled to The Hague, where she was a delegate to the International Congress of Women, some of whose members thereafter formed the International League for Peace and Freedom (WILPF), still going strong today.

Prominent among Balch's fellow WILPF founders were Jane Addams and Alice Hamilton; together the three women co-authored the extensive report, *Women at the Hague: The International Congress of Women and Its Results*.

Balch was already a full professor at Wellesley, but her peace activities and her opposition to the US entering the war earned her the label of "dangerous peace radical." Her contract with the college was not renewed.

In 1918 her book *Approaches to the Great Settlement* was

published. Throughout the Great War, she personally tried to persuade neutral governments to intervene, stop the war, and work for a fair settlement.

In the late nineteen-thirties, thinking her peace work had been done, she prepared the manuscript of a book of poetry, *The Miracle of Living*, which was published in 1941. But once again a world war left her no rest. The US entered the war that year, and she "went through a long and painful struggle, [but never] reached a clear and consistent conclusion." She did not oppose America's entry into the war, yet she worked for refugee resettlement internationally, opposed interment of Japanese-Americans, and supported conscientious objectors (COs).

In 1946, at age 79, she was awarded the Nobel Peace Prize, an honor never recognized by the US government, not even a simple congratulations. Undeterred, she nominated Mohandas Gandhi for the Peace Prize It was the last of five nominations he had received, but again, he was denied.

Here, we will offer a final tribute to Emily Greene Balch as a Peace Hero.

Mohandas K. Gandhi (1869–1948)

Educated in England as a lawyer, Gandhi developed a successful practice in South Africa but gave it up to return to his native India; there he became the ascetic Gandhi we all know. He eschewed Western ways beginning in the early 1900s and, not many years thereafter, organized a satyagraha (truth force) movement and ashram to advance India's independence. He viewed nonviolence as a way of life and as a political tool, urging protesters to use civil noncooperation and disobedience to achieve their goals.

In 1921 Gandhi's essay, "Disaffection a Virtue," promoting those approaches, appeared in *Young India*. He and the editor, S.

Banker, were arrested and put on trial for spreading hatred and contempt for the British government by preaching disaffection and encouraging much civil disobedience.

In his opening remarks before the court, Gandhi was unequivocal about the ways disaffection should be expressed: "I wanted to avoid violence. Nonviolence is the first article of my faith. It is also the last article of my creed."

In the statement that followed, he recalled his initial voluntary and hearty cooperation, both in South Africa, then England, and finally in the early years after his return to India. But, then in 1919, the Rowlatt Act was passed, which allowed the government to imprison anyone without a trial, and Gandhi changed his position completely to one of total opposition. He condemned the denial of justice in the Punjab under the imposition of martial law following the 1919 massacre at Jallianwala Barg; he accused the British Indian government of destroying the widespread cottage industry that had once supplied the populace with fabric and clothing, reducing them to poverty; and he held them responsible for widespread semi-starvation among the masses.

The judge gave Gandhi a sentence of six years of "simple imprisonment."

In another essay, "The Doctrine of the Sword," Gandhi had addressed strength, fear, cowardice, and forgiveness. He wrote, "Strength does not come from physical capacity [or weapons].... I believe that non-violence is infinitely superior to violence and forgiveness is more manly than punishment.... We in India may in a moment realize that 100,000 Englishmen need not frighten 300 million human beings.... I do not believe India to be helpless ... and forgiveness would therefore mean definite recognition of our strength.... And so I am not pleading for India to practice non-violence because it is weak. I want her to practice nonviolence conscious of her strength and power. No training in arms is required for realization of her strength.

"The religion of non-violence is not meant for the Rishis and saints. It is meant for the common people as well. Non-violence is the law of our species as violence is the law of the brute.... The dignity of man requires obedience to a higher law—to the strength of the spirit."

Mohandas Gandhi saw the end of colonial rule in the Indian subcontinent in 1947. He was a Peace Hero not only in his own time but for all time.

George Bernard Shaw

George Bernard Shaw (1856–1950) lived at a time of enormous changes in the world. Yet many realities of social, political, and moral nature are not very different today. He used his talent as a writer to weigh in on a wide variety of issues, as diverse as the hypocrisies of society and the staging of Shakespeare's plays.

He achieved worldwide fame, and the Nobel Prize in Literature, as a playwright. His other activities regarding many economic, political, and moral matters dwelled in the shadow of his prodigious output of plays. As a socialist, he was a charter member of the Fabian Society and wrote and spoke in their behalf on political and economic theory and practice. He was instrumental in establishing the London School of Economics and Political Science, a major institution today for study of the social sciences and international affairs. He was one of the founders of *The New Statesman*, a progressive intellectual journal, both then and now.

In addition, he used his expressive talents and none-too-subtle wit to oppose war in general and, in 1914, the Great War in particular. His articles were published prominently in British and American newspapers, among them: "Common Sense About the War," "The Peace of Europe and How to Achieve It," and "An Open Letter to the President of the United States of America." He addressed the Fabian Society several times.

Nor did he hold his tongue until 1914. In 1894, he wrote the now classic *Arms and the Man*, a farce set at the time of the Bulgarian-Serbian war of 1885. Predictably, it ridiculed both war and romantic ideals of love.

A few quotations from his writing will leave no doubt as to where he stood. From *Arms and the Man*:

> *My rank is the highest known in Switzerland: I am a free citizen.*
>
> *War as a school of character and as a nurse of virtue must be formally shut up and discharged when this war is over.*
>
> *Militarism is not to be treated as a disease peculiar to Prussia. It is rampant in England and France ...*
>
> *... my insistence that this war was an imperialist war and popular only in so far as all wars are, for a time, popular ...*
>
> *... the obsolescence and colossal stupidity of modern war.*

We should not hold George Bernard Shaw to task as an anti-war activist and peacemaker, and deny him his success as a playwright. He deserves listing as a Peace Hero, as well.

Bertrand Russell

For just two small islands off the Atlantic coast of Europe, England and Ireland have produced an inordinate number of remarkable individuals, among them artists, inventors, physicists, poets, and philosophers. Bertrand Russell (1872–1970) was in good company. He was a leading mathematician, philosopher, and writer of the 20th century.

His *Principles of Mathematics* of 1903, which equated mathematics with logic, led to a collaboration with Alfred North Whitehead in the now classic *Mathematica Principia* published in three volumes from 1910 to 1913.

With the advent of WW I, his activities as a social critic markedly increased. He was a Socialist, having joined the Fabian Society in 1914, and was outspokenly opposed to the war. In 1916, the Military Service Act was passed, and Russell, who had played a key role in the No Conscription Fellowship, was accused and convicted of violating the Defense of the Realm Act. In 1918 he was sent to jail for six months for the conviction.

In the 1920s, Russell joined other worldwide notables in opposing injustice wrought by the US government in the murder trial of anarchists Sacco and Vanzetti.

In the '30s, he returned to philosophy with two publications, *The Conquest of Happiness* and *Religion and Science*, and began work on *A History of Western Philosophy*.

The 1940s, World War II, and the use of atomic bombs on Hiroshima and Nagasaki seemed to bring about aberrant thinking in Bertrand Russell. On the one hand, he spoke before the House of Lords and warned about the enormously destructive power of nuclear bombs, especially the hydrogen bomb, as was soon enough demonstrated at Bikini atoll. He predicted that the Russians would soon have them, too, and supported the Baruch Plan for an International Atomic Authority. In a speech he gave in 1948, however, he noted the aggressive actions of the Soviet Union in Eastern Europe and advised that the Western Alliance act while the US was the only nation that possessed the atomic bomb. Some interpreted that speech as advocating first use by the West in a war with the USSR; others interpreted the speech to suggest that the

A-bomb would just be a deterrent. Russell published articles and wrote letters, though, presenting the position that the US would be justified in using the bomb in a conflict with the USSR. The question became moot when the Soviets tested an atomic explosive device in 1949, and Russell changed his position to one of abolition of all nuclear weapons. Thereafter, he became more and more resolute that nuclear weapons presented the greatest danger the world has ever faced.

In 1955, he wrote to Albert Einstein, "War may well mean the extinction of life on this planet." He added the simple deduction in an age of nuclear weapons that nations must learn to live in peace. Einstein said he agreed. Russell drafted a statement of purpose, which he tried to persuaded other leading scientists to sign. Einstein signed it just before his death. So did nine other illustrious scientists, representing six nations. The Einstein-Russell Manifesto, as it became known, started worldwide momentum to ban nuclear weapons. There followed the Mainau Declaration of 1957, organized by Otto Hahn and Max Born and signed by eighteen Nobel Laureates. Also in 1957, the Pugwash Conferences were founded by Joseph Rotblat and Bertrand Russell; the Campaign for Nuclear Disarmament was led in the US by Linus Pauling. For their efforts, Rotblat and Pauling were each awarded a Nobel Peace Prize.

In 1963 Russell also established the Bertrand Russell Peace Foundation. In 1966, he wrote *Peace Through Resistance To US Imperialism* and called for a War Crimes Tribunal to accuse the US of war crimes in Vietnam. Over the next two years Russell and Jean Paul Sartre organized such an International Tribunal and formally accused the United States of many war crimes committed in Vietnam. The proceedings were published in *Against the Crime of Silence*.

At age 98, Russell publicly condemned Israel's aggression

against the Palestinians, despite his early support of statehood for Israel in 1943, and sent it to the International Conference of Parliamentarians in Cairo in February 1970.

Let us forgive Bertrand Russell for his short lapse in moral thinking within a long life devoted not only to mathematics and philosophy but to social and political activism. He opposed war as early as WW I and as late as the Vietnam-American war. In his last twenty years he worked incessantly to abolish nuclear weapons. He is deserving of designation as a Peace Hero.

Vera Brittain

Vera Brittain (1893–1970) was an unlikely peace activist-to-be. In 1914 she was a 21-year-old whose close circle of friends included her brother Edward and their three best friends Roland, Victor, and Geoffrey. When the Great War broke out, the four young men patriotically enlisted and left Vera to herself in college. After completing only one year, she left her studies in English Literature to become a Voluntary Aid Detachment (VAD) nurse.

She kept up a correspondence with the four, and solidified her affection for Roland, and he with her, by becoming engaged. Roland was the first of the four to be killed in action (their deaths came in 1915, 1917, 1917, and 1918). Vera's journals voiced her anger and agony and expressed her disillusionment in the best way she knew.

Her book of poetry, *Verses of a VAD*, was the beginning of her antiwar conversion. Four years later, she followed with a novel, *Dark Tide*. Then, she published *Testament of Youth*, her memoir of the war years and the difficult times that followed. The poignant expression of her personal pain and the betrayal of the youth of the nation struck a nerve with the public, and the book became a best seller. Vera became a sought-after speaker who could tell of her first-hand experiences along with the stories of the "lost generation" and of the futility of war.

In 1937, she joined The Peace Pledge Union and spoke to as many audiences as possible about her personal losses and the horrors of war for society. She lent her then well-known name in support of conscientious objectors, much to the dismay of both the British and German governments.

War broke out again in 1939, and the US joined the Allied side in 1941. After the Allies started a campaign of saturation bombing of German cities that resulted in the deaths of many civilians, she became vociferous in her condemnation of the mass bombings. She published a small book, *Seed of Chaos: What Mass Bombing Really Means*, published in the United States under the title *Massacre By Bombing*, which earned her the enmity of both governments and the charge of disloyalty. Brittain contributed regularly to *Peace News* magazine, often focusing on the special responsibility of women and on the need for nuclear disarmament.

Vera Brittain's life and her book, *Testament of Youth*, has, in the 21st century, been adapted for film. But she was a Peace Hero in her own lifetime.

Wilfred Owen

Wilfred Owen (1893–1918) was brought up in the tradition of the English Romantic Poets, and as a young man his own poetry reflected their style. In 1915 he took a break from poetry and enlisted in the Officers Training Corps; two years later he received a commission as a 2nd lieutenant with the Manchester Regiment serving in France. In combat on the front lines, he suffered a concussion and was additionally diagnosed with "shell shock." He was sent back to England for treatment at a military hospital in Scotland. While recuperating there, he met follow poet Siegfried Sassoon.

Sassoon was only seven years older, but already well established and recognized as a war poet. He was happy to introduce Owen to the artistic and literary community in Edinburgh.

Owen so admired Sassoon's direct style of writing that his own poems took a sharp turn away from the Romantic and brought him to speak of the "Pity of War." Owen then addressed the horrific realities of war in new work much wider and deeper in implication, and often metaphorical, as well.

Owen's oeuvre of war poems was written in the briefest time, between August 1917 and September 1918. In that time, more than thirty intense poems that fit the genre of war poems (or, more accurately, antiwar poems) were composed, often with revisions.

A few of the titles will give some idea of the scope of the work: "Anthem for Doomed Youth"; "Dulce Et Decorum Est"; "Asleep"; "Mental Cases" (alternate title, "Deranged"); "Futility"; and "The Next War." Let's sample a few lines:

No mockeries now for them; no prayers nor bells,

Nor any voice of mourning save the choirs,

The shrill, demented choirs of wailing shells;

And bugles calling for them from sad shires.

— from "Anthem for Doomed Youth"

My friend, you would not tell with such high zest,–

To children ardent for some desperate glory,

The old lie: Dulce et decorum est

Pro patria mori.*

— from "Dulce Et Decorum Est"

*It is sweet and fitting to die for one's country.

We laughed, knowing that better men would come,
And greater wars; when each proud fighter brags
He wars on Death—for lives; not men—for flags.

— from "The Next War"

Although Wilfred Owen would spend the remainder of the war in the British Army, it could have been in England, safely away from the front lines. It is said he chose duty at the front, wanting to earn the Military Cross and thus be recognized as a war poet. Silly man—the Military Cross conveyed no skill in fine writing, and he already had the experience of the stinking trenches, the poison gas, and explosions of the shells, on which to draw. Perhaps he valued recognition as a "war poet" more than life itself.

We certainly recognize Wilfred Owen as a pre-eminent war poet. The effect of his poems on future generations of Brits and others is inestimable. Let us honor him with the further designation as Peace Hero.

Frank B. Kellogg

Frank Kellogg (1856–1937) was largely self educated, but he passed the bar in Minnesota and came to the notice of a cousin at an established law firm. With talent and a strong work ethic, he succeeded as a lawyer and was able to represent some major industries in Minnesota. Theodore Roosevelt asked him to prosecute a few industrial giants, such as the Union Pacific Railroad and Standard Oil, under the Sherman Anti-Trust Act. Much to everyone's surprise, the prosecutions were successful.

Kellogg entered politics as a Republican and was elected to the US Senate representing Minnesota. He was soon appointed Ambassador to Great Britain and then Secretary of State under Calvin Coolidge. As Secretary of State, he favored legal arbitration in international disputes between nations and signed many pacts and agreements.

He guided the 1928 Pact of Paris, which became known as the Kellogg-Briand Pact, to international affirmation and signature by sixty-two nations. In the US, it was signed by the President and ratified by the Senate by a vote of 85-1. It still stands as the law of the land, though few Americans alive today ever heard of the accord.

The Kellogg-Briand Pact, which outlawed war as an instrument of any nation's foreign policy, was considered so significant that Kellogg received the Nobel Peace Prize only one year after its adoption. That can be contrasted to other Peace Prize Laureates who had to wait an undue time until they were so recognized.

Kellogg received a final honor in his life when he was appointed as a Judge of the Permanent Court of International Justice. But, he always considered the Pact of Paris his greatest achievement. "I know of no greater work for humanity than in the cause of peace, which can only be achieved by the earnest efforts of nations and peoples." To note that favoring peace was not enough, he also said, "Competition in armament, both land and naval, is not only a terrible burden upon the people, but I believe it to be one of the greatest menaces to the peace of the world."

We concur, and name Frank B. Kellogg a Peace Hero.

Kathe Kollwitz

Kathe Kollwitz (1867–1945) was an artist who worked in many mediums including painting, drawing, sculpture, printmaking, etching, lithography, and woodcuts. Her work was in the style of the German Expressionists, with dark line and vivid contrast, and expressed strong emotion about several social and political issues.

She was well regarded in the art community and became the first woman elected to the Prussian Academy of Arts, an achievement that brought to her a paid position of instructor.

Her son had enlisted in the Army early in The Great War and was killed in 1914 at the front lines in Flanders, still just 18 years old. It was an event that sharpened Kollwitz's antiwar views and and influenced her artistic work.

She said, "The war has been going on for two years, and five million young men are dead and more than that number are miserable, their lives wrecked. Is there anything at all than can justify that?" She questioned further, "Has it been a case of mass madness?"

Kollwitz's life work in sculpture, drawing, and print making deeply expressed human emotion: suffering, sorrow, grief, hunger, and the plight of the poor. The titles she gave to some of the individual works are illustrative: a pair of sculptures titled *The Grieving Parents*, a series of seven woodcuts called *War*, a series of lithographs labeled *Death*, a poster titled "War – Never Again," a sculpture named *Mother with her Dead Son*, another, *Tower of Mothers*, of mothers protecting their children, and more than a dozen other works. She said, "I am in the world to change the world."

Kollwitz was recognized for her work throughout Germany and in Europe in her own lifetime. In the 1960s, especially in the US, she was also revered as a pacifist and antiwar activist.

For this thesis, Kathe Kollwitz is a true Peace Hero.

Will Rogers

Will Rogers (1879–1935) was an American original: a cowboy, newspaper columnist, movie star, folksy social commentator, and brilliant political wit and satirist. More notable quotes are attributed to Rogers than almost any other American, even his contemporary Mark Twain. If we include English-speaking notables, Shakespeare might provide a little competition.

Rogers was often ahead of his time, his earthy wisdom as relevant today as in the 1920s and '30s. One of his best-known quips, for example, is, "Everything is changing. People are taking their comedians seriously and the politicians as a joke."

Nor did war escape his pointed wit:

You can't say that civilization doesn't advance; for in every war they kill you in a new way.

Sometimes it takes two or three conferences to scare up a war, but generally only one will do it.

I have a scheme for stopping war. It is this—no nation is allowed to enter a war till they have paid for the last one.

There is two things that can disrupt business in this country. One is to enter a war and the other is a meeting of the Federal Reserve Bank.

People talk peace, but give their life work to war.

These five quotes were all that an extensive search turned up among more than a hundred otherwise memorable ones. They are clever, funny, and all too true. But, none condemn war for its human costs: the death, physical injury, and often long term mental & emotional harm. Nor are the costs to society addressed. Can we consider Will Rogers a peace hero? Perhaps a 5% Peace Hero.

Albert Einstein

Albert Einstein (1879–1955) was the most famous scientist in all the world over the last 100 years. As a theoretical physicist, he worked on scales very large—gravitation and light—and very small—the motion of molecules and particle theory. He developed the General Theory of Relativity and, in 1915, deservedly earned the Nobel Prize in physics. In 1921 he showed the power of turning matter into energy with the equation $E=MC^2$.

Yet he was a lifelong pacifist and found time to work for peace. He signed the Manifesto of the Peace Pledge Union in 1955, saying: "… educated people should use their influence to bring about a peace treaty that will not carry the seeds of future war." In 1922 he appeared publicly at a No More War rally. He renounced German citizenship in 1933 when Hitler came to power.

In 1955 he and Bertrand Russell issued the Russell-Einstein appeal: "We are speaking not as members of this nation or that nation, continent, or creed but as human beings, members of the species Man whose continued existence is in doubt." The statement goes on to discuss nuclear weapons and ends with a resolution that urges all governments of the world "to find peaceful means for the settlement of all matters of dispute among them."

The Appeal was so powerful that Linus Pauling and eight other prominent scientists asked to sign it. The Manifesto was a fitting capstone to Einstein's productive, world-changing life as a Peace Hero.

Smedley Butler

Gen'l Smedley Butler (1881–1940) was a commissioned officer in the US Marine Corps who rose through the ranks from 2nd Lieutenant to Major General. He was highly decorated for his leadership and bravery in action many times during his 33-year career, and by the time he retired, he had serious doubts about the purposes of war. He had seen up close the collusion between the government and the corporations that produced the weapons for wars and the banks that also profited from financing war. In 1935 he wrote *War Is a Racket*, which has as much relevance today as when it was written. He made many speeches railing against war profiteering and against Fascism. He knew war, first hand, for what it really was.

Smedley Butler must be counted a Peace Hero for all time, as much as he was a war hero during his career.

Jeannette Rankin (1880–1973)

In 1916, well before passage of the 19th Amendment giving American women the right to vote, Jeannette Rankin became the first to serve in Congress, elected at the age of 36 to represent Montana. She wasted no time in establishing herself by voting against US entry into WW I. As one of only fifty members of the House to vote "No," she was not too popular, even among her fellow suffragists, but one significant voice applauded her antiwar stand: Fiorello LaGuardia, also a congressman and later, famously, Mayor of New York City. After the vote she said, "I felt the first time a woman had a chance to say 'No' to war, she should say it."

After her term in Congress, Rankin continued her work for women's suffrage and against child labor. She worked as a field secretary for WILPF (Women's International League for Peace and Freedom) and started the Georgia Peace Society. She also advocated for an antiwar Constitutional Amendment. In 1937, she used her rhetorical skills to address many audiences about peace—93 speeches in ten states.

In 1940, Rankin again ran for Congress and was again elected to represent her district in Montana. In the House, she cast the only vote against declaring war on Japan, believing Roosevelt has provoked the Japanese.

She said in casting her lone "No" vote, "As a woman I can't go to war, and I refuse to send anyone else." The other four Congresswomen voted for declaring war.

In 1968, at the age of 88, she led the Jeannette Rankin Brigade, a coalition of women's peace groups who marched, 5,000 strong, from Union Station in Washington, DC, to the US Capitol, where they served House Speaker John McCormack (Mass) with a petition against the war in Vietnam.

Another couple of her statements confirm Jeannette Rankin as an autocrat of peace partisans:

> "You can no more win a war than you can win an earthquake.
>
> "There can be no compromise with war: it cannot be reformed or controlled; cannot be disciplined into decency or codified into common sense; for war is the slaughter of human beings, temporarily regarded as enemies, on as large a scale as possible."

Jeannette Rankin—suffragist, social worker, member of Congress, and pacifist—deserves the title of Peace Hero. Today, the Jeannette Rankin Peace Center continues her work from Montana.

Linus Pauling (1901–1994)

Linus Pauling was one of the most innovative chemists of the 20th century. By using the principles of quantum mechanics, He was able to define the electronic structure of atoms and the bonds between the atoms of molecules. His book, *The Nature of the Chemical Bond and the Structure of Molecules and Crystals*, published in 1939, became the standard text in the field of inorganic chemistry.

During the late 1930s, Pauling became interested in the

structure of organic molecules, and from the '40s worked on the structure of proteins. In the '50s, his interest in and work on the structure of nuclei brought him to a cluster-of-nucleons model, which became accepted in scientific circles.

Even as he made ground-breaking discoveries and published many papers in the scientific literature, the US was evolving a war culture and war economy. The Manhattan Project, brought to a culmination at Hiroshima and Nagasaki in 1945, engaged his attention and moral sensibilities. His wife, Ava, was a pacifist and would not have let him escape into his work anyway. In 1946, he joined Einstein's Emergency Committee of Atomic Scientists in opposition to nuclear weapons and, more widely, to war itself. Thereafter, he signed the Russell-Einstein Manifesto and the Mainau Declaration.

Pauling also calculated the frequency of congenital deformities to be expected from the radioactive chemicals released into the atmosphere in nuclear testing, and then publicized the results across the entire United States. In 1958, he gathered signatures from over 10,000 scientists in fifty nations on a petition opposing nuclear weapons testing, and presented it publicly to Secretary General Dag Hammarskjold at the United Nations. The same year his book *No More War* was published.

Pauling supported the work of fellow activist Barry Commoner and the Citizens Committee for Nuclear Information, which published a study of Strontium-90 in baby teeth resulting from nuclear testing. Wide publicity of the study and heightened public pressure helped lead to the subsequent Test Ban Treaties ending atmospheric testing of atomic and nuclear bombs (though underground and undersea testing continued.

Pauling had received the Nobel Prize for Chemistry in 1954. Then, in 1962, in recognition of his efforts to end nuclear testing and to banish war entirely, he was awarded the

Nobel Peace Prize. We can do no less than count Linus Pauling as a Peace Hero.

Joseph (Josef) Rotblat

Joseph Rotblat, born in 1908, lived through both World Wars and well into the nuclear age, dying in 2005 at age 96. His expertise in nuclear physics and his work on the Manhattan Project—until 1944, when he resigned—eminently prepared him to become the conscience of the world.

Rotblat, an innovative physicist, had shown as early as 1939 that during the process of fusion, uranium atoms released neutrons from their nuclei, freeing considerable energy. He calculated that if many uranium atoms all underwent fusion in a fraction of a second, the result would be an enormous nuclear explosion. The possibility of Nazi Germany developing an atom bomb convinced Rotblat to accept an invitation to work on the Manhattan Project. In 1939, Rotblat was studying nuclear physics in England with Nobel Laureate James Chadwick. Rotblat's wife, Tola, planned to join her husband in Liverpool, but the outbreak of WW II trapped her in Warsaw. As a Jew, she was seized by the Germans and sent to the Majdanek concentration camp, where she later died. Joseph, meanwhile, received a fellowship and was able to remain in England, but the loss of his wife affected him deeply.

When invited to work on the Manhattan Project at the Los Alamos National Labs, he felt the need to win the race against the Nazis to develop a thermonuclear bomb, and so consented.

Physicists were in high demand at the Manhattan Project, and Rotblat was given a key role. But when, in 1944, it seemed certain that Germany would never develop an A-bomb, Rotblat resigned on grounds of conscience. Before leaving, he heard Gen. Leslie Groves, the Director of the Manhattan Project, mention in conversation that the bomb was no longer needed to defeat Germany or to avoid an invasion of the Japanese mainland, but to keep the Russians in line. Rotblat was shocked. The unneeded explosions of the uranium and plutonium bombs over Hiroshima and Nagasaki, respectively, turned Rotblat into a zealous campaigner against nuclear weapons and war itself. With one year, he had organized the British Atomic Scientists Association to oppose the use of science for such destructive purposes.

In 1955, he was an early signatory of the Russell-Einstein Manifesto. He was also the organizing force behind the Pugwash Conference on Science and World Affairs. The first meeting of the Pugwash Conference drew over 100 participants from more than 40 countries, several from the U.K., US, and USSR. Rotblat was the Pugwash Secretary General from 1957 to 1973. He also was the first to propose a Hippocratic Oath for all chemists, biochemists, and physicists. The wording of such an oath was thereafter offered by the Pugwash Conference to the Nuclear Age Peace Foundation and other peace groups.

Soon after the hydrogen bomb test at Bikini Atoll, Rotblat traveled to Japan and obtained first-hand reports from witnesses and samples of water from the site. He then calculated the power of the explosion to be 1,000 times as great as the Hiroshima uranium bomb. He brought this information to public attention; the media went to town with an Armageddon story by a nuclear physicist who had worked on the development of America's first atomic arms.

In the years from 1962 to 1964, he published four important papers on the harmful effects of radiation on amino acids (the building blocks of proteins), and in 1962 his book *Science and World Affairs* was published. In later books he addressed nuclear war more directly. All told, his papers and books on the dangers of nuclear radiation from testing and especially from nuclear war would fill a couple of library shelves.

In the 1990s, some half a century after Hiroshima was destroyed, he was recognized officially. In 1992, Rotblat was awarded the Einstein Peace Prize; in 1994, he was elected a Fellow of the Royal Academy, and in 1995, he received the Nobel Peace Prize. His Nobel Lecture informed the world of the danger that nuclear weapons could render the entire Earth uninhabitable. In 1998, he accepted a knighthood from the Queen of England with the citation, "For services to international understanding."

Bertrand Russell, the inaugurator of the Russell-Einstein Manifesto, wrote of Rotblat's "courage, integrity and complete self abnegation to give up his career and devote himself to combat the nuclear peril as well as other allied evils."

We can do no less than designate Joseph Rotblat a Peace Hero.

José Figueras Ferrer (1906–1990)

As a young man José Figueras Ferrer studied at the Massachusetts Institute of Technology (1922-1926), but he felt he learned more from reading in the Boston Public Library. He returned to Costa Rica to work as a coffee grower, though he considered himself a philosopher-farmer. He became a revolutionary when the Cost Rican Army, aided by the communist-led guerrillas, prevented the just-elected President from taking office. With a force of 700 irregulars (the Caribbean Legion) he led a successful revolt, restoring democracy, in just forty-four days.

Figueras became the head of the revolutionary Founding Council and served as Acting President in 1948–49, and in that brief time he brought about radical change in Costa Rica. The Council:

- abolished the army
- nationalized the banks
- instituted women's suffrage
- guaranteed public education for all
- established a civil service replacing the spoils system for government jobs
- provided Social Security for the elderly
- outlawed the communist party

There were close to 840 reforms in all, the major ones being written into the new Constitution.

After eighteen months, he stepped aside for the originally elected President Otilio Ulates Blanco. In 1953, Figueras formed the Natiuonal Liberation Party (PLN) and was elected president himself. Democracy flourished. He tried to maintain friendly relations with the US, but opposed dictators in neighboring states of Nicaragua, Venezuela, Cuba, and the Dominican Republic. He said in an interview, "Your hands are not clean to fight communism when you don't fight dictatorships." He promoted democracy at home and, by example, abroad.

In 1970, he ran again and was elected to another full term. Two years later, when Costa Rica suffered an economic crisis with the collapse of the Central American Common Market, Figueras Ferrer quickly found a new market for the country's principal export, coffee. A trade deal for 30,000 tons of coffee beans was struck with USSR. The Russians may have thought to gain some political advantage with the opening of a Mission as well as aiding the Costa Rican economy, but Figueras Ferrer was able to hold good diplomatic relations with both the US and the Soviet Union.

José Figueras Ferrer exemplified the best of human social-political potential. He promoted both private enterprise and a wide range of governmental social services. He was a champion of democracy and an opponent of dictatorship and corruption. He kept his country peaceful with no standing army, and the funds that would have been devoted to the military were used for education and other domestic purposes, resulting in prosperity for all. He joins the legion of all-time Peace Heroes.

Vasili Arkhipov

Vasili Arkhipov (1926–1998) was a USSR naval officer known to few outside the Soviet navy. In 1961 he was serving aboard a K-9, one of the early nuclear subs when a reactor started to overheat and a meltdown was imminent.

Arkhipov, with an engineering background, did not hesitate to enter the radioactive compartment with a few key others to repair the cooling system, thus saving the lives of the entire crew. His reputation spread throughout the Soviet navy.

The following year he was aboard a class B-59 submarine heading toward Cuba during the Cuban Missile Crisis between the two superpowers. His submarine, spotted by a US carrier-led task force, immediately dived. When American destroyers starting dropping depth charges to force it to the surface, the captain of the sub thought that open war had broken out and was ready to order the launch of their nuclear-tipped torpedo aimed at the carrier. To launch that nuclear weapon, however, required three unanimous votes. The captain and political officer voted to launch. Arkhipov, the fleet commander, thought the order should come from Moscow, and voted no.

Had the nuclear torpedo struck the carrier and the US

retaliated, it would have started WW III. Though the captain, the political officer, and even the rest of the crew supported launching the nuclear torpedo, Arkhipov stood up to all of them in favor of precaution.

In fact, the depth charges were not meant to strike the sub but only force it to the surface, where its officers would see it was outclassed by the US task force. And indeed, the sub did surface and headed for European waters; it was not attacked when it came up, but allowed to proceed eastward. The crisis was averted.

Vasisl Arkhipov, little known to the American public, is surely a Peace Hero.

Martin Luther King, Jr. (1929–1968)

Martin Luther King, Jr. was the major figure of the Civil Rights movement of the 1950s and '60s. The movement, and especially the horrendous reaction to it by law enforcement in the South, led to the passage of the Civil Rights Act of 1964. That Act rendered unconstitutional the various laws of states and municipalities that had previously legalized segregation. The year before, in 1963, King had received the Nobel Peace Prize, awarded in recognition of the fact that Civil Rights was an issue whose time had come and no longer could be delayed and obstructed.

King was awarded the Peace Prize not for an antiwar stance which was yet to come, but for his nonviolent approach to civil disobedience—based on Ghandian principles of nonviolence—that the movement used in demonstrating against the de jure and de facto segregation in the United States.

Every ordinary person, and many extraordinary ones, would consider the Nobel Peace Prize and the passage of the Civil Rights Act the capstone of a towering life, but King was only 35, and there were still many wrongs in the world that needed his leadership.

The Vietnam War was heating up with the US reaction to the alleged Gulf of Tonkin incident in the waters off North Vietnam. Martin Luther King had privately expressed opposition to the war, but was told by friends and enemies alike to limit his attention to civil rights here in the US. His conscience, however, did not allow him to keep silent. In 1967, he traveled to New York and ascended to the pulpit of Riverside Church where, before an audience of 3,000 he gave a speech/sermon titled, "Beyond Vietnam: Time to Break Silence." It was called by many his greatest speech. King was not about to give in to mere mortals when he felt compelled to express his deeply held, God-given convictions. In the address he said, "The Nobel Prize for Peace was also a commission—a commission to work harder than I had ever worked before for the brotherhood of man." He then called for an end to "one of history's most cruel and senseless wars."

Martin Luther King Jr, always linked justice, peace, and righteousness, calling himself a "drum major" for all three as essential to humanity. For his activities in a too-short life of 39 years, and for their effect on society after his death, we count him as a Peace Hero.

Recent Peace Heroes

Peter Ackerman, born in 1946, was a founder and is a Visiting Scholar at the International Center on Nonviolent Conflict. His entire career has been centered on dispute resolution and nonviolent strategies. He cowrote the study, published as a book, *Strategic Nonviolent Conflict: the Dynamics of People Power in the Twentieth Century*. In it he documented fifty of sixty-seven transitions to democracy that occurred nonviolently during the century. He was also a principal editor for the film, *A Force More Powerful: A Century of Nonviolent Conflict*. Peter Ackerman is a working Peace Hero. May he live long and prosper.

Eqbal Ahmad (1933–1999) was a Pakistan-born political scientist who studied and then taught in the United States but kept up with his contacts in Pakistan. He came to know such political dissidents as Edward Said, Daniel Berrigan, Noam Chomsky, Howard Zinn, and Arundhati Roy.

Though a secularist he expressed admiration for the Sufi tradition and attempts to bring the Muslims and Hindus together, and for helping the poor while giving them a sense of self-respect.

Ahmad was a theorist and original thinker, not an ordinary academic. He opposed all colonialism and militarism. During the Vietnam War, he opposed it publicly and considered it an American war. He was a man of action as well, and with Philip Berrigan was indicted as one of the "Harrisburg 7" for planning to kidnap Henry Kissinger. In a well-known quotation of his political beliefs, he said, "We are living in modern times throughout the world and yet are dominated by medieval minds."

Eqbal Ahmad fully deserves to be listed as a Peace Hero.

Martti Ahtisaari (1937–) is the former president of Finland who received the Nobel Peace Prize in 2008. Upon leaving office as President in 2000 he formed the Crisis Management Initiative (CMI), which has gone on to resolve disputes around the world, even violent ones. CMI has a strong focus on women's participation in its work as a peace broker.

With his personal experience in helping to resolve the disputes in Kosovo, Namibia, and between Acchi and Indonesia, Ahtisaari is ever more certain that "all conflicts can be resolved" using dialogue and mediation. His leadership in conflict resolution has earned Martti Ahtisaari a Peace Hero title as well.

Tadatoshi Akiba, born in 1942, was only three years old in 1945 when the first atomic bombs were dropped on Hiroshima and Nagasaki. His education was in mathematics, but his real work was as an advocate of peace and disarmament. He entered politics and became a member of the Japanese House of Representatives and then Mayor of Hiroshima. As a politician, he won several prestigious peace awards. As Mayor he was elected as president of Mayors for Peace, and increased membership from 480 cities in 104 countries to 4,680 members in 150 countries and regions.

As both a worldwide advocate and as a political leader, Tadatoshi Akiba deserves the title of Peace Hero.

Widad Akreyi (1969–) was brought up in a secular Kurdish family and has identified with the plight of the stateless Kurds since she was a small child. But today, she is far from a one-issue activist. She has taken on human rights, women's rights and gender equality, and peace and social justice both in the Near East and, more recently, in the world. With a background in public health, she has worked with medical researchers to improve the health of communities. She has worked to heighten women's involvement in peace building and to press the United Nations to enact an Arms Trade Treaty to Control the Trade in Small Arms and Light Weapons, currently valued at $70B (US) annually. The Treaty passed in 2013. That same year, largely due to her efforts, the UN also passed a Declaration of Commitment to End Sexual Violence in Conflict which was signed by 113 countries.

She has received multiple prestigious awards: Pacem In

Terris Peace and Freedom Award; FOR's Pfeffer Peace Prize; and Amnesty International's appointment as its Stop Torture Ambassador. When she takes on an issue, especially when it concerns women, Akreyi also has the ear of the UN, thanks to her appointment as its Stop Torture Ambassador.

In her spare time—she is not yet 50 as of this writing—she has written an accurate historical novel, *The Viking's Kurdish Love—Zoroastrians' Fight for Survival*.

Akreyi left Amnesty International to cofound Defend International, whose mission is "to respond to grave violations of human rights and international humanitarian Law, monitor the implementation of preventive measures that are designed to end impunity for the perpetrators of these crimes, conduct medical research that may either directly or indirectly improve the health standard of communities, and to promote peace and democracy through cultural relations and diplomacy." Her Pacem In Terris statement is especially relevant today: "We must remember compassion is contagious. The more we spread it, the more people will cherish it and share it, We must replace the culture of war with the culture of Peace."

Widad Akreyi is a Peace Hero for today and years into the future.

Randall Amster (1966–) teaches peace and justice at Georgetown University, and edits the *Peace Chronicle*. He concentrates his research and writing on Peace Ecology as the Path to Peace. He insists that Peace Ecology is not just a synthesis of two terms, but shows the relationship between war against the Earth and war between each of us. He indicts mankind's inclination towards competition and conflict, and the glorification of war. He warns that many other forms of life would flourish with the extinction of mankind. Randall

Amster continues to be the voice of wisdom and a Peace Hero.

Annot (1894–1981) was a painter and a peace activist. Born in Germany, she and her husband, Rudolf Jacobi, established an art school in Berlin but left under the Nazis and emigrated to the United States.

She had been an antiwar activist since her early twenties, having worked for the German League for Human Rights and for WILPF (Womens' International League for Peace and Freedom (still a force for peace today), and in the US she became a Quaker.

She studied with well-known artists and became an accomplished artist herself, receiving many awards for her work and several solo exhibits. But for her lifelong advocacy for peace—in Germany, Norway, and the US, and particularly Puerto Rico—we must also remember her as a Peace Hero.

Jerica Arents (1986–) is an Adjunct Professor in DePaul University's Peace, Justice and Conflict Studies Program. In addition to teaching peace studies, she has worked as an organizer for Witness Against Torture and has written about America's post-9/11 policies of indefinite detention and torture, and traveled to Guantánamo Bay, Cuba, in 2015 to raise awareness about the prison. She was a co-coordinator of Chicago's Voices for Creative Nonviolence, and has participated in two peace delegations to Afghanistan. A board member of the War Resisters League since 2016, in 2011 Arents received the Mary Elsbernd OSF Social Justice Award from the 8th Day Center for Justice, for her "exceptional passion for the journey of justice and peace, grounded in a sense of relationship marked by mutuality, nonviolence, and cooperation, and ... rooted in a sense of imagination for creative systemic change."

Arents, who considers Kathy Kelly (see p. 216) "an incredible mentor, teacher, and role model," is a true Peace Hero.

Emile Arnaud (1864–1921) was a lawyer who often spoke out opposing war; we may rightly call his frequent rhetoric a campaign. Indeed, he founded the Ligue Internationale de la Paix, and in 1902 authored the Code de la Paix which defined the mission of the Peace Movement of his time. He is credited with coining the term "pacifism." For that alone he deserved to be listed as a Peace Hero, but his whole life was so devoted, and we need not quibble over words and terms.

Klaus Pontus Arnoldson (1844–1916) was a self educated Swede who started life as a railway man, but after wide reading he became a Humanist, believing in freedom of conscience and thought.

Norway and Sweden were joined in a union for 90 years beginning in 1814. When Norway, feeling it was treated unequally, threatened to end the union, Sweden responded with threats of military action. Arnoldson campaigned for peace, distributing handbills with the slogan "Peace with Norway, whether the Union sinks or swims." He felt that Norwegians and Swedes were "brother people and must never go to war with each other." Though the Union was dissolved in 1905, he was awarded the 1908 Nobel Peace Prize. In his Nobel address, he said "Education is the only certain road to the final goal of peace."

Arnoldson went on to co-found the Swedish Peace and Arbitration League and headed the campaign to extend the League's work to all international disputes. He also promoted the concept of permanent neutrality of the Scandinavian nations. So, world peace would begin in Scandinavia. The process is already underway. Klaus Pontus Arnoldson certainly deserves to be a Peace Hero.

Vittorio Arrigoni (1975–2011) was an Italian journalist and activist who last worked with the International Solidarity Movement at the Gaza Strip before he was assassinated. Arrigoni said activism was in his genes—his grandfathers fought against Mussolini and the Fascists.

When Israel blockaded the Gaza Strip, he was part of the Free Gaza Movement and was on the first boat to break the blockade. He called his blog Guerrilla Radio, and his writing was followed by left-wing as well as fundamentalist Arab groups. Several of his posts, advocating direct action but not physical violence, were picked up by Electronic Intifada.

When "Vic" was abducted and murdered, the outpouring of grief and outrage came from the whole world: Italy of course, Europe, the International Solidarity Movement, the Hamas Government and throughout Gaza, but also by Fatah, Islamic Jihad, the Palestinian People's Party and the Popular Resistance Committees. He was called "The Hero of Palestine." All would agree, and we would further name Vittorio Arrigoni a Peace Hero.

Arrigoni leads a long list of others in Palestine & Israel including Rabbi Arik Ascherman, Mubarak Awad, Ali Abu Awwad, Ghassan Andoni, Rachel Corrie, Rabbi Menachem Froman, Jeff Halper, Shaul Judelman, Rabbi Aryeh Levin, Ilan Pappe, and dozens of others—some ordinary farmers and fishermen, Palestinians, Israelis, and a Christian—all Peace Heroes.

Joan Baez (1941–) is world-renowned as a folk singer and songwriter, with over thirty albums to her credit. She performed fourteen songs at the Woodstock Festival in 1969, where she introduced Bob Dylan to the world of music and poetry. But, she is just as well known as a social and political activist, working for the causes of civil rights, the antiwar movement, and more recently Occupy Wall Street. She has recorded not only her own songs but also those of Woody Guthrie, Phil Ochs, and Pete Seeger, among others, but for us she is a Peace Hero for all time.

Russell Baker (1925–) Even though he classed Korea, Vietnam, and the Cold War as terrible wars, and opposed capital punishment "except for the killing of time," the issues of war and peace occupy a small percentage his voluminous total output of writing. We classify Baker as a first-rate satirist, but also a less noted Peace Hero.

David Barsamian (1945–), the host of Alternative Radio, interviews well-known peace heroes and records their speeches. A progressive social-political voice, he is a bona fide Peace Hero.

Archibald Baxter (1881–1970) was born and reared in New Zealand. In the Second Boer War, he refused to enlist on the British side. He had listened to speakers and read much literature, then decided with conviction that war would not solve national policy problems and that war was wrong.

With the NZ Military Service Act of 1916, which included conscription, he refused to register on the basis that "all war was wrong, futile, and destructive to victor and vanquished alike." But he was refused Conscientious Objector status and imprisoned. Archibald and two of his brothers were court-martialled.

It was determined after being subjected to Field Punishment

#1 that he and other COs were to be sent to the front in France as punishment. The issue of those claiming CO status being sent to the dangers of the front was taken up by an MP in Parliament, by the Women's International League (WILPF), and the press. It led to the No More War movement, started in New Zealand (in 1931), and to the Peace Pledge Union there during WW II.

After WW II, Baxter and his wife continued their pacifist ways, opposing nuclear arms and the American Vietnam war. Baxter was not a journalist or academic; indeed he had only a primary school education, but his pacifism was deeply held. He said in an interview, "We make war chiefly on civilians, and respect for human life seems to have become a thing of the past. To accept this situation would be to accept the Devil's philosophy."

Let us remember Archibald Baxter as a Peace Hero, not just in New Zealand but the world over.

Medea Benjamin (1952–) is co-Founder of Code Pink; author of *Drone Warfare: Killing by Remote Control* and *How to Stop the Next War Now: Effective Responses to Violence and Terrorism*; and winner of the 2012 Peace Prize (US Peace Memorial). She was and is everywhere, it seems, from the streets leading protests to hanging a peace banner from the gallery of Congress—a veritable one-woman gang. She is a Peace Hero and more.

Dan Berrigan (1921–2016) received the War Resisters Peace Award, the Gandhi Peace Award, The Pax Christi Peace Award, Pacem in Terris Award, and the Peace Abbey Courage of Conscience Award after a lifetime devoted to the Catholic church, poetry, and promotion of peace.

He and his brother Phil, also a priest, were leaders of the Cantonsville Eight and the Plowshares Nine. During these years they both were nonviolent—though not averse to destroying draft records with home-made napalm, or damaging nuclear warheads with hammers, or pouring blood on Selective Service records.

Dan Berrrigan has also had numerous books published, including most recently, *To Dwell in Peace: An Autobiography*.

Philip Berrigan (1923–2002), also a peace activist, felt that the times he lived in demanded effective activism and leadership, and more than simple protest. He blazed a trail of protests and civil disobedience against the Vietnam War and against nuclear arms. He was arrested, tried, convicted, and imprisoned a number of times; but there were some acquittals and other trials that resulted in no jail time.

Phil Berrigan led groups in signature raids on draft boards and defaced records with their own blood or destroyed them with homemade napalm. He was one of the Baltimore Four, the Cantonsville Nine, the DC Nine, the Milwaukee Fourteen, the Boston Eight, the Buffalo Five, and the Camden 28.

Front-page news reports accompanied the arrests and trials of the Berrigan brothers.

Following the series of draft board protests, and the subsequent end of the Vietnam War, the Berrigans turned their attention to war armaments, and in particular nuclear weapons. The first protest was at the town of King of Prussia, PA, where they raided the GE nuclear plant and hammered on the two nose cones of missiles. More than seventy other Plowshares protests involving civil disobedience followed in the years thereafter.

The Berrigans' aim was to bring the insanity of war to the attention of the public in concrete ways. Their successes were evidenced disparate ways: their inclusion on the FBI's Ten Most

Wanted List in the late 1960s and their appearance on the *Time* magazine cover in 1971, under the headline "Rebel Priests: the Curious Case of the Berrigans."

Both Dan and Phil Berrigan were true Peace Heroes.

Leah Bolger (@1960–) retired in 2000 from the US Navy after twenty years of active duty. She is president of Veterans for Peace, a member of the Drones Watch delegation to Pakistan, and "Secretary of Defense" in the Green Shadow Cabinet. She must have learned all that peace stuff when on duty in Iceland, Japan, and Bermuda.

She learned it well, retiring to full time time work waging peace. That is worth designation as a Peace Hero.

Kenneth E. Boulding (1910–1993), academic, Quaker, and mystic, was a scholar and prolific author in many disciplines, but especially: economics, philosophy, history, peace studies, and poetry. As a peace activist, he founded the International Peace Research Association and also the *Journal of Conflict Resolution*. He brought peace to the forefront with a short thesis "How to Establish A Stable Peace," designed to be applied between states and all social groups, even marriage partners.

Though most of his scholarly work was concerned with economics and systems research, his peace work was significant enough to make him a Peace Hero.

Fred Branfman (1942–2014) was assisted into maturing into an antiwar activist by the conduct of the US military, the CIA, and the governments they are supposed to represent during the US wars in Vietnam, Afghanistan, and Iraq. He is best known as the whistleblower on the illegal bombing of Laos, which caused such a high rate of civilian death and injury in a country that wasn't at war with anyone. His book, *Voices from the Plain* *of Jars–Life Under an Air War,* read widely and well reviewed, brought news of the secret war in Laos to the American Public. Congress, too, took note and called on him to testify.

More recently, he wrote about the torture carried out at Abu Ghraib in his essay "Good Americans in a Time of Torture." The ever-increasing drone warfare in Pakistan, Afghanistan, Yemen, and Eastern Africa, coupled with the high percentage of targeting errors, did not escape his biting tongue in national journals.

Branfman died in 2014, but he will always be a Peace Hero.

Hugh Brock (1914–85) was a British pacifist and driving force behind the anti-war movement and opposition to nuclear weapons in that nation in the mid-20th century. He himself was a conscientious objector in WW II.

In 1946 he was assistant editor of *Peace News*, which published over 100 articles showing how Gandhi's non-violent direct action related to Western nations. In 1955 he became editor and shifted the focus to opposing nuclear weapons. The protests throughout Britain made worldwide headlines when the British protested their H-Bomb tests on Christmas Island in the Pacific, in double irony.

When he was arrested at Aldermaston and any of the other protest sites, he always pleaded guilty with pride. Hugh Brock was a Peace Hero in the time of many of us.

Viscount James Bryce (1838–1922) was a barrister, historian, Member of Parliament, and cabinet officer. He served the UK government in various elected and appointed positions, and came to know many notable historical figures.

For many men, these achievements would have brought fulfillment to an extraordinary lifetime. Bryce, however, was not finished. He changed direction in 1914 when he accepted the position of Jurist on the International Court of Justice at the Hague. In 1918, he published *Essays and Addresses In Wartime*, and that same year spoke out to advocate for the League of Nations. His most notable quotation speaks volumes: "Patriotism consists not in waving the flag, but in striving that our country shall be righteous as well as strong."

Viscount James Bryce must be considered a Peace Hero, although he would have had greater backing from the women listed in this chapter as Peace Heroes, if he had not opposed suffrage rights for all women.

Helen Caldicott (1938–) is an Australian physician. As a 19 year old, she was so affected by reading Neville Shute's novel *On the Beach* about a nuclear holocaust, that it gave direction to her entire adult life.

France had begun a series of atmospheric tests on some of the Polynesian islands in the late 1960s, incurring the wrath of the the indigenous populations and the political opposition of activists in nearby New Zealand and Australia. Caldicott was instrumental in getting Australia to join New Zealand in bringing suit against France in the International Court of Justice.

In 1977, she was in the US practicing pediatrics at the Children's Hospital in Boston and teaching at Harvard Medical School. Physicians for Social Responsibility had been dormant, but was reborn when Caldicott organized 153 chapters with over 20,000 active members. Parallel groups of physicians were formed in several other countries under the umbrella of International Physicians for the Prevention of Nuclear War. They were a force for the countries of the "Nuclear Club" to reckon with. Then in 1980, the Three Mile Island nuclear power reactor in Pennsylvania had a partial meltdown. Caldicott decided to leave the clinical practice of medicine to expand her efforts in opposing not only nuclear weapons and war, but civilian nuclear reactors as well. She wrote medical papers, published books, wrote newspaper op-ed articles, gave interviews, and organized seminars and lectures for anyone who would listen. In 1985, the Nobel Prize for Peace was awarded to International Physicians for the Prevention of Nuclear War (IPPNW). It was a tribute to Helen Caldicott and the founders of that organization, the American Bernard Lown and the Russian Yevgeniy Chazov.

Caldicott continues to be hyperactive in opposing nuclear weapons and civilian nuclear power, bringing both medical knowledge and common sense to bear. (Splitting the atom to produce steam to drive turbines to generate electricity is outrageous, and can only generate good satire.) Helen Caldicott fully deserves to be designated a Peace Hero.

Peter Carnley (1937–), Archbishop of Perth and Primate of the Anglican Church of Australia, strongly opposed Prime Minister John Howard's support of the American war in (against) Iraq. He wrote, "Churches have to demonstrate that they can live together in Peace for the world to live by the same values." He is a Peace Hero for all of us.

Paul K. Chappell (1980–) evolved during his youth from West Point cadet and commissioned officer, to veteran of the Iraq war, to peace activist. He spoke in many venues across the across the nation and wrote a series of books opposing war, including *Will War Ever End?*, *The End of War*, *Peaceful Revolution*, and *The Art of Waging Peace*. Chappell, the Peace Leadership Director of the Nuclear Age Peace Foundation, is unquestionably a Peace Hero.

Erica Chenoweth (1980–) is a Peace Hero if for no other accomplishment than her well-researched book, *Why Civil Resistance Works*, which shows that nonviolent civil resistance is twice as effective as armed resistance against repressive regimes.

Noam Chomsky (1928–) linguist, scholar, and political activist, has opposed many of the wars since the early 1970s. Highly informed about a full range of national and international issues, he speaks and writes with authority in such books as *Who Rules the World*, *Profits over People*, and *Failed States*. A political dissident who sometimes seems more interested in how many arguments he can fit on the head of a pin than on leading a protest, at 92 Chomsky is an activist as well as academic (emeritus) Peace Hero.

Ramsey Clark (1927–) served as Attorney General under President Lyndon Johnson, but after leaving that powerful office became known for his representation of unlikely clients and documenting US aggression throughout the 20th and into the 21st centuries. His list of major aggressions by both major political parties includes:

- the 1953 overthrow by the CIA and British Secret Service of Iran's elected president Mohammed Mossadegh in favor of American ally Shah Mohammad Reza Pahlavi
- 1954, when Guatemala's democratically elected President, Jacobo Arbenz, was removed and death squads roamed both cities and countryside
- 1961 and thereafter, the secret, and then overt, US involvement in Vietnam
- the 1961 assassination of President Patrice Lumumba in the Congo instigated by Belgium and the CIA

- America's attacks, wars, and invasions of Granada, Panama, Libya, Somalia, Iraq ("the First Gulf War"), Afghanistan, and a few others

In 1992 Clark was a recipient of a Gandhi Peace Award, and also initiated Clark's International Action center in NYC. He represented Native American activist Leonard Pelletier, founded "votetoimpeach," and accused President George W. Bush, VP Richard Cheney, and some American generals of crimes against peace, against humanity, and of war crimes. He also wrote the three-part analysis, *Torturers In the Mirror*, published in 2010. Ramsey Clark is a Peace Hero of our time.

William Sloane Coffin (1924–2006), as a youth, was a member of Yale's secret society Skull and Bones, and then became a CIA agent. He matured to become an activist in the Civil Rights movement and a major figure in the peace movement. He opposed the Vietnam War and all the others the US became entangled in, including the Iraq War promoted by George W. Bush and Dick Cheney. Toward the end of the Vietnam War era, he had preached civil disobedience and encouraged young men to turn in their draft cards. He was arrested and jailed for conspiracy to aid and abet young men to resist the draft.

At each step of the theological ladder, he gain more credibility and influence on the national stage: Chaplain at Williams College and then at Yale University, and a signatory of "A Call to Resist Illegitimate Authority," along with Dr Benjamin Spock, Michael Farber, Marcus Raskin, and Mitchell Goodman.

In 1968, Coffin was named senior minister at Riverside Church in New York, but in 1987 he resigned, to become president of SANE/Freeze. In this position he could work full time at disarmament, lecturing nationally and internationally, participating in interviews, and writing three books. A 2004 biography by Warren Goldstein, *William Sloan Coffin: A Holy Impatience*, was an in-depth portrait of a Peace Hero.

Jeremy Corbyn (1949–) is a leader of the Labor Party in UK. He has been an MP with the support of the labor unions in his home district since 1983. He also has the backing of the young voters for his antiwar and antinuclear policies. As he describes himself, he is a Social Democrat, a member of Old Labor. He is also an environmentalist and a peace proponent.

As a peace activist, talking the talk and also walking the walk by leading numerous antiwar rallies, Jeremy Corbyn's political pursuits in the Labor Party and in Parliament may overshadow his peace activism. but he is a full-fledged Peace Hero.

David Cortright (1946–) is a scholar, educator, and peace activist. As a soldier in Vietnam, he spoke out against the war, much to the displeasure of the government. After the withdrawal of US forces, he continued his activism through protesting the development of nuclear weapons as Executive Director of SANE.

Currently he is Director of Policy Studies for the Kroc Institute for International Peace Studies at the University of Notre Dame. He has written and/or edited many books on nonviolent social change, nuclear disarmament, and diplomacy to prevent international conflicts. He was awarded a Gandhi Peace Prize with Karen Jacob for six years from 2004 to 2010, and is a presence on the international stage of building peace, although he carried out no antigovernment protests and no illegal actions. Yet, he is worthy of being a Peace Hero.

Frances Crowe (1919–2019) became a peace activist with a vengeance after the bombings of Dresden, Hiroshima, and Nagasaki. Active since 1945 in the War Resisters' League, Crowe cofounded the Taprock Peace Center, and has worked with WILPF, SANE, and Women against War. In 1967 she served as a counsellor for over 2,000 young people applying for Conscientious Objector status early in the Vietnam War. She was arrested at the Yankee Nuclear Power Plant and at the Seabrook Nuclear Power Plant. Indeed, she has been arrested numerous times in her peace and anti-nuclear activities, most recently at the age of 98, on June 24, 2017. She has also been a tax resister since the beginning of the Iraq War.

Not just a protester, but also an effective organizer of coalitions and alliances in Massachusetts, Crowe was honored with the Courage of Conscience Award at the Peace Abbey in 2007. She has been been a Peace Hero for three-quarters of a century, and might well continue to be a role model for others.

George Maitland Lloyd Davies (1880–1949) was born into a well-to-do Welsh family and, as a young man who believed in an all-volunteer army, took an officer's commission with the Royal Welsh Fusileers. But soon he resigned his commission and joined the Fellowship of Reconciliation and became a pacifist.

In 1923 he was elected to British Parliament as an Independent Christian Pacifist. He lost his seat in the next election to the Liberal candidate but never turned his back on pacifism. He came to lead Heddychwyr Cymu, the Welch branch of the Peace Pledge Union. He believed each of us should be "an Island of Peace."

In Jen Llywelyn's biography, *Pilgrim of Peace*, Lloyd Davies was noted particularly as a pacifist, Conscientious Objector, and peace builder. One of his own books, *Pilgrimage of Peace*, was published posthumously.

The Welshman, George Maitland Lloyd Davies joins our own list as a Peace Hero.

Nicolas J.S. Davies has written numerous articles on the disasters, secrecies, and illegalities of war, published in different journals of the alternative press. A recent article, "How America Spreads Global Chaos," is worthy of a keynote address, taking on the CIA and Special Forces operations. His well known book, *Blood on Our Hands: the American Invasion and Destruction of Iraq*, would, alone, make Nicholas J.S. Davies a Peace Hero.

Garry Davis (1921–2013) was born in Maine, a state that often goes its own way. A peace activist who decided that wars could not be abolished as long as there were nation-states, he thereupon renounced his American citizenship and became a World Citizen, spending his time and energy promoting the World Citizen movement. He designed a flag, issued passports, and established a registry of World Citizens. He also had several books published and attracted the notice of some illustrious figures around the world. Here, we name him as a Peace Hero.

Dorothy Day (1897–1980) lived a multifaceted life, best known for her work with the destitute and the homeless. She established two hospitality houses to help the poor of New York City, which served as models for shelters around the country. Because the city did not care for their own homeless and indigent, she took up the task.

In doing so, she continued her earlier work as a crusading journalist, who in 1933 had cofounded *The Catholic Worker*, which still sells for a penny a copy.

Day was, at the same time, a committed pacifist who knew from her personal experience that the poor and destitute never profited from war or its military preparations. She opposed US entry into both World Wars. She was also active with the War Resisters League, the Fellowship of Reconciliation, and the Plowshares Movement. All three organizations passionately opposed US entry in WW II, and the Plowshares activists were especially avid in condemning nuclear weapons. After the War, she herself was arrested for nonviolent disobedience in refusing to participate in civil defense drills to prepare for a nuclear attack.

Dorothy Day was widely recognized as saintly for her care of the poor and needy. Just as rightly, she was a Peace Hero for her anti-war activism.

David Dellinger (1915–2004) lived through several wars and seems to have been born to be a Peace Hero.

In the Spanish Civil War, his sympathies were with the leftist Populist Front that was democratically elected in 1936. He was strongly opposed to the Army plotters and to self-styled Generalissimo Francisco Franco, but unlike many Americans who fought on the side of the Republic, he could do no violence: instead of bearing arms, he drove an ambulance.

During WW II, he refused to register for the draft, both before and after the Pearl Harbor attack. He said he refused "to "fight for General Motors [or any other general], US Steel, and Chase Manhattan Bank," and was imprisoned as a Conscientious Objector.

In 1956, Dellinger, along with Bayard Rustin, A.J. Muste, and others founded *Liberation* magazine, and became its (long-serving) editor. In it he condemned the use of atomic bombs on Hiroshima and Nagasaki.

He vehemently opposed the Vietnam War when the US took over from the French, and in 1967 led the "Encircle the Pentagon" protest at which Abbie Hoffman, the leader of the Yippies, led the group in exorcism rites in ancient Aramaic. The following year, during the 1968 Democratic National Convention in Chicago, he was one of the leaders of the protests against the war. Arrested as one of the Chicago Seven, and charged with conspiracy with the intention of starting a riot, he became well known as a radical pacifist.

When the US-Iraq War began with the "Shock and Awe" bombing of Baghdad in 2003, David Dellinger was 87 years old. He was suffering from Alzheimer's Disease, though his long-term memory was still sharp. However, he still managed to attend nearby vigils against the war.

Two years before his death, he attended a gala celebration of his life and work held by his friends in Burlington, VT. David Dellinger was a Peace Hero his entire life and shall ever more remain so.

W.E.B. Du Bois (1868–1963) was a brilliant intellect and an irrepressible activist for black rights but also, in his middle and later years, for peace. He was the first Black to receive a PhD from Harvard and made his career as a scholar, writer, and teacher. His thesis examined the shameful details of the "Slave Trade to the United States of America, 1638-1870." He never accepted and, indeed, opposed the policy of accommodation and political politeness. At the same time, he disapproved of the policies of Booker T. Washington (The Atlanta Compromise) and Marcus Garvey of Jamaica. Though he opposed all forms of racism in education and employment, he did not favor an all-Black state in the US.

Du Bois attended a Peace Meeting in Paris and declared

"Colonialism has been the chief cause of war." He was involved in many other international peace causes as well. At the Boston Community Church, he gave a talk titled "Peace Is Dangerous." He was Chair of the Peace Information Center, attended a meeting of World Partisans of Peace in Stockholm, and helped gather about two million signatures on the Stockholm Peace Appeal petition asking all world governments to ban nuclear weapons. He joined Linus Pauling and O. John Rogge in asking the American Congress to endorse World Peace. For his efforts, he was placed on an FBI watch list, and the Department of Justice brought a criminal indictment against him for failure to register as an agent of a foreign government. The case was dismissed, but his passport was not returned to him for a number of years.

W.E.B. Du Bois deserves the designation of Peace Hero as well as that of a civil rights leader.

Muriel Duckworth (1908–2009) was a Nova Scotian, one of the founders of Voice of Women, later called the Canadian Voice of Women for Peace. She believed "There are no good wars or bad wars," that all war is simply war. She was also a proud and active member of the Halifax branch of the Raging Grannies.

One would never know that she was afflicted with chronic shyness, what with all her efforts at social reform, educational development, and creating a more equitable and better world.

Muriel Duckworth was a worthy Peace Hero.

Peter van den Dungen – who established the Center for Non-Violence.

Shoghi Effendi (1897–1957) As the 20th-century Leader/Guardian of the Baha'i faith, he professed "permanent and universal peace as the supreme goal of all mankind." He believed that there could be unity through diversity and preached that Peace would be achieved through love and kindness. The Leader of such a faith should surely be a Peace Hero.

Daniel Ellsberg (1931–) is an economist, a former member of the State Department, and one of the authors of the report that came to be known as the Pentagon Papers. He was later a member of the Campaign for Peace and Democracy and a senior fellow of the Nuclear Age Peace Foundation.

His 1971 decision to make and leak copies of the Pentagon Report that told of the futility of remaining in South Vietnam and of the false claims of the Gulf of Tonkin Resolution is well known.

For his courageous efforts at releasing the Pentagon Papers to Congress, and in book form to the American public, Ellsberg was given the Right Livelihood Award, known as the alternative Nobel Peace Prize, but not until 45 years later, in 2006.

Long after the Paris Peace accord was signed (largely because of his efforts) he continued to protest war and the militarism that accompanies it. In 2010, Ellsberg and Veterans for Peace were arrested outside the White House, where many of them had chained themselves to the surrounding security fence to protest new wars in the Middle and Near East. The following year he was part of the group arrested at the Marine Corps Brig in protest of the imprisonment of Bradley Manning, and in 2013 he co-founded the Freedom of the Press Foundation.

Surely we have not heard the last of Daniel Ellsberg. He was and is a Peace Hero.

Jodi Evans (1951–) is a cofounder of Code Pink and has been an antiwar activist and advocate for justice of many sorts. She wrote the book *Stop the Next War Now* and produced several documentary films including *Rooted In Peace* and *The Most Dangerous Man in America: Daniel Ellsberg and the Pentagon Papers*. She collected signatures from rural Afghani women on a petition that asked President Obama not to send more American troops to Afghanistan. She won a Peace Award from The East-West Vision of Peace.

Although of lower profile than Medea Benjamin, her Code Pink cofounder, Jodi Evans, too, deserves to be a Peace Hero.

David Fabbro (1978–), for his publication of "Peaceful Societies: An Introduction" in the *Journal of Peace Research*.

R. Brian Ferguson (1951–), author of *How Can Anthropologists Promote Peace?*

Randall Caroline Forsberg (1943–2007) spent her entire adult life as an antiwar activist. She started by working at the Stockholm International Peace Institute and, in the US, founded the Institute for Defense and Disarmament Studies (accent on disarmament). Later she was instrumental in the Nuclear Weapons FREEZE Campaign, writing "Call to Halt the Arms Race," which became the Manifesto of FREEZE.

Forsberg was active in her peace efforts internationally not only in the United States but also in S. Korea, Sweden, Norway, Germany, Russia, and China. In her spare time, she wrote several articles and books. In her too-short life of 64 years, she was a force to reckoned with. She unquestionably deserves a designation of Peace Hero.

Ursula Franklin (1921–2016) was a physicist, educator, metallurgist, and technology philosopher—and a champion of peace throughout her life. A feminist and a pacifist, she and her family were practicing Quakers (Society of Friends).

She participated in the Baby Tooth Survey for Strontium 90 and thus helped to ban above-ground testing of nuclear weapons by the US in 1953. She wrote many papers and books on her field of metallurgy, but beyond that she wrote *Nuclear Peace, Pacifism as a Map* (a collection of papers, talks, and interviews on the subject), *Pacifism and Conscience*, and an important paper titled "Reflections on Theology and Peace." She was also active with Voices of Women (VOW) and urged Canadian withdrawal from the North Atlantic Treaty Organization. A vocal supporter of conscientious objectors, she publicly advocated for US withdrawal from Vietnam as early as 1969.

In her numerous speeches she insisted that war and violence were morally wrong, ineffective, and costly. One of her well known quotes tells the story: "Peace is not the absence of war; peace is the absence of fear."

Of course, she received many awards including the Pearson Medal of Peace. Here, we note her as a Peace Hero.

Johan Galtung (1930–) is a Norwegian mathematician, sociologist, and principal founder of peace and conflict studies. He established *The Journal of Peace Research* in 1964 and was the founder of the Peace Research Institute in 1959. He developed theories on peace and conflict resolution, structural violence, and the concept of peace building.

In 1987 he won the Right Livelihood Award, and has received numerous other awards, honorary degrees, and distinguished professorships in many universities around the world.

He is the author of over one hundred books and even more hundreds of papers in journals and newspapers. A small sampling of the titles tells the tale of the prodigious output of this extraordinary intellectual figure.

> 1969: *Violence, Peace, and Peace Research*
>
> 1975: *Peace: Peace Research — Education — Action*
>
> 1996: *Peace by Peaceful Means: Peace and Conflict, Development and Civilization*
>
> 2008: *50 Years: Peace and Conflict Perspectives*

Johan Galtung has done more than enough in his lifetime to be a Peace Hero several times over, and he is still going strong.

Amy Goodman (1957–) was born to be a protestor of injustice and war. Her father, George, was a founding member of the Long Island Chapter of of Physicians for Social Responsibility, and her mother, Dorothy, cofounded a chapter of SANE/Freeze.

After ten years as a director of WBAI (Pacifica Radio), Goodman launched the radio (and later television) show *Democracy Now*. In 1998, she covered Chevron in Nigeria in which Chevron provided helicopters to the Nigerian navy to remove protesters from an off-shore drilling platform, killing two of them.

In 1991, she and Allan Nairn reported on an attack by Indonesian troops on a peaceful assemblage of East Timorese at a prayer meeting in a cemetery. The worldwide news of the massacre led in time to East Timorese independence.

In 2000 she interviewed Bill Clinton, who wanted to make a turn-out-the-vote announcement. The president later called her "hostile and combative" after Goodman turned it into a confrontational half-hour interview.

Two other times, Goodman retreated into the official narrative on major issues. Once, when sanctions were applied to Iraq and caused undue hardship (restricted importation of food and medication) among the civilian population, causing the deaths of 500,000 children, she supported sanctions, much like Madeleine Albright who famously said, "It's worth it." Then, upon publication of David Ray Griffin's book *The New Pearl Harbor*, which rasied many questions about the official government story of the 9/11 bombing of the World Trade Center, she invited a conspiracy denier to join her and used the tactic of character assassination, rather than the facts presented by Griffin, to challenge his conclusions.

Yet, for all the good she has done in *Democracy Now* reporting, she deserves to be a Peace Hero in our time.

Greenham Common Women's Peace Camp (1981–2000), the RAF base in England where the US was to emplace cruise missiles in addition to silos for nuclear missiles, was where a group of thirty-one Welsh women chained themselves to the perimeter fence in 1981. The next year, 30,000 answered a chain letter and arrived at Greenham Common to Embrace the Base, joining hands around its nine-mile perimeter. Other creative protests continued at the site: 70,000 women joined hands in a human chain from the military base to an ordinance factory fourteen miles away at Burghfield; 200 women dressed as Teddy Bears entered the base for a protest picnic; forty-four women scaled the base fence on New Year's Eve and climbed atop the missile silos, then danced past midnight; while another human chain joined hands to replace sections of fence that they had cut away and removed.

Presidents Reagan and Gorbachev signed an Intermediate Nuclear Forces Treaty (INF) in 1987, essentially removing cruise missiles in NATO and Warsaw Pact countries.

The Greenham Common Women's Camp inspired other women in Great Britain, Continental Europe, and the US.

A notable Peace Camp in the US was the Seneca Women's Encampment for a Future of Peace and Justice in 1983.

All the women of the Greenham Common Peace Camp deserve to be Peace Heroes.

Otto Hahn (1879–1968) was a top theoretical academician as well as a laboratory scientist working empirically in the field of nuclear chemistry, later called applied radio chemistry. In 1938, Hahn discovered the natural fission that occurs in uranium, and with that discovery brought in the nuclear age.

Many years before, in 1905, he had discovered a radio isotope of thorium that he named mesothorium (or radiothorium), before isotopes were known. In following years, he discovered a host of new "elements," but it was when fission of the uranium nucleus with the great release of energy was confirmed, that the excitement in the scientific world occurred.

Nuclear chemistry was an exotic field at the time, and there were few scientists in it: Lise Meitner, Fritz Strassmann, Ernest Rutherford, William Ramsay, among them. Otto Hahn, like Albert Einstein, was politically aware and a staunch opponent of Jewish persecution under the Nazis.

During WW II, Hahn continued to work in his field of expertise (he had received the Nobel prize in 1944), but avoided any work to develop a nuclear weapon or even an atomic reactor. When the War ended in 1945, a few leading German scientists were taken to England. It was there he heard of his Nobel Prize, and soon afterward, of the nuclear weapons that destroyed Hiroshima and Nagasaki. He became psychologically distraught, feeling that his discovery of nuclear fission led to the terrible weapons.

After Hahn had recovered from the shock of learning

about the use of the weapons based on his theories, and on his return to West Germany, Hahn's social responsibility came to the fore fast and furiously. With the war over he was free to act.

In 1955, he signed the Mainau Declaration never to use nuclear chemistry and physics to produce nuclear weapons. He was instrumental in bringing the Gottingen Manifesto of 1957 into effect, not to arm the new West German military forces with nuclear weapons. The same year, Hahn signed the Vienna Appeal which warned of the dangers of any atomic weapons experiments. In 1958, he publicly supported the Pauling Appeal which was signed by over 9,000 scientists and sent to the United Nations and calling on all nations to stop all testing (air, water, and underground) of nuclear weapons. In 1959, he founded the Federation of German Scientists which was committed to the ideals of responsible science.

Because of his key scientific discoveries that led to nuclear destruction, Otto Hahn felt a personal duty to speak out in opposition to development, testing, and stockpiling of all nuclear weapons on planet Earth. He did so for the remainder of his days. Otto Hahn remains a truly important Peace Hero.

Jonathan David Haidt (1963–) wrote and published an essential study of the psychology of morality, *The Righteous Mind: Why good people are divided by politics and religion*.

Judith Hand is a Peace Hero for her books *A Future Without War*, *Women, Power, and the Biology of Peace*; and *Shift: The Beginning of War, The Ending of War*.

Brian Haw (1949–2011) was an English pacifist who lived out of a tent in a peace camp in Parliament Square in London for ten years. He thus put his actual life into a protest against whatever war the US and UK were pursuing at the time. He held and wore signs to express his displeasure, and he spoke out through a hand-held loudspeaker for all to hear. His posters said "My country – Right Its Wrongs," "Stop Killing Our Kids," and "Truth." He called for peaceful resolution to international conflict on the basis of justice and equality.

The government tried to remove him and so prevent his public protest. The courts upheld his rights of expression. His protests were pointedly aimed against then-Prime Minister Tony Blair and media mogul Rupert Murdoch, and also future PM David Cameron.

Brian Haw set an example for all ordinary people. He is hereby declared a Peace Hero.

Tom Hayden (1939–2016) was a born social-political activist, seeking to change the world for the better, as early as his college days. In the early 1960s he joined of SDS (Students for a Democratic Society) and drafted the Port Huron Statement, their Manifesto. He was one of the Chicago 8 arrested for disrupting the 1968 Democratic National Convention, for which he was convicted of inciting a riot.

By the mid-sixties he was actively opposing the Vietnam War, and made trips to Hanoi in 1965, 1967, and other years. He was in the good graces of the North Vietnamese and was asked to bring three POW airmen who were suffering medical problems back to the US. He was quickly placed on an FBI watch list—a secret government observation program that became permanent. He also founded the IndoChina Peace Campaign (IPC) and helped mobilize dissent in the US against the Vietnam (American) War.

In the 1980s and '90s, he ran for, and won, seats in the Assembly and the state Senate. But he continued to write (a total of nineteen books written or edited) and to speak publicly. [I once sent him a satirical piece from my GADFLY column; he replied that he didn't think it was so funny. Maybe he had an overly serious personality or was too caught up in the current issue of the day.]

Tom Hayden was an original, and we need more of his kind. Despite his lack of a well-tuned sense of humor, he certainly was a Peace Hero and was not with us long enough.

Hamilton Holt (1872–1951) wrote an important editorial titled "A Way to Disarm: A Practical Proposal" in 1914, and was a member of The League to Enforce Peace.

Hannah Hallowell Clothier Hull (1872–1958) was a Pennsylvanian when to be so harkened back to the days of William Penn. She was a Quaker, a pacifist, and a feminist, and though not an extraordinary person such as Gandhi or Erasmus, she devoted her life to peace. She was one of the founders of the Women's Peace Party and of the Women's International League for Peace and Freedom, and she attended the Second Hague Conference for International Peace in 1907.

Her papers now reside in the Swarthmore College Peace Collection, her alma mater. She was an ordinary person but an extraordinary Peace Hero as well. We need more of her kind.

John Hume (1937–), a schoolteacher as a young man, entered the fray of politics in Northern Ireland in the 1960s as a Catholic and civil rights leader. He was also a founding member of The Irish League of the Credit Unions.

Hume soon was in the leadership of the Social Democratic Labor Party. Because his major influences were pacifists

Mohandas Gandhi, Martin Luther King, Jr., and Nelson Mandela, he did not support the armed IRA and its willingness to use violence. Rather, he encouraged both the British and Northern Irish to meet and negotiate with the IRA, placing him in the good graces of both the British government and Sein Fein.

He was instrumental in the agreement between the UK and the Republic of Ireland that ended the "Troubles," the 1994 cease-fire between the IRA and the Northern Ireland Nationalists, and finally the "Good Friday" agreement of 1998.

The Nobel Peace Prize, awarded jointly to John Hume and David Trimble, sealed an end to the conflict which had proved to be one of the most intractable of all. John Hume and his reputation for fairness and nonviolence was felt by all sides to be the key. All would agree that John Hume deserves the label of Peace Hero.

Daisaku Ikeda (1928–) is a Buddhist philosopher, educator, and campaigner for nuclear disarmament. He leads Soka Gakkai International, the largest Buddhist lay denomination with 12 million followers worldwide. It is described as Buddhist humanism that respects all life.

Beginning in the 1970s he embarked on over fifty international exchanges with scholars, peace activists, and world leaders. Each year he submits a peace proposal to the UN, proposing the elimination of nuclear weapons.

In 1975, Ikeda presented Kurt Waldheim, then Secretary General of the UN, with a petition calling for total abolition of nuclear weapons; it was signed by 10 million people, both ordinary and famous.

Ikeda is a superb organizer and has tried to associate his name not just with Peace Heroes, but together with Gandhi and King. Nor has he shied away from association with Henry

Kissinger and George HW Bush. Nevertheless, on balance overall, we must name him a Peace Hero.

Japanese academics, in a group, who have renounced any military research—not only nuclear research that could be used for weapons—are also Peace Heroes.

Chalmers Johnson (1932–2010) served in the US Navy during the Korean War. A scholar by nature, he gathered many observations about China and Japan, served as a consultant to the CIA, taught political science on a university level, and authored several books.

He was a self-admitted cold warrior, highly critical of the Soviet Union, but when the USSR broke into separate nations, he took note that the budget of the US Department of Defense (de facto Department of War) went up rather than yielding the promised "peace dividend."

Johnson became disillusioned with the American political-economic system and military culture when no diversion of budget from the military to education/infrastructure/health/civilian research needs took place.

From 2000 to 2006 he wrote a series of books he called the "Blowback Trilogy": *The Costs and Consequences of the American Empire; Nemesis: The Last days of the American Republic;* and *Dismantling the Empire: America's Last, Best Hope*. The last one was required reading for CIA agents.

Though he had been known for his scholarship on China and Japan, it was as critic of American imperialism and its dependence on the well over 700 foreign military bases around the world and the US military "solutions" to political and economic questions, that his writing became known. It is also why Chalmers Johnson is considered a Peace Hero.

Kathy Kelly (1952–) is and, it seems, always has been a social activist, outspoken critic of war, and advocate for peace. She was a founder of Voices in the Wilderness, and continued to be creative in showing war and militarism for what it is by the more newly formed Voices For Creative Nonviolence.

She has remained in combat zones during the early days of both Iraq wars and the war in Afghanistan displaying the activities of Americans that would benefit the citizens—not guns and bombs, but food, medicine, and blankets. She has in person opposed deadly drone activity in the US, at Creech, Nevada, Syracuse, NY, Beale, CA, and Whiteman, MO. Wait till she hears of the piloting bases in Texas, Arizona, and New Mexico!

When Kelly wrote to Attorney General Janet Reno of her plans to bring medicines and food to the people of Iraq in violation of the sanctions, she was threatened with jail and a $1 million fine. Wherever there was peace work to be done, there was Kathy Kelly—in Nicaragua against American-supported Contra murders and violence; in the Missouri Peace Planting at the Nuclear missile site near Kansas City; at the School of the Americas Watch at Fort Benning GA; at the Gaza Strip on behalf of Palestinian rights; at the US Capitol with Witness against Torture to conduct a mock funeral for prisoners at Guantanamo who were reportedly tortured to death; visiting with Afghan Youth Volunteers in Kabul and Bagram (near the Air Force Base and Prison)....

In her spare time she has written many essays, op-eds, and books. Her best known work was *Other Lands Have Dreams*. In addtion to many speaking engagements around the country, she has received dozens of awards—and has been arrested more than sixty times for her peace activities and sentenced to significant prison time. Her friends have noted that "jail is the only place she can rest."

Kathy Kelly is without question a Peace Hero.

Colman McCarthy (1938–) was a journalist and columnist for *The Washington Post* for thirty years. Then, without stopping to catch his breath after retirement, he became a teacher and lecturer in a wide variety of schools, teaching peace and nonviolence. Founder and Director of the Center for Teaching Peace, he is so avid in this second career, we must count him as a Peace Hero.

David Fraser McTaggart (1932–2001) was a Canada-born environmentalist who used his own boat to protest French nuclear tests in the South Pacific in 1972. The French military damaged his boat and injured him, but France ended atmospheric nuclear testing two years later.

His next project could be summed up in a sound byte: Save the Whales. He and singer Byran Adams toured the world to gain support for the Southern Ocean Whale Sanctuary. The Sanctuary was established in 1994 by the International Whaling Commission, with only Japan voting in opposition. In 1979, he was the principal force in the formation of Greenpeace International, and in 1987 he founded the Third Millennium Foundation to continue his work for disarmament and Peace.

David Fraser McTaggart showed that one individual can be politically effective. He was an exemplary Peace Hero.

Moriori culture of Chatham Island, NZ are, is an entire community of Peace Heroes for their culture of nonviolent, passive resistance.

A.J. Muste (1894–1964) was a Quaker, a labor organizer, and a leader in the peace movement of the mid-20th century. He is probably best known for his assertion, "There is no way to Peace: Peace *is* the way." But, we may also point to his great influence on Martin Luther King, Jr., James Farmer, and Bayard Rustin. Muste also was successful in getting Albert Einstein to convince the scientific community to renounce all work that the military might use. He was a central figure in Fellowship of Reconciliation and the War Resisters League. He lived a life of conscience, but went further to show that being a pacifist was by no means being passive. He was a true Peace Hero.

Abie Nathan (1927–2008), born in Persia (now Iran) and growing up in Bombay (Mumbai), India, entered he British RAF in 1944 at age 17 as a pilot. It was a time when there were no machine guns and bombs were thrown out of windows by hand. If the pilots were too emotionally disturbed about the resultant deaths and injuries of civilians caused by the wanton bombing, they would often ditch their bombs in the sea.

In the 1948 Arab-Israeli War, Nathan volunteered as a pilot. Afterward, he resided in Israel and formed the Nes (Miracle) political party and ran for a seat in the Knesset. Not elected, he turned his attention to humanitarian work and peace advocacy. It was the beginning of his real life's work.

In 1966 he flew his plane *Shalom 1* (*Peace 1*) to Egypt to deliver petitions to President Nasser calling for peace between Egypt and Israel. It was the beginning of a series of actions to wage peace between Palestinians and Israelis, including meeting with Yasser Arafat, who was classified as a terrorist at the time. Then, in 1973, after many financial difficulties, he celebrated the inauguration of the Peace Ship, which sailed off the coast in international waters and broadcast "Voice of Peace" programs. The Voice of Peace also had a humanitarian purpose to aid children and civilians in natural and man-made disasters around the world, from Biafra to the earthquake in Guatemala.

Abie Nathan seemed to be everywhere at once. He often stretched his resources too far, and when, in 1993, the date of the Oslo Peace Accords, he decided to call an end to the Voice of Peace after twenty years. The last program was Pete Seeger's "We Shall Overcome."

Even after suffering a stroke in 1996, he attended public functions from his wheelchair to lend moral support, and in 1997 he received the Nuremberg International Rights Award—which he attended in person.

Abie Nathan was an indefatigable Peace Hero who overcame adversity and often succeeded in his peace efforts.

Thich Nhat Hanh (1926–) is a Vietnamese Buddhist peace activist. He was ordained a monk in 1949, and is a prolific author, having published over 100 books, forty of them in English. He is also a superb organizer who has founded many meditation centers, monasteries, and schools, issued declarations, and attracted followers—all in his quest for non-violent solutions to conflict.

In 1961 he came to the US to teach comparative religion at Princeton University (he is fluent in seven languages). Two years later he briefly returned to Vietnam to assist fellow monks in their peace efforts. Back in the US, he met with Martin Luther King, Jr. in 1966 to convince him that his voice was needed to oppose the war publicly. The following year King made his now-famous address to the American people at Riverside Church. Meanwhile, the CIA named Nhat Hanh as the leader of Thich Tri Quang, a dissident [their term] group. In 2005 and 2007, he led two peace marches in Los Angeles to oppose the Iraq War.

All his life, he would not use any animal products, either for food or for wearing apparel; his Buddhist beliefs rejected engaging in violence against non-human animals.. The "mindfulness" that he is so well known for is a personal quest for peace, but in the 1960s he called for Engaged Buddhism, to require the individual to actively engage in creating change.

He has received many awards, including The Courage of Conscience award and the Pacem in Terris Peace and Freedom Award. Let us add another: Peace Hero.

Phil Ochs (1940–1976) was a singer and song writer known for his sharp wit and his songs of protest. He was most active and recognized in the 1960s and early 70s.

His musical talent showed up when he was a teenager: at age 16 he was the principal clarinet soloist for an Ohio Conservatory orchestra. He studied journalism at Ohio State, and the two interests came together in the way of folk songs, where his major influences were Bob Gibson, Woody Guthrie, and Pete Seeger.

His songs included: "I Ain't Marching Anymore"; "Draft Dodger Rag"; "Love Me, I'm A Liberal"; and "I Declare the War Is Over." He always described himself not as a protest singer, but as a singing journalist. In the early 1970s, believing his music was ineffectual in bringing the Vietnam War to an end, he took up country music and early rock and roll. He described himself as a combination of Elvis Presley and Che Guevara. In spite of the change, his followers would not abandon him. His concerts at Carnegie Hall, "Gunfight At Carnegie Hall," were eminently successful.

His most popular song, "I Declare the War Is Over," was written in 1967 and first performed publicly at the Lincoln Memorial in Washington, D.C. When the war finally ended in 1975, a great rally was held in New York's Central Park. Over 100,000 people came to hear Ochs, Harry Belafonte, Odetta,

Pete Seeger, Joan Baez, and others in concert, ending with Ochs performing "I Declare The War Is Over." True at last! The rally was followed by a peace march from Washington Square to Times Square to the UN.

Phil Ochs was a bone fide Peace Hero, though a tragic figure who was not with us long enough.

Martin Niemöller (1892–1964), a German Lutheran pastor, wrote one of the most famous Peace Poems in history. It alludes to silence in the face of war and violence, and he spoke it, in various versions, from shortly after the war in 1946 well into the nineteen-fifties.

> *First they came for the socialists, and I did not speak out – because I was not a socialist;*
>
> *Then they came for the trade unionists, and I did not speak out – because I was not a trade unionist;*
>
> *Then they came for the Jews, and I did not speak out – because I was not a Jew;*
>
> *Then they came for me – and there was no one left to speak out for me.*

Niemoller was imprisoned in two concentration camps over a period of eight years for not supporting the Nazi takeover of the churches, and after the war became an antiwar activist and advocate of nuclear disarmament. But there is some amount of dispute for his being called a Peace Hero.

The quotation, often called a poem, is worthy of being remembered as a Peace Poem.

Frederic Passy (1822–1912) grew up in a family of political notables. He became a lawyer, then an economist, and was an active member of the French Société d'Economie Politique

(Political Economy Society) for seventy years. For his unceasing work in the Peace Movement he became known as the "Apostle of Peace."

He tried by his personal efforts to prevent war between France and Germany in 1870. These efforts and those of William Randal Cremer in England led to the formation of the Inter-Parliamentary Union. Passy founded La Société Francaise Pour l'Arbitration entre Nations (French Society for International Arbitration) and promoted the Hague Conference. The idea of solving conflict through diplomacy if possible and arbitration if necessary met with international acceptance and earned both men Nobel Peace Prizes in 1901 (Passy) and 1903 (Cremer).

Passy was known throughout France as the dean of the Peace Movement. May we keep the momentum going by naming Frederic Passy a Peace Hero.

Peace Pilgrim (1908–1981) was born Mildred Lisette Norman, but in 1953 decided to do something about the military and war culture that had afflicted the world under the leadership of the US. She renamed herself Peace Pilgrim and started on a pilgrimage up and down and across the country "until mankind has learned the way of peace, walking until I am given shelter and fasting until I am given food."

Her journey was cut short in 1981 when she was killed in an auto crash, but for twenty-eight years she spread the message of inner peace to achieve world peace. She spoke to people individually along the way and to groups in churches, colleges, and the media.

Her friends published a book *Peace Pilgrim: Her Life and Her Work*, and the booklet "Steps Toward Inner Peace." In them is her best known quote: "Overcome evil with good, falsehood with truth, and hatred with love."

Posthumously, she received the Peace Abbey Courage of Conscience Award. Peace Pilgrim was certainly worthy of being a Peace Hero.

Albert Schweitzer (1875–1965) was first an organist, then a philosopher and theologian, and last a medical missionary. He earned his PhD in 1899, and one of his earliest quotes showed his direction: "The highest insight man can attain is the yearning for peace, for the union of his human with God's will." He opposed every form of cruelty. Two other quotes are notable: "All life is sacred, even life we may consider lower than our own," and "Reverence for life is the highest court of appeal."

Schweitzer was best known for the hospital that he and his wife started in Lambarene, Gabon, in Africa. A gifted musician, he gave organ concerts in Europe to fund the hospital.

After WW II Schweitzer joined Bertrand Russell and Albert Einstein in denouncing the testing and stockpiling of nuclear weapons as well as the threat of their use as national policy. In 1953 he won the Nobel Peace Prize.

Albert Schweitzer will live on as a Peace Hero.

Pete Seeger (1919–2014) was far more than an iconic musician, and his life was taken up with far more than music. He played the 12-stringed guitar, the 5-stringed banjo, and his own longneck banjo with three more frets and tuned two steps down. He was also a prolific songwriter and was interested in labor rights, civil rights, social equality, peace or war; and he opposed all militarism.

He was associated with some of the great ones who preceded him such as Malvina Reynolds, Woody Guthrie, and Leadbelly, and many others who came later and were more associated with him but who became famous in their own right, such as Tom Paxton, Johnny Cash, and Bob Dylan.

Although he often sang his own songs, he would just as soon sing those of others that he deemed worthy.

His songs included "Where Have All the Flowers Gone," "Turn, Turn, Turn," "If I had a Hammer," "Which Side Are You On?" "Waist Deep In the Big Muddy," and "Bring Them Home, Bring Them Home."

The 1960s were salad days for Seeger and the Weavers, but in the Fifties he had been accused of being a Communist and was summoned to appear before the House Un-American Activities Committee. Seeger appeared but would not name fellow Communists, citing not the Fifth Amendment, but the First Amendment to the Constitution. Seeger continued his wicked ways to the dismay of the committee, until Joseph Welch, Counsel for the Army, had the courage to ask Joseph McCarthy publicly, "Have you left no sense of decency, sir?" However, Seeger was blacklisted, had his contracts and concert dates canceled, and was convicted of contempt of Congress and sentenced to several years in jail.

In the Sixties he became one of the of the leading voices against the Vietnam War and visited North Vietnam in 1972 [the year after my own essay "The Grand Plan to End the War in Vietnam" was published in *WIN* Magazine].

Seeger, who lived until his mid-nineties, made good use of his years to promote social, political, and environmental goals. One, the Clearwater project, was successful in raising awareness of the pollution of the Hudson River with PCBs from the GE plant upstate. The Clearwater inevitably led to a cleanup of the River. In 1977, the US Environmental Protection Agency finally banned the manufacture of PCBs. The Clearwater Project and the young people involved with Pete provided the political pressure.

Many of Pete's followers had their own favorite song that he performed. Mine was "The Bells of Rhymney," a collaboration between Seeger and the Welsh poet Idris Davies. Whatever their favorite, all would vote to count Pete Seeger as a giant of a Peace Hero.

Gene Sharp (1928–2018) was a political theoretician who promoted nonviolent activism to foster peace and progressive social change. He wrote many books in his career including: *Exploring Nonviolent Alternatives* (1970), *The Politics of Nonviolent Action* (1973), and *Waging Nonviolent Struggle: 20th Century Practice and 21st Century Potential* (2005).

Sharp pointed to Gandhi, A.J. Muste, and Henry David Thoreau as major influences in the formation of his philosophical beliefs. His theoretical political writing has been claimed as the basis of the liberation of the Baltic countries in 1991 and the Arab Spring in Egypt in 2011 (though some of the Egyptian activists who overthrew Mubarak say they did it on their own).

Sharp founded the nonprofit Albert Einstein Institution in 1983, and in 2012 he received the Right Livelihood Award, a loud voice in his behalf.

Whether theoretical or pragmatic, Gene Sharp must be listed in the Annals of Peace as a real Peace Hero.

Robert Shetterly is a painter who has established an on-going series of portraits: *Americans Who Tell the Truth* (AWTT). The series comprises more than 200 portraits, including many who are or were antiwar activists and are listed in this chapter as Peace Heroes.

The Sikhs were founded by their first Guru, Nanak, at the time of the Renaissance in the West. As a young man, he claimed divine revelation and set an example by helping the poor and feeding the hungry—leading a life of moral character, good behavior, and piety. Nanak was a monotheist, living among Hindus and Muslims, but taught tolerance for all religions. Human rights were primary. Though the men wear turbans and the women head scarves, they are equal before God.

Sikhs, to this day, pray for the well-being of all humanity. They work actively for peace and to uphold justice.

Next comes the difficult part. Guru Sanak was nonviolent and peace-loving. Guru Gobind Singh, the tenth and last guru, was known as the warrior leader. He is often depicted wearing a long, curved sword and is known to have fought many battles against the Mughal rulers in northern India. Yet he was a scholar, and he composed a large body of poetry. He said, "In my poetry, I have praised acts of valor, but I have also said that the sword should be drawn only when all other means have failed. Using a sword is not always heroic, and not wishing to fight is not always cowardly."

Let us give Guru Gobind Singh special dispensation and call him a conditional Peace Hero. The first Guru, Nanek, remains an unconditional Peace Hero.

Lawrence S. Wittner (1941–) wages peace as his life work. He is an active member of Peace Action, the Peace History Society, and the International Peace Research Association. He has written nine books and edited another four. A few of the titles tell us of his sympathies re: *War or Peace: One World Or None; Resisting The Bomb;* and *Toward Nuclear Abolition*. But the subtitles give us insight into his context: *A History of the World Disarmament Movement*.

Wittner is a historian and academic (PhD and all). He has spoken at many colleges and universities, nationally and internationally, and has addressed the UN and the Norwegian Nobel Institute. He may not have been on the protest lines or unfurling banners in the gallery of Congress informing everyone about the mistakes of military drones, but the Peace Movement can use all the help it can get. Peace needs those willing to perform civil disobedience as needed, and the historians and other academics, too.

Lawrence Wittner hereby joins the ranks of Peace Heroes.

Abdulkadir Yahya Ali (1957–2005), known as "Yahya," was a prominent Somali peace activist. With all the militias, jihadists, and interference by foreign governments both in Africa and abroad, it was almost impossible to be a peace activist in Somalia. Nevertheless, he was a public figure advocating for peace, having founded the Center for Research and Dialogue which was widely respected in Somalia and internationally.

Somalia was and is as much a failed state as could be imagined, with the government mostly in the North, no legal system, and the capital of Mogadishu largely in anarchy. The US was active, not diplomatically, but in counter-terrorism (militarily). Yet, Yahya was an indefatigable optimist.

Assassinated by jihadists in 2005, one of his speeches was read at his memorial service. It called on diverse groups of Somali society to act together: "traditional leaders, spiritual leaders, intellectuals, artists, mothers and all women, students, and ordinary people, the 90% of the population who needed to bring on a peaceful uprising to achieve a peaceful and harmonious society." His was a call for courage.

Yahya was offered residence in a foreign country but turned it down because he wanted to rebuild his nation from within. He was arguably the most courageous Somali of all. We must label Abdulkadir Yahya Ali a Peace Hero.

Howard Zinn (1922–2010) was a professor of history, and in view of his *People's History of the United States*, still is. Zinn was a bombadier in WW II, then educated under the GI Bill. As a natural historian, he returned after the war to a town he participated in bombing and reviewed municipal records and newspaper clippings from 1945 and interviewed survivors.

In his career as a historian, Zinn wrote over twenty books, many covering the labor movement in the US, the Civil Rights era (still going on), and antiwar protests through all the direct and proxy conflicts.

In 1979, he was personally involved in a strike of clerical workers at his university, refusing to cross their picket lines.

As to antiwar efforts, he published *Vietnam: the Logic of Withdrawal*. He also supported the GI campaigns against the war such as the Veterans March from Lexington, MA, to Bunker Hill, and the Winter Soldier hearings in which former GIs testified about the atrocities they witnessed or may have participated in. When the US under Bush and Cheney invaded Iraq in 2003 against public opposition, Zinn opposed the "Shock and Awe" bombing and occupation of that ancient country on both moral and legal grounds.

Zinn received many awards including the Peace Abbey Courage of Conscience Award, the Thomas Merton Award, and the Eugene Debs Award. His *People's History* was also honored by being banned from being taught in Arkansas and Indiana public schools.

We, too, pay tribute to Howard Zinn, with the designation of Peace Hero.

Chapter 8

Human Aversion to Killing

The great majority of archaeologists agree that hunting-gathering groups of humans in the Upper Paleolithic (about 60,000–10,000 BP) were egalitarian and cooperative, and that troublesome individuals were ostracized, not killed. There were neither population pressures nor competition for resources, either of which could have led to group conflict or war. In fact, violence between small bands would have been costly and a threat to the survival of the groups ... and to the new species itself, given the low total population. Survival must have been difficult enough, what with accidents, difficulties of childbirth, infections, diseases, and large carnivores.

Among the hundreds of cave paintings dated to the Upper Paleolithic era, there are none that show humans attacking other humans. Indeed, there are very few showing animals intersected by lines, a questionable representation of hunting. These lines could more likely have been meant as waves or lines of force or design elements.

There have been merely six skeletons discovered with embedded stone points among a few thousand skeletons found at hundreds of sites dated to the Paleolithic period. Such evidence of violence (or perhaps accident) is the rare exception.

The Upper Paleolithic period, beginning about 60,000 or

70,000 BP, was the time of cognitive changes in the human brain and the defining of our genetic heritage. We could think of past and future as well as the present and were able to plan ahead. We had a sense of self and a realization of death. We could employ conceptual and symbolic thought, and were aware that others of the species had these same attributes. Let us call it the conceptual brain.

All the great apes—orangutans, gorillas, chimpanzees, and bonobos—have ancestors in common with humans, and all have DNA structures that are over 95% alike. *Australopithecus, Homo habilis*, and *Homo erectus* all preceded *Homo sapiens* and had genomes even more alike. The primatologists can be of some help with the question of whether we are inherently violent or whether we are more social beings guided by empathy, morality, and cooperation. They invariably are on the side of the latter.

The paucity of evidence of violence in the social species called mankind through the 190,000-year-long Middle and Upper Paleolithic speaks of a genetic heritage that is not violent, but cooperative. The next period, the Neolithic, was defined by early farming and herding as well as advances in ceramics, the fashioning of sophisticated stone tools, and the first use of copper. The archaeological record from the Neolithic is far more extensive, and provides insights in the life of *Homo sapiens* living at that time.

A particular type of artifact that is especially instructive is the stamp seal carved in stone. Agriculture enabled Neolithic mankind to produce surpluses that could be stored or traded for other goods such as flint, obsidian, shell, or copper. The stamp seal impressed in the clay wrapping of the goods stored or traded would identify the owner and insure honesty in any transaction. There have been a few thousand seals and many imprints in clay tablets found from the Neolithic period, indicating that trading and commerce was the order of the day.

Compared to the very limited number of sites with evidence of violence, some of it equivocal, the thousands of seals and sealings demonstrate that commerce and cooperation were ubiquitous. It is a given that one does not attack a trading partner. The fermentation of barley to produce ale was surely a part of establishing celebration as an important part of social life of those early times. Occasional seals of drinking parties from the following Bronze aAge period are well known. Perhaps ale was an integral part of diplomacy of those times.

Populations increased markedly with permanent settlements, as men were not away on a hunt for days at a time. There seemed to be time and technologies to produce surpluses of food, fiber, various types of stone, and other resources available to trade, obviating any need, and the risks, of attacking other settlements for "spoils."

That mankind is capable of violence, individually and in groups, has been all too well documented from the mid-3rd millennium and thereafter up to the present day. Yet, no serious researcher has proposed that *Homo sapiens* underwent a sharp mutation of the species around 3,000 BCE to become violent and warsome, following the peaceful Paleolithic period. Indeed, we are genetically the same *Homo sapiens* today that evolved millennia ago as modern humans. Our *culture* was responsible for the change to violence. Cultures can change in less than a generation, and they can change to a culture of peace and conciliation just as rapidly.

We have been adroit in avoiding conflict and violence, as we have, at other times, in inciting or acting in violence. Mankind has been able to avoid violence and war in any of several different ways, and there were consequently long periods of time when the great majority of humans were peaceful and cooperative.

The innate reluctance to kill or seriously harm another of the species may well be in our genetic heritage. 20th-century studies of soldiers during warfare confirm this aversion.

S.L.A. Marshall was a general and Dave Grossman a lieutenant colonel in WW II. Both did extensive interviews of soldiers after battle and reported their findings in the lay literature as well as in official reports. Marshall and Grossman both found that most soldiers did not fire their rifles at the enemy. Marshall's figures were astonishingly high: 80% to 85% of soldiers failed to fire with the enemy clearly in sight. Grossman interviewed as many as he could as soon after battle as possible. He, too, found widespread reluctance to kill the enemy. Grossman also quotes other writers who confirm an aversion to killing. His own grandfather was a member of a firing squad in the Great War (WW I) who told the family that he never killed a prisoner, always aiming to miss.

The writings of Sun Tzu of ancient China and Charles Ardant du Picq in the 19th century are instructive. Sun Tzu, a general and philosopher who wrote *The Art of War*, advises emperors to avoid prolonged war, to subdue the enemy without force if possible, and to consider politics and economics as much as military strategies. He speaks of warfare not in terms of *killing* the enemy but of *convincing* him (winning hearts and minds).

Du Picq notes in *Battle Studies* that most soldiers fire just to fire but not to hit the enemy. He states that human nature and the way men react to war can be more important than technology and military tactics. The WW I story of the Christmas Truce is widely known. At that time soldiers in opposing trenches spontaneously joined in singing "Silent Night" ("Stille Nacht") and then exhibited enough trust to meet their enemies in no-man's land, exchanging small gifts and photographs. It was not one isolated incident at one location, but at many points along the defensive lines of trenches. In one area, the Germans and Scots opposing them even had an impromptu football game (soccer).

Other historians have confirmed soldiers' reluctance to kill. Military historian Gwenne Dyer analyzed the air war in WW II. A tiny minority of USAF pilots did much of the air-to-air killing, and the majority of pilots never even tried to shoot down an enemy plane. Roy Swank and Walter Marchand, both psychiatrists, found that after sixty days of combat, 98% of surviving soldiers became psychiatric casualties. The 2% who were able to endure the sustained combat had the common trait of a psychopathic personality to start with.

Another author, military historian John Keegan, points out the incongruity between the death and destruction of two World Wars and the civilian climate of family, school, and cultural life. He notes the antipathy to violence and conflict that followed WW II. Keegan quotes Shakespeare's *Henry V*, in which Henry orders his troops to slaughter the prisoners but the knights refuse to do so.

The national mood in England when WW II ended was described by Kay Summersby, a personal friend of Eisenhower:

"No one laughed, No one smiled. We had won, but victory was not anything like what I thought it would be. There was a dull bitterness about it. So many deaths. So much destruction. And everybody was very, very tired."

The poet Patrick Dickinson was even more succinct: "There are no words to be said … tomorrow night a war will end."

Paul Fussell was an infantry lieutenant in WW II. After the war he became a social historian and wrote, "The culture of war is dominated by fear, blood, and sadism, by irrational actions. It has more relation to absurdist theatre than to actual life."

Fussell more recently told of a Pentagon official clarifying why he censored a clip of TV footage that showed an Iraqi on the ground being cut in two by automatic fire from an American helicopter: "If we let people see that kind of thing, there would never again be any war."

Although there has been some complaint about S.L.A. Marshall's methodology, and that his report falls short of the standards of true research, his credibility at the Pentagon was total. In the post-WW II era, training camps for new recruits used several conditioning techniques to make killing an unthinking reflex. On the firing range, bulls eye targets were replaced by pop up silhouettes that left no time for thinking before firing. At the end of a marksmanship training session, accuracy scores were recorded in the number of "kills." At some boot camps, the drill sergeants instructed recruits to yell "Kill!" with each round fired. In addition the cultural differences with the enemy were emphasized: our foes were called "gooks" in Vietnam and "ragheads" in the Near East.

The innate reticence of humans to kill partly explains the extremely high rate of PTSD (post-traumatic stress disorder) among returning veterans of the Iraq and Afghan wars. The other reason must be cultural. They left a civilian life of obedience to the rule of law and to the Ten Commandments, both of which forbid murder, and they entered the armed forces to be trained as killers. It is no wonder that so many veterans start to exhibit some combination of the classical signs of PTSD: they become depressed; they get divorced; they can't hold down a job; they succumb to alcohol and drug abuse and to smoking; they become homeless; they engage in crime; or they commit suicide. The figure of 20% of veterans is accepted as the minimal incidence of PTSD, but less than half the true number of cases is reported. That makes the real figure to be at least 40%.

All in all, war appears to be an artificial construct. Margaret Mead wrote, "Warfare is only an invention, not a biological necessity." Once established, war becomes a cultural norm and develops its own traditions. People assume that war has always been with us and always will be. But a number of authors and social thinkers disagree. John Horgan, Joshua S. Goldstein, Douglas P. Fry, Paul Fussell, John Mueller, Jonathan Haas, Matthew Piscitelli, David Fabbro, and Randall Forsberg are but a sampling of the many who, like Margaret Mead, say that if war was invented by societies of men, it can be abolished by them. As we will see in chapter 9, 21st-century society has already abolished nine-tenths of the formerly violent, cruel, and inequitable practices of the past 5,000 years. We no longer burn witches at the stake....

Two Moons

Evening sky and water surface —
  the miles reduced to two
dimensions each. The Earth's lone

  satellite finds many forms in
  all the metaphors and
images evoked in this

newly conceptual brain of our
  Second Coming: sculpture,
philosophy, poetry...

Military—Politary

    Mumble,
fumble
    moneyrolls, but
    not to worry: honey
holds the overruns. So

    rubber
stamp the
    brass and ribbons,
    ask no calendars,
just pass the vote right down

    the aisle
say "aye"
    to arms, and dash
    the decimals. Let John Q
    know that castles cost.

> *War is easy, almost mindless, just pull the trigger or, nowadays, press the button. Peace is difficult. It requires patience, forbearance, understanding, creativity, and wisdom.*
>
> —Gadfly Zeeks

Chapter 9

RESOLUTIONS OF CONFLICT

Violent conflict, often outright war, has been the default method to resolve conflict since about 2500 BCE. A satisfying sense of immediacy and completeness seems to come from wielding swords, shooting guns, or, nowadays, pressing buttons. War is easy, and warriors too often equate revolution with resolution.

More difficult is the resolution of conflict by means of peaceful methods. Such methods include statecraft and diplomacy, negotiations and conciliation, patience, persistence, and creativity. Often, such resolution of conflict doesn't yield a sense of victory. Yet, in the previous half century, many seemingly irreconcilable conflicts have been settled by nonmilitary means. The oppressed have resorted to many methods of redress: petition of grievances, demonstrations, banners, use of the alternative media, sit-ins, strikes, occupations of space, boycotts, noncooperation with regulations and orders, civil disobedience, street theater, flowers, chocolates, humor ... whatever he creative spirit can bring to bear.

The experience of mankind with two world wars in the first half of the century, especially at the nuclear-horrific end of WW II, did not seem to turn everyone into a pacifist. Yet, despite the police and military power of many authoritarian governments and outright dictators, and their willingness to use cruelty and murder, the will of the people for justice, freedom, and democracy was attained through *satyagraha*, or truth force. Yes, many times, the blood of some of the people seeking change has been shed, but the loss of life was nowhere near what it would have been were there open warfare or protracted military conflict. The large number of instances of the success of nonviolent action was beyond the expectations of the governments of the world. Let's looking at a sampling.

Philippines

In the Philippines, a nation that has known foreign rule (of Spain), attempted annexation (by the US), corrupt and brutal dictatorship (of Ferdinand Marcos), and assassination of a popular opposition leader (Benigno Aquino), the united and imaginative actions of hundreds of thousands of citizens accomplished the seemingly impossible.

The opposition was led by the Church, aided by the defections of key government officials and refusal of orders by several units of the Army and Air Force. Aquino's widow Corazon, the Cardinal and bishops of the Catholic Church, clandestine radio, and an independent polling commission all called for active, nonviolent resistance to the point of civil disobedience. The people responded, even protecting the disobedient units of the military, not with guns but with numbers of civilians massed on the streets, singing and praying. Finally, when Marcos could no longer count on the loyalty of the Armed Forces, his dictatorship collapsed in a matter of four days. He called on the US to protect him and was flown by American helicopter to Clark Air Base and then to Hawaii.

Latin America

Active but peaceful revolutions occurred throughout Latin America through the 1980s and '90s. In Chile, the military regime of General Augusto Pinochet routinely arrested, imprisoned, and tortured anyone who possibly might question his rule. In 1986, matters came to a head. After an assassination attempt on Pinochet in which five bodyguards were killed, the military retaliated against well known political opponents. One, a human rights lawyer, thwarted an attempt by hooded men to abduct him in the early morning hours by turning on all the lights in his house and banging pots to alert the neighbors, who then joined in the clamor. The hooded men quickly drove off before they were seized by the crowd that had formed. Other tactics were used to protest, as well. One such was to unfurl large banners in the streets around prisons announcing "Here They Torture People." It was entirely truthful. In 1988, Pinochet called for a plebiscite to ratify his continued rule. The plebiscite was accompanied by threats and none-too-subtle intimidation against all those who advocated a "no" vote. Nevertheless, "No" won.

Similar nonviolent efforts to bring justice and democracy to country after country in Latin America came under the banner of "firmeza permanente" (relentless persistence). In Brazil, many centers sprang up in the rural countryside to demand land reform whereby the government would take over large unproductive landholdings of absentee owners and distribute parcels to landless peasants. In Uruguay, the office of Serpaj (Service for Peace and Justice) was unrelenting in its efforts to publicise the horric abuses of the military junta. In Argentina, the mothers of "Los Desaparacidos" (The Disappeared) kept vigils and organized demonstrations to bring their plight to the attention of the world. Movements for justice and democracy were also active in Nicaragua, Honduras, Guatemala, and Peru. Today, in much of South and Central America—Chile, Brazil, Argentina, Bolivia, Venezuela, Peru, Ecuador—free and fair elections are held, and popularly elected governments serve the people.

One nation, Costa Rica, was at peace during the political turmoil ravaging the rest of Latin America. Costa Rica did not have an army to keep the peace, having abolished its standing army in 1948, instead relying on the cooperation and good will of its people.

Indonesia

On the other side of the Pacific Ocean in Indonesia, the military regime of its president, General Suharto, reacted to student protests against corruption and dictatorial rule with harsh crackdowns. The student demonstrations continued. By the 1990s, the situation in Indonesia became more uncertain, and relations with China worsened with the treatment of large population of Chinese expatriots. The 1991 Santa Cruz massacre in East Timor caused the US Congress to suspend aid to Indonesia's military, and in 1997, cracks developed within the military, itself. Then, that same year, an international monetary crisis occurred, hitting Indonesia particularly hard. The resultant higher fuel and energy prices set the stage for widespread protests led by university students. In early 1998, those protests were met with lethal violence that killed thirteen students, and rioting engulfed the nation over the next few months. By May 1998 Suharto was forced to resign.

The southern island of the Indonesian archipelago, Timor, has had its own struggles during and after the repressive and sometimes bloody regime of Suharto. The division of the island goes back to colonial times, when the Dutch and

Portuguese fought over the Island. In 1849 the two European powers settled by splitting control of the island into a Dutch western half and a Portuguese eastern half.

Having been "East Timor" for nearly a century, the colony was administered by the Portuguese again following WWII. But twenty-five years later, in 1974, Portugal itself underwent a revolution that was led by the army and the lower-ranking officers who took to the streets where the people offered them carnations to place on their uniforms and in the muzzles of their rifles. As a result of the peaceful Carnation Revolution, the colonies in Africa, and including East Timor, were promised independence: in 1975, the Portuguese administrators withdrew from the island. Then, after a few military skirmishes, one of the political parties of East Timor declared independence. A month later, the Indonesian army, under the Suharto administration, invaded and annexed East Timor as a province. Greg Shackleton, an Australian journalist and his crew reporting on the invasion, were seized and executed the following day.

Resistance to the occupation, active but mostly nonviolent, continued. In 1991, at the Santa Cruz cemetery near Dili, troops fired on the mourners at a memorial service, killing more than 250. At the cemetery, two American journalists, Amy Goodman and Allan Nairn, were beaten with the stocks of American-made M16 rifles. They survived and reported the massacre, raising awareness in international community. The following year the US Congress, after hearing from Indonesian officials that the Santa Cruz attack was a matter of Indonesian policy, cut off all military assistance.

In 1993, '94, and '95, groups of East Timorese entered foreign embassies in Jakarta to seek political asylum. In 1996, Carlos Belo, the bishop of Dili, was awarded the Nobel Peace

Prize. Meanwhile, Suharto faced widespread opposition and disorder in Jakarta over his murderous repression of student protestors, and, as noted, in 1998 he was forced to resign. The following year, Indonesia and Portugal signed an agreement allowing the East Timorese to vote on whether to become independent or remain part of Indonesia. 99% of the eligible voters participated in the UN referendum, with 78% voting for independence, a result recognized by the Indonesian parliament. An Australian peace-keeping force was dispatched to put down a short-lived campaign of terror by the anti-independence militia, and a UN transitional administrational team arrived. Finally, in 2002, East Timor declared its independence, elected Xana Guzmao as president, and was admitted to the UN as a full member. Pressure from the international community was a critical factor.

Myanmar

In nearby Southeast Asia, Myanmar (called Burma for much of its modern history) has a past that extends back to 13,000 BCE. Records were sparse of the earliest times, and invasions were known for much of the historical era, but there were peaceful periods, as well. The period of the Pagan (Bagan) dynasty, 1044 to 1287 CE, was a golden age in which Theraveda Buddhism became widespread in the country. During this time, 10,000 temples and pagodas were built, over 2,000 of which still remain. Much of the Pagan dynastic rule was peaceful. During the 17th and early 18th centuries, under the restored Taungoo dynasty, reforms of government brought prosperity and peace.

In 1886, British colonial rule was established throughout Burma after a series of three Anglo-Burmese wars. Burma became part of the British Raj of the Indian subcontinent until WWII. After the Japanese surrender, negotiations between the British and a nationalist group led by U Aung San brought independence in 1947-48. The first ten years saw a gradual economic recovery in spite of the assassination of Aung San and a great deal of political infighting. Then U Nu headed the government until 1962, when a military coup led by General Ne Win was carried out.

Myanmar (Burma) remained under repressive military rule that lasted from 1962 into the 21st century. Suu Kyi is prevented from running for president by a clause in the Constitution, but in 2016 she was appointed State Counselor, akin to Prime Minister. In this position, and with a seat in the Assembly, she has considerable political power, but has come under widespread criticism for the treatment of Muslims in the province of Rohingya.

Suu Kyi must still be considered a Peace Hero for her many years of work while under house arrest as she opposed the military junta non-violently. Perhaps the country will return to being called Burma.

S. Korea

Further north on the eastern coast of Asia, South Korea has has had a succession of dictatorial or authoritarian governments since WWII. Syngman Rhee was the first strongman president, serving from 1948 to 1960. He was repressive in the face of dissent and protest. After the Korean war, Rhee maintained his hold on the presidency through rigged elections, and by 1960 student-led protests became insistent. The protests were brutally suppressed, causing significant bloodshed. In reaction, the students were joined by professors and large numbers of ordinary citizens. In the end, Rhee was forced to resign and was flown out of the country by the CIA.

In 1961, a military coup by General Park Chung-hee

continued the tradition of authoritarian governments. Park ruled until 1979, and his regime was followed by other military coups, by Chun Doo-hwan in 1980 and Roh Tae-woo in 1988.

Beginning in the 1970s, a Korean activist named Kim Dae-jung emerged as an opposition figure who fought for justice and human rights. He was jailed in 1976 and came to the attention of Amnesty International, which designated him a "Prisoner of Conscience." He was arrested again in 1980 accused of the serious charges of sedition and conspiracy. Sentenced to death, he received the support of Pope John Paul II, who pleaded for clemency for him.

In 1998 Kim campaigned for the presidency again and was elected. As president, he instituted a "sunshine policy" to establish closer ties with the north and arranged a summit meeting with Kim Jong-Il in Pyongyang. He became known as the Mandela of the East and was awarded the Nobel Peace Prize. Kim Dae-jung served his full five year term and established for the Korean people the heritage of free and fair elections. His presidency was followed by that of Moh Moo-hyun elected in 2003, Lee Myung-bak in 2008, and Park Guen-hye, Korea's first woman president, in 2013.

In 2018 Moon Jae-in succeeded Park, and has been active in pursuing better relations—if not total reconciliation—with N. Korea, which is ruled by the dynastic president and "Supreme Leader" Kim Jong-Un (son of Kim Jong-Il and grandson of founding president Kim Il-sung).

Taiwan

The Island of Taiwan lies off the eastern coast of mainland Asia, south of Korea and north of the Philippines. It has its own history, still ongoing. After WWII, Taiwan was declared a province of the Republic of China, ruled uneasily by Chiang

Kai-shek and the Kuomintang. General Chen Yi was appointed Chief Executive of Taiwan Province. Under the Japanese, Taiwan was given a great deal of autonomy and government was largely under local control. Chen Yi, in contrast, established central control, and his government was riddled with corruption. A black market flourished, and as inflation rose the entire economy sank and disaffection of the populace spread.

Protests and demonstrations against the government arose in 1947, and were violently suppressed. Student leaders and dissidents called for open rebellion. In the resulting uprising, control of several cities was taken over by rebels. The mainland government responded with Kuomintang troops who carried out a bloody repression, the 228 massacre.

In 1949, the Nationalist government suffered a major defeat in the Chinese Civil War on the mainland and retreated in entirety to Taiwan. Chiang Kai-shek and the Kuomintang instituted martial law on the island and presided over an authoritarian regime. No opposition or dissent was permitted. Although Chiang Kai-check died in 1975, martial law was retained by Chiang Ching-Kuo, his son and successor.

Only in the mid-1980s did popular political pressure cause the one-party state to move toward democratic rule. In 1986, the opposition Democratic Progressive Party was formed, and the following year Chiang Ching-kuo removed martial law, just a year before his death. Lee Teng-hui, the chair of the Kuomintang, became president. Democratic reform proceeded further, and in 1996 a popular election was held, the first in modern times. By 2000, the candidate of the Democratic Progressives, Chen Shui-bian, won the national election.

All the political change to democratic rule from the 1980s onward occurred nonviolently. Were there political squabbles and shifting tactics? Yes, but no military coups, no murders, no tortures, no burning down police stations—like in "the good old days." Now, if only the political disputes between The People's Republic of China and the people of Taiwan can be settled diplomatically...

Sri Lanka

In South Asia, the efforts of Mohandas Gandhi to bring India from the era of colonialism to the modern world of democracy is well known. Less high profile, the large island of Sri Lanka, just to the south of the subcontinent, was the focus of conflict from the beginning of the colonial period in the early 16th century. Hostilities regularly arose between the Portuguese and the Dutch, then with the British; between the Europeans and the natives; and between the different ethnic groups who had been there for centuries.

Sri Lanka was inhabited by humans as early as 35,000 BCE, the time of the Paleolithic. Those original hunter gatherers were known as the Veddahs. As of the first millennium BCE, Anuradhapura (dated to 900 BCE) had begun, and over the next two hundred years the settlement expanded in size to what we would call a city. By 500 BCE, advanced hydrology such as dams and reservoirs were utilized for agriculture. It was no primitive Neolithic culture.

For many hundreds of years, Sri Lanka has been populated by mainly two cultures—the Sinhalese who were first established in the 6th century BCE and the Tamils in the third century BCE. The differences in culture, skin color, religion, and language have fed into any social and political conflicts between them ever since their independence in 1948. The Tamils were located mainly in the North and East, the majority Sinhalese in the South and West. In 1983, the riots of Black July began a civil war in earnest. The LTTE (Tamil Tigers, a militant group, which had previously been formed to promote a separatist state for the Tamils) participated in the violence.

The civil war continued despite Indian peacekeepers who had been brought in. After eighteen years, in 2001, intense international pressure brought about a ceasefire. The Tamil Tigers had suffered large losses and gave up their demands for an independent Tamil nation. International mediation achieved the model of a more moderate, united nation the following year. All citizens—Buddhist Sinhalese, Hindu Tamils, Muslims, Dravidians, and a few Christians left over from colonial times—could participate in Sri Lankan affairs. The indigenous people, the Veddahs, who lived in the forests and maintained a hunting-gathering way of life, were to be respected.

No, it is not a large love-fest so soon after the seemingly endless civil war, and the fate of some of the journalists who dared question the majority Sinhalese Government is especially troubling. But the long military conflict has ended.

If the Sinhalese and Tamils, with so many centuries-long differences and historical antagonisms could, under the weight of universal international pressure, find peace in the same nation, what conflict could not be solved?

Ireland

Another island where animosities had a long history and 20th-century conflict seemed insoluble was Ireland. The island, north and south together, is about the same size as Sri Lanka, but the differences with Ireland are in culture and religion, not race or language. (The Irish and Northern Irish can tell each other apart from their accents, though each speaks the same English language.) It is helpful to know the history of the Island to more fully appreciate the long-standing, confused conflict and its eventual resolution.

The island of Ireland was first inhabited in the Mesolithic Period, about 10,000 BP. The first people likely had traveled there by boat or raft from Britain, which was still connected geologically to continental Europe, and they made their living by hunting and gathering. The Neolithic age of farming and herding is dated there to about 4,000 BCE. Their Bronze Age began in 2,000 BCE, and Celts began arriving about 500 BCE, bringing with them a pagan religion intertwined with Nature. The Celts were divided into small communities called tuaths, but all were guided by Brehon Law.

Britain and its inhabitants were conquered by the Romans, but not the the Picts and Scots north of Hadrian's Wall and not the Celts west of the Irish Sea. In the 5th century CE, St. Patrick arrived on the Emerald Isle, bringing Christianity and the Roman alphabet to the Celtic people there. By the 6th century, several monasteries had been built and were occupied by learned monks who produced beautiful illuminated manuscripts, notably the Book of Kells.

Later in the 1st millennium, Ireland endured Viking invasions, extreme weather, and plagues. In 1169 CE, under Henry II, the Duke of Normandy and first Plantagenet king, several barons invaded Ireland and seized Irish lands. Two years later, alarmed as a Norman nobleman, the Earl of Pembroke (Richard "Strongbow" de Clare), increased his power and reputation in Ireland, Henry led a large military force across the Irish Sea and established personal control of the area around Dublin and Waterford. Over following generations, however, there was a resurgence of Gaelic dominance, not least because the descendants of the Anglo-Norman barons considered themselves Irish rather than English.

Fast forward to the 16th century—Henry VIII (he of the six successive wives) quarreled mightily with the Vatican, in large part over his desire to annul his marriage to his brother's widow; and the Church of England no longer remained under Papal authority. In the 1530s Henry sought to establish his control over Ireland with an expeditionary force seizing the lands of the pre-eminent FitzGerald clan, and killing their men. His offer to introduce the Reformation made the Irish more determined than ever to remain Catholic, and they declined Henry's overture. Henry had already had Parliament pass the Act of Supremacy, whereby as king, he was the "Supreme Head of the Church of England." In 1541, Henry tried to settle the religious question in Ireland by declaring himself Monarch of the New Kingdom of Ireland, thus removing Ireland from the control of the Vatican.

Elizabeth I, Henry's last daughter, became the English Monarch in 1558 on the death of Mary I, her older half-sister. Mary was a Catholic and oversaw the Restoration of Roman Catholicism during her brief five-year reign.

Elizabeth was a Protestant and she re-established her father's Act of Supremacy under which English subjects were required to recognize the Crown as the Supreme Governor of the Anglican Church. The Act of Supremacy forbade any allegiance or payment of monies to the Holy See in Rome. The Act of Uniformity, passed earlier under Henry's rule, was also reinstated by Elizabeth.

Elizabeth was not as combative with Rome as her father had been, and she was somewhat tolerant of those subjects who privately practiced religions other than Church of England Protestantism. But in Ireland, the people were not willing to give up Catholicism, even though Elizabeth was Queen Regnant of England and Ireland. There were a few rebellions in the North of Ireland, which became more insistent in the Nine Years' War in the 1590s. The English forces numbered as many as 18,000 at one point. Most of the Irish rebels surrendered in 1602, and the remainder in 1603, six days after Elizabeth's death. With the loss of the Nine Years' War and the crowning of James I as monarch of Great Britain, several Irish chieftains left Ireland for the Continent — the flight of the Earls. These "escheated" lands were then confiscated and formed the basis of the Plantation system.

James I arranged a large scale migration of lowland Scot Protestants to His Majesty's Plantation in Northern Ireland in 1607. James had some influence over the home crowd in that he was James VI of Scotland before he was James I of Great Britain (England, Scotland, and Ireland). The Plantation in Ireland proved to be successful economically and was the beginning of the Protestant majority in Ulster.

After James, his son Charles I took the throne and was kept too busy quarreling with Parliament to pay much attention to Ireland. In 1641 the Irish, under the banner of the Irish Catholic Confederation, rebelled and controlled much of the countryside. Back in England and Scotland, a full-fledged civil war erupted between the Presbyterians in Scotland and the high Anglicans backing Charles. Oliver Cromwell's forces in Parliament, backed by their new model army, were victorious; Charles was tried, found guilty of treason, and executed as the result of their "Glorious Revolution."

Cromwell—now the "Lord Protector"—then turned his attention to the Irish, who had supported Charles and had stubbornly retained their Roman Catholic faith. As commander of a cavalry regiment, he led the army into Ireland, resulting in devastation of the land and widespread famine. Cromwell, to this day, is a detested historical figure in Ireland.

In 1660 the monarchy was restored under Charles II, eldest son of Charles I, and a Protestant. Known as the "Merry Monarch" for his hedonism, he was taken up politically with the

Anglo-Dutch war. On his death in 1685, his younger brother James II, a Catholic, took the throne. James's son was born in 1688, and a group of Protestant nobles, none too friendly toward the new king and now fearing a Catholic succession, invited the Protestant William of Orange (with an army) to England.

On his arrival, William was welcomed by many Englishmen, including nobles and many Protestant army officers who refused to fight for the Catholic James II. James gave up without a fight and fled to France.

Parliament declared that James had abdicated and offered the crown jointly to William and Mary. (William of Orange was the maternal grandson of Charles I through his mother, Mary; his wife, Queen Mary, was Charles's paternal granddaughter through her father, James II.)

The following year Louis XIV supplied a detachment of troops for James to lead an Irish invasion. In reaction to James's landing in Ireland, William raised a large force to defeat the Jacobite forces and, as well, to re-establish British sovereignty over Ireland. The Battle of the Boyne in 1690 was a decisive defeat for the French forces and for the native Irish army. The treaty of Limerick ended the war with the Protestants in control of Ireland, but under favorable terms for the French troops, who were allowed to return home, and for the Irish Catholics who could stay or go but who had to swear allegiance to William and Mary in order to retain their property and remain Catholic. The Protestants in Ireland, however, thought the Treaty was far too lenient on the Catholics.

Over the next century, even into the early 1800s, a series of penal laws made life more intolerable for the Catholic majority of the Irish population and reduced much of the country to abject poverty. As the 19th century went on, there were many small conflicts, with various gangs riding the countryside and creating random destruction of properties of large landowners. In 1791, first in Belfast, then in Dublin, the Society of United Irishmen was formed.

Inspired by the emerging American democracy, they sought Parliamentary reform, universal male suffrage and, not a few of them, separation from Great Britain. In reaction, the loyalist Orange Order was organized. A full-scale insurrection followed in 1798. The rebellion was brutally put down: any rebels captured alive were sent to penal colonies in Australia. Moreover, the Irish Parliament was abolished.

The 19th century saw the natural disaster of a three-year potato blight, intensified by the agricultural selection of a single variety of potato, the Lumper potato. The years 1845, '46, and '47 saw the Great Famine, during which as many as one million people died from starvation or from typhus and other famine-related diseases, and up to two million emigrated, most to America. In general, the English would never eat potatoes when bread was available, and even during the famine wheat was exported from Ireland to England; nor could potatoes be traded as a commodity, as they do not keep the way grains do. Thus there was enmity in all directions. Toward the end of the 19th century, the first and second Gladstone Laws were proposed for granting a measure of home rule for Ireland (1886, 1893) to calm down the Irish impetus for Independence.

Both bills failed in Parliament. In 1898, however, a Local Government (Ireland) Act was passed. The Unionists, especially in Ulster, opposed the campaign for home rule. In 1903, the Wyndham Land Purchase Act allowed tenant farmers to purchase their plots from landowners, and the 1906 Boyce Laborers Act protected the new small property owners. Yet the unrest in Ireland continued. Sein Fein (We Ourselves) organized around this time with the goal of full Irish independence.

In 1914, the British Parliament passed an Irish Home Rule Act, but it was put on hold because of the "Great War" that had started the same year.

Irish soldiers, irrespective of domestic politics, served with British forces in the Great War. Nonetheless, 1916 saw an armed rebellion by the Irish Republican Brotherhood aided by the Irish Volunteers in an attempt to establish an independent Irish Republic. Known as the Easter Uprising, it was crushed by British troops in six days. There followed a conscription crisis in 1918, the same year that Sein Fein won 73 of 105 possible Irish seats but refused to sit in the British House of Commons. In 1919, an elected Assembly (Dail Eireann) issued a Declaration of Independence, proclaiming an Irish Republic. The UK Parliament passed the Fourth Home Rule Act in 1920, and in 1921 an Anglo-Irish treaty was negotiated which at last recognized the Irish Free State as a Dominion—but gave the six counties of Northern Ireland the right to remain part of Great Britain. In 1922, Northern Ireland so chose.

A semblance of stability in Northern Ireland existed until the mid-nineteen sixties, when ethno-religious-nationalistic conflict increased, and by 1969 turned to violence. Riots became widespread, pitched battles were fought, and the Royal Ulster Constabulary had to be reinforced by British troops. The period from 1969 to 1998, known as "the troubles," was punctuated by demonstrations, speeches of incitement, paramilitary groups on both sides, and sporadic shootings and bombings, even in England (including the 1979 bomb assassination of Lord Louis Mountbatten, the Queen's second cousin).

Finally, in 1998, the bitterest of enemies made peace in the Good Friday Agreement, by which the different factions would engage in electoral politics free of violence. Now they argue over the flying of flags and the wearing of uniforms.

What brought about the settlement of 1998? Betty Williams and Mairead Corrigan started the process in the darkest days of 1976 following personal tragedy as a result of violence between Loyalists and Republicans involving the British Army.

The Good Friday Agreement may serve as a model for other nations to wage peace—in particular, Iraq (Sunnis and Shiites) and the Holy Land (Palestinians and Israelis). Many skeptics say the Holy Land has been an exception to all rules—Diplomacy, Law, Peace Conciliation—from ancient times. But, they have their own skeptics—the political satirists. Our home satirist writes a column called Gadfly and has tackled the Holy Land problem in a couple of pieces:

The first was at the time of the Oslo Accords, known as the Two-State Solution. The Gadfly column was called "The Holy Land: The No State Solution."

Gadfly

The HolyLand – The No State Solution
By Mort Malkin

Hereafter, it will be called the Holy Land, not Palestine, not Israel. The name change is necessary to bring about the only possible solution to the Arab-Israeli conflict – the No-State Solution.

Before there were Jews and Muslims, before there was a Yahweh, the Near East was well settled by different peoples. The Sumerians, having migrated from Central Asia, settled in Mesopotamia. Bedouins from the desert were accepted into their midst. Earlier, some 9,000 years ago, population centers had developed at Catal Huyuk in central Anatolia (Turkey) and at Jericho in the Levant. Different races (by skull type) apparently got along together. On the Mediterranean coast only a little later, cities developed at Byblos, Sidon, and Tyre. Many people and many peoples cultivated crops and herded animals in the Near East. They became craftsmen using materials found in the earth. Trade existed from earliest times in the Neolithic – obsidian and pottery are but two examples.

In these ancient times, most folks worshipped many gods: Utu (Samas) the sun god, Nanna (Sin) the moon god, Ea the god of sweet water, Enlil the god of air and wind, Ninhursag (Nintu) the goddess of the earth, and scores more. You could call upon Innana the goddess of love, but after Sumerian times, it was a little trickier as she became Ishtar, who was in charge of both love and war. Perhaps that's when Nanshe the goddess of morality stepped up to keep some balance among mortals.

Around 1900 BCE, a Semite named Abram, who lived in the city of Ur on the Euphrates, had a vision and made a covenant with a God who said He was in charge of everything. Abe changed his name from Abram to Abraham and set off for Canaan on the Western Sea.

Abraham had some major doubt when this new God asked him to sacrifice his #2 son, Isaac. When the request was rescinded at the last moment, Abraham kept his half of the deal. God, over the following generations performed a few tricks (miracles) to convince the skeptical who still had favorites among the other gods. Soon, or maybe not so soon, monotheism among the Semites became established. There followed a few centuries of wandering around the Near East – once a nomad it's hard to cleanse your blood of the inclination – before three major branches of monotheism grew:

Judaism, Christianity, and Islam. The denominations of each will wait till later in our discussion.

Today, there is great animosity between Jews and Muslims, especially between Israelis and Arabs. Some pundits say the conflict has always existed and never will be resolved. But, past history tells us otherwise and professional seers say the future isn't writ is stone. Here's the story.

At the western end of the Mediterranean, the Moors converted to Islam and established their rule in southern Spain. In Andalusia, the city of Cordoba became the preeminent center of intellectual activity: science, medicine, mathematics, literature, and philosophy. Scholars were attracted from the entire world of the time. Jews were tolerated and even served in high posts in government. Some change occurred from one caliphate to the next, but Islamic rule began in the 8th century and lasted almost 800 years. The great Jewish philosopher-physician-rabbi Maimonides lived under Islamic rule in Spain, Morocco, and Egypt during this time (12th century).

At the eastern end of the Mediterranean, Jews and Muslims had lived together peaceably in the Levant for centuries. When Pope Urban II launched the First Crusade and his forces captured Jerusalem (1099), Jews and Muslims were slaughtered with equal fervor. Fighting over political and economic power makes for strange friends and enemies – strange to us today.

Let us go back further to Sumerian times in Mesopotamia – many Bedouins from the Arabian desert settled in and around the Sumerian city-states of the Fertile Crescent and a few integrated with the urban populations. By 2300

BCE, Sargon, a descendant of these nomadic tribes, took power and embarked on a series of military adventures by which he established the Akkad empire. War became an established way of doing business thereafter. Before Akkad rule, the city-states – Ur, Uruk, Kish, Babylon, Larsa, Eridu, and others – were each ruled by a king. But one city, Nippur, was considered neutral ground. It was a holy city under the protection of the great god Enlil and respected by all. When kings of different cities would send their ministers to Nippur to confer (or confront), they were not allowed to bring warriors with weapons. Agreement was easier without spears and swords for distraction. Archaeologists have found many documents in clay (hard copy, then) stamped with seals of several cities in common agreement. Nippur is a fine model for a no-state solution for Israel and Palestine.

Jews and Muslims can start integrating the cities one after another:

Jericho, Jerusalem, Gaza, Askalon, and Hebron – all the oldest cities first. They would live side by side and even welcome Christians and Pagans. Integration of the countryside would follow in short order.

Arabs and Jews working in the olive groves and raising figs and pomegranates – the deserts would bloom. Muslims and Jews have a common tradition. They both speak of Abraham as their common Patriarch. Their dietary habits are similar to this day. In the Levant, many Israeli Jews speak Arabic and Israeli Arabs all speak Hebrew. We know opposites attract and can expect there to be a few who fall in love and marry. The Holy Land will be the new land of man & womankind. The Holy Land currency will be written in Arabic, Hebrew, and English, just as it was in the early 20th century. The tradition of Isaiah will attract diplomats, negotiators, and conciliators. Enemies here and there around the world will become only adversaries, and then it's just a short thought to collaboration. Jerusalem, in the spirit of Solomon, will be the place for resolving world conflicts peacefully.

What work could be more holy?

A more recent Gadfly column was called "Our Origins In Ancient History."

Our Origins in Ancient History

Jews and Palestinians are both Semitic people – originally from the Arabian (not necessarily the Saudi Arabian) desert.

In the 5th to 3rd millennia BCE, the Sumerians migrated from Central Asia to the Mesopotamian Valley of the Tigris and Euphrates Rivers where they became farmers and herders. Between farming and trading, the Sumerians became prosperous and built towns and cities.

Some of the nomads from the nearby dessert became attracted to the life in the settlements and were welcomed, even as the Semites and the Sumerians exhibited different physiognomies.

The centuries went by: the Sumerian Early Dynastic time from 3000 BCE to mid-millennium, the Akkad period of Empire, the invasion of the barbaric Gutian mountain tribes and dark times, and then the Third Dynasty of Ur resurgence. It was 2000 BCE, the time that Abraham lived – a thousand years into the Bronze

Age. Religion had been polytheistic among the people in all the cities: Shamash, the sun god; Enlil, god of wind and storm; Inanna, goddess of love; Ea, god of sweet water; and a patron god of each city-state. People liked the idea of choice, and they especially liked the stories about the relations between the gods.

At the time of Ur III, God revealed Himself to Abraham (then called Abram) as the one true God and promised a land for his descendants. The story went through Moses and the Ten Commandments, Jesus and the New Testament, the Prophet and Islam. The bottom line is that Abraham was and is the Patriarch of both Jews and Muslims, both having been desert nomads and of Semitic origin.

So why are the Jews and Arabs forever fighting with each other? As Rabih Alameddine, the Lebanese writer told us, "At the heart of most antagonisms are irreconcilable similarities."

> Snow opaque, but ice as cold in
> its lucency. Water moving
> in the River underneath the
>
> freeze as if the fish wrote that Law.
> Lives of sea creatures use different
> Laws to live through Winter's worst.
>
> Life, unknowing, from octopus
> to shark, learned many Laws of the
> universe — cosmologists, we.

H₂O

Water, snow, and ice — so
   mundane of substances, though
rarest in the galaxy, even

counting lives of primates,
   insects, and plants. OK, add
bacteria, but are viruses

admitted to the list?
   And what of derivatives
created inside our brains — theories,

games & sports, fellowship
   or ostracy, treaties for
outlawry to make Peace permanent?

Chapter 10

The Tradition of Cooperation and Caring

America is proud of its tradition of rugged individualism. It is a land known for individual initiative, entrepreneurship, and self-made millionaires, where people have pulled themselves up by their own bootstraps.

At lower profile, however, there is a long tradition of cooperation and caring. Let us count a few of the ways that often date to the nation's beginning and are still going strong.

- The new country was largely forests and countryside with far less urban life than today. Family farms and rural granges were a trademark of the young nation.
- Barn raisings have a long tradition, a joint effort by a group of neighbors in counties where small farms are still viable.
- Quilting bees were and are another staple of small towns.
- Choral and chamber music groups spontaneously organize everywhere (not just barbershop quartets).
- Printmakers, watercolorists, potters, woodworkers, and blacksmiths form their own organizations and guilds for specialty crafts and fine arts.

- Poets find each other in towns and cities and form workshops.
- Farmers' markets have seen a resurgence in recent years.
- County fairs are going strong in rural communities, and attract city and suburban folks.
- Pancake breakfasts and potluck dinners are a staple in rural communities and are well attended.
- Block parties celebrate events and holidays in both towns and cities.
- Every city and many towns have a central square or plaza belonging to the people, where citizens may spend a spring afternoon in the outdoors, gather a music group, or bring a soapbox to address a political or social issue.
- Our nation was founded on a shared sense of fairness—no taxation without representation.
- City parks are more to the purpose of an area set aside for people to enjoy the natural world in the midst of concrete and glass buildings with rivers of asphalt between them. If paved drives cross or circle within a large park, they are often reserved for runners and walkers on weekends. The parks represent The Commons.
- Churches in small towns organize monthly Community Cafés to offer free luncheons to promote fellowship. In my own village (population 500), Katie's Café and Two Franks Café each attract 25 to 50 people. In one, the pastor participates regularly. I myself can usually be found at one or the other.

- Throughout the nation, there are community service organizations such as Rotary Clubs, Lions Clubs, Elks Lodges, and Masonic Lodges which serve worthy groups and individuals in need.
- Town meetings are held in a number of Congressional districts, even in residential neighborhoods of cities.
- Folk dances and square dances are still held everywhere, from community centers to granges to churches.
- Women in local neighborhoods may cooperate in sewing garments for the dowry of an engaged girl. It is an old tradition which still persists.
- Volunteer fire departments today respond to fires in rural areas, towns, and smaller cities.
- Habitat for Humanity volunteers gather building materials and actually construct houses for needy people. Eventual owners contribute sweat equity (labor).
- In schools of both cities and towns, PTAs connect parents with each other and with teachers.
- Food banks, soup kitchens, and Thanksgiving dinners for the poor illustrate the American tradition of caring for people in need. It is also true of organizations that collect coats and sweaters for them for cold weather. Some churches will set aside a community room for the homeless of a community in cold weather.
- Communities large and small celebrate the nation's founding with public Fourth of July picnics, fireworks, and parades.

- Many cities turn vacant lots over to neighborhoods for community gardens, much along the lines of cities in England where the Town Councils allocate allotments for citizens to grow their own produce. Needless to say, there is much cooperation such as the sharing of tools, labor, and experience.
- In the country, many small farms have adopted a CSA (community sponsored agriculture) structure whereby members purchase a share of the farm's harvest. Each week, the farmer brings whatever vegetables and fruits are ripe to distribute to the farm sponsors at an outdoor parking area or indoor community center.
- A new movement of cooperation and caring has appeared in the citizen sector, completely separate from government. It is called "Random Acts of Kindness" that I recall from the late 1960s, but officially dates from 1995. It started with ten suggestions, and more recently went under the name of "Pay It Forward," and expanded the suggestion list to fifty, retaining many of the same original ones. such as #6: smile and say hello to someone next to you in the elevator or someone you pass on the the street; or #44: take cookies to your public librarian; or #1: buy coffee for the person behind you at a take-out line.

Volunteerism is also a tradition in the US—strong evidence of cooperation and caring being inherent in the human spirit. A few typical organizations that encourage volunteerism are:

- the Red Cross
- public libraries, hospitals, schools

- literacy volunteers
- museums
- churches, temples, and othe faith communities
- Shalom Communities of the United Methodist Church (open to noncongregants)
- ASPCAs
- local historical societies
- the Boy and Girl Scouts
- Little League teams and other sports clubs
- YMCA, YWCA, YMHA, and YWHA
- consumer food co-ops where members do volunteer work in exchange for food at cost
- health foundations (American Cancer Society, American Diabetic Association, American Heart Association)
- National Public Radio stations and PBS TV channels.

There are, as well, many categories of NGOs that advocate for the environment, civil rights, civil liberties, scholarship funds, medical and surgical free clinics—volunteers are active in all of them. For "conservative" people who consider "environmental" groups too controversial, they call them "ecological," but it's still cooperative.

In the economic sector, in high profile, the US has been known for its individual-centered corporate culture. Examples of free-for-all capitalism abound, from the robber barons at the turn of the 20th century to "vulture capitalists" of more recent days. Yet, at very low profile, US economic life is also cooperative across a wide swath of enterprises. In North Dakota, the State Bank keeps its considerable assets invested almost entirely in-state. Across the country, over 7,000 credit unions hold $1 trillion in assets. These public banks are owned by more than 90 million depositor-members. In Maine, with a population of less than 1.34 million, the Maine Credit Union League boasts 175 branches with 250 ATMs and 680,000 members who do their banking there.

Also, across the nation, some 2,000 public utilities supply electric power to 46 million consumers. Some large cities are engaged in capitalistic enterprises but are owned by their citizens. Boston owns Faneuil Hall Marketplace and Hartford owns its Civic Centre—two examples of public ownership of commercial properties. Similarly, New York City, Los Angeles, Cincinnati, San Antonio, and Louisville all own commercial space in the name of the citizens of those cities.

Many municipalities, states, and the federal government (We the People) own and operate parks and beaches, public transport, streets and roadways, public schools, and public libraries. The Postal Service, the FAA, FDA, EPA, FCC, NSA, correctional institutions (prisons), police, armed forces, and all the agencies that carry out these public functions, do so on behalf of the people. The National Parks are very high profile, but there are many state parks that are noteworthy, and town parks are popular everywhere. Even rural township parks such as the sixty-acre Damascus Forest, where I live, have well-used trails. London set an example centuries ago with Hyde Park and its Speakers' Corner. New York did it one better with Union Square Park, where speakers are not consigned to one corner. Society, by its very nature, is cooperative.

Individuals of the species who are violent are restrained, ostracized, and instructed in the ways of cooperation.

If there was any doubt about the nature of the US—cooperative or conflictual—the first president, George

Washington, set the question to rest in his Farewell Address. Four key quotes toward the end of the speech summarize the sense of his sentiment:

Observe good faith and justice towards all nations; cultivate peace and harmony with all.

It will be worthy of a free, enlightened, and ... great nation, to give to mankind the magnanimous and, too, novel example of a people always guided by an exalted justice and benevolence.

Harmony, liberal intercourse with all nations, are recommended by policy, humanity, and interest.

...maintain inviolate the relations of peace and amity towards other nations.

Homo sapiens, even in the nation of rugged individualism called America, is cooperative and often understanding. Most days, random acts of kindness appear among the denizens.

So many millennia to
get it right ... or wrong. The universe
just is — even the nearby solar

planets: Mercury, Venus, and
Mars missed out. Only Earth found promise
in recent days of trial-and-error:

we were gatherers and hunters
in that Paleolithic Era.
Soon came monarchy, empire, and all.

Bully Thistles

Last week of August, the weather
still in the eighties — too hot for
strong workouts till evening. One new
blossom has appeared — the thorny
thistle — the flower of Scotland,

one with the Ancient Picts, saviors
of their land, and unconquerable.
Ask the Romans who built a wall
to keep their legions away from
the ways of those painted people.

Chapter 11

SOCIAL–CULTURAL EVOLUTION

"If we could analyze various wars and identify the causes of war, we could eliminate these causes and live in perpetual peace," said the antiwar movement for over a century in all earnest.

Many candidates for elimination have been proposed:

- An arms race, up to and including nuclear missiles and bombs
- A military culture
- Standing armies
- Violent video games
- Fear of "others"
- Religion (Christianity, Islam, Judaism, Buddhism, Hinduism …)
- Atheism, anarchism
- Capitalism and greed, socialism under central control
- War for resources ("spoils")
- Poverty
- Population density

- Imperialism, colonization
- Dictatorship, even authoritarian government
- Leaders who seek after hero status
- Injustice
- Inequality
- The Y chromosome, or at least testosterone that causes aggression
- Patriarchy
- Leaders with psychopathic personality
- Tradition and the notion that war builds men
- National honor or prestige
- The hubris that assures one side that it can win quickly and easily. Two examples are ancient Assyria and the United States from 1950 to the present (Korea, Vietnam, Panama, Granada, Iraq, and Afghanistan).

Wars are caused by differing circumstances. Some start over a misunderstanding, some by miscalculation.

Throughout history, we can add slavery and the "need" for slavery to sustain the economy. Now, that reason is moot, though its repercussions are still with us a century and a half after its abolition. War for spoils was once common, too. Nowadays, nations have to be more circumspect about starting a war over the lure of resources. Lewis Fry Richardson, after researching dozens of wars ("deadly quarrels") came up with over 200 random causes of war.

Moreover, studying past wars and their causes may not be instructive if we are to eliminate war in the future. War may occur despite establishing democracy, or capitalism (which are not the same thing). War can also occur with women in charge; with a strong judiciary that stands against injustice; in the face of treaties that bring about (relative) disarmament; under an economic system that precludes poverty and financial inequality; in a nation whose populace will not accept fear that its leaders try to instill... Many of these factors that are cited as causes may well be intimately tied in with the pursuit of war, but their elimination may not prevent war.

Would the world be a better place without weapons of war? Without standing armies? Without poverty? Without inequality and injustice? Without imperialism? Add your favorites from the list on the preceding pages. Some nations have started to lead the way.

New Zealand has for many years declared its territory, including its coastal waters, a nuclear-free zone. Nuclear-powered ships and vessels carrying nuclear weapons are banned. New Zealand's army is tiny, as is its navy, (though the Kiwis are always contenders for the America's Cup). Replacing the armed forces, to an extent, is the National Guard, who are trained to assist victims of natural disasters.

In Central America, Costa Rica has been at peace since 1949, the same year its armed forces were abolished permanently. In the US, there is a precedent for army service without ever handling a weapon: it's called the Army Corps of Engineers.

Historian Howard Zinn advised us "to find a substitute for war in human ingenuity, imagination, courage, sacrifice, and patience." Anthropologist Margaret Mead, too, saw the need to find a replacement for war. Nelson Mandela and others have suggested that sports can challenge our youth who need to prove themselves. Still others have suggested that service to the nation can be met with a year or two in the Peace Corps, a Conservation Corps, Teaching for America in an inner city school, service in AmeriCorps, a family farm internship, working at an urban community garden, a library apprenticeship ... all worthy work to benefit the individual and the nation and to contribute to a culture of peace.

We need not only to disassemble the war culture of society including the defense (war) establishment of both government and private industry, we must establish a peace culture in all its facets. We need to establish:

- classes and courses in peace history in all public schools and colleges
- libraries with sections devoted to books and writing on various aspects of peace, to include such authors as John Horgan, Joshua Goldstein, John Mueller, Paul Fussell, Douglas Fry, Randall Forsberg, Jonathan Haas & Matthew Piscitelli, Linus Pauling, Howard Zinn, Gene Sharp, Peter Mayer, Peter (Pyotr) Kropotkin, Barbara Deming, Jonathan Schell, Peter Ackerman & Jack DuVall, Samuel Bowles and Herbert Gintis, Marija Gimbutas, Jill Cook, and others
- Peace Academies in place of the present Military Academies
- a cabinet-level Department of Peace
- a diplomatic corps trained in negotiation, mediation, conciliation, the creative arts

Anthropologists point to the social-cultural advances of civilization over the last few hundred years. In fact, it has been a slow evolution since the 3rd millennium BCE. Let us see what progress we have made.

Over the past 5,000 years, mankind has engaged in many practices that today are unacceptable at best and barbaric at worst. Here is a list of what we have outlawed or deleted from our playbook, at least by law:

Murder and wanton killing

Genocide

Burning witches (or anyone else) at the stake

Stoning to death (as in "The Lottery")

Assassination (perhaps someday)

Piracy

Lynching

Slavery

Torture

Dueling

Rape

Human sacrifice (to appease deities)

Military conscription of children (still happening in some places)

And though most nations and international law have banned the following practices, some nations and regions still impose them, either legally or extralegally:

Absolute Monarchy or "Divine Right of Kings," wherein a subject can be imprisoned, or even executed, for such good and sufficient reason as the monarch's whim (still occurring in some absolute monarchies)

Female genital mutilation

Blood feuds

Honor killings of women

Capital punishment (abolished in most nations and in 20 American states so far)

The abolition of war is the final step in mankind's social-cultural evolution. Perhaps, a couple of small beginnings have already been made. A few nations have been at peace long term, and they do not seem to miss any benefits of the military conflicts of yesteryear. Sweden, Iceland, Switzerland, and the Edo period in Japan—all for more than 100 years—stand out as good examples. As well, there have been no hundred years wars since the 15th century, no major thirty years war since the 17th century, and only a few conflicts—like the US fighting in Afghanistan—lasting twenty years or more. Are we evolving? Or is it simply that our attention span is diminishing?

Soon, we may attain the state of peace known to several present-day "primitive" societies that: do not engage in organized violence internally or externally, have no military organization, and experience only the rarest instances of inter-personal lethal violence. Examples are: the !Kung of the Kalahari desert of Africa, the Mbuti Pygmies of equatorial Africa, the Copper Inuit of northern Canada, the Siriono of eastern Bolivia, the Hutterites of north central United States and south central Canada, the Semai of Malay Peninsula, and the Islanders of Tristan da Cunha of the South Pacific.

If war is a cultural matter, and not genetic, there should be no reason we cannot establish a culture of peace in all countries. A few countries have already shown us the way.

References

Albert, Michael. *Parecon: Life after Capitalism*.

Alexander, Gene, and David Raichlen. 2016. "Runners' Brains Have More Connectivity." *University of Arizona News*, Dec. 2016.

———. 2017. "Brains Evolved To Need Exercise." *University of Arizona News*. June 2017.

Aron, Raymond. *Peace and War: A Theory of International Relations*.

Augusta, Josef, and Zdenek Burian. *Prehistoric Man*.

Boehm, Christopher. *Moral Origins: The Evolution of Virtue, Altruism, and Shame*.

Bowles, Samuel, and Herbert Gintis. *A Cooperative Species: Human Reciprocity and Its Evolution*.

Butler, Smedley. *War Is a Racket* – Speech to American Public.

Cook, Jill. *Ice Age Art and the Arrival of the Modern Mind*.

Darwin, Charles. *The Descent of Man*.

Deats, Richard. 1996. "The Global Spread of Active Nonviolence." *Fellowship* magazine.

Deming, Barbara. *Revolution & Equilibrium*.

de Waal, Frans. *Primates and Philosophers: How Morality Evolved*.

———. *Are We Smart Enough to Know How Smart Animals Are?*

Dunbar, Robin. *Human Evolution: Our Brains and Behavior*.

Ferguson, R. Brian. 2018. "War Is Not Part of Human Nature." *Scientific American*, Sept. 2018.

Founts, Roger. *Next of Kin: My Conversations with Chimpanzees*.

Fry, Douglas P. *Beyond War: The Human Potential for Peace*

Fussell, Paul. *Doing Battle: The Making of a Skeptic*.

Gitting, John. *The Glorious Art of Peace: From the Iliad to Iraq*.

Haas, Jonathan, and Matthew Piscitelli. *The Prehistory of Warfare Misled by Ethnography*.

Hawkes, Kristen. "The Grandmother Thesis." several papers

Horgan, John. *The End of War.*

Hrdy, Sarah Blaffer. *Mother Nature: Maternal Instincts and How They Shape the Human Species.*

———. *Mothers and Others: The Evolutionary Origins of Mutual Understanding.*

Isaac, Glynn and Richard E. F. Leakey, eds. "Human Ancestors." from *Scientific American Readings.*

Keltner, Dacher, Ed. *The Compassionate Instinct: The Science of Human Goodness.*

Kropotkin, P. *Mutual Aid: A Factor in Evolution.*

Leakey, Richard E. F., and Roger Lewin. *People of the Lake: Mankind and Its Beginnings.*

Life Magazine. "The Harrisburg Conspiracy: The Berrigans & the Catholic Left." *Life.*

Malkin, Mort. 1971. "The Grand Plan to End the War in Vietnam," *WIN* magazine.

———. 1997. "Walk for Peace." *Fellowship* magazine.

———. 2007. "Homo Sapiens: War and Peace." *Connections* magazine.

———. 2007. "Human Evolution, Genetic and Cultural." *Connections* magazine

Marx Brothers, The. *Duck Soup.* film.

Mayer, Peter, Ed. *The Pacifist Conscience.*

O'Day, James. *Cultivating Peace.*

Pinker, Steven. *The Better Angels of Our Nature: Why Violence Has Declined.*

———. *The Blank Slate: The Modern Denial of Human Nature*

Schell, Jonathan. *The Unconquerable World: Power, Non-Violence, and the Will of the People.*

Share International Foundation. *The Ageless Wisdom Teaching.*

Singh, Parkash. *Community Kitchen of the Sikhs.*

Swanson, David. *War No More: The Case for Abolition.*

———. *When the World Outlawed War.*

Williams, A.C., and L. J. Hill. 2017. "Meat and Nicotinamide: A Causal Role in Human Evolution History, and Demographics." *International Journal of Tryptophan Res.*

Wrangham, Richard. *The Goodness Paradox: The Strange Relationship between Virtue and Violence in Human Evolution.*

Zinn, Howard. *A People's History of the United States.*

Can the imagined be more real
than what the brain knows in all its
connections, the five senses and
feed-back loops of every movement.

A sixth sense: comfort or less than
as risk aversion finds meaning.
Of late, Quantum Mechanics has
had us deal with Schrodinger's Cat.

About the Author

Mort Malkin has been a polymath throughout his life. He has been, in turn—and sometimes simultaneously—a decathlete, a surgeon and teacher of others, an artist, a poet, an archaeologist, and a collector of artifacts from the Neolithic and Sumerian periods.

He is also an ardent canoeist and kayaker, the lyricist for *Danser's Inferno*, and a speaker at several national conferences, most recently The De-Aging Lecture Series.

He has published many papers in the medical literature, and is the author of numerous books, including the following:

Psyching up for Tennis (co-author). Basic Books, 1977.

How to Eat Like a Thin Person (manuscript preparation). Simon and Schuster, 1982.

Walking—The Pleasure Exercise. Rodale Press, 1986.

Aerobic Walking, the weight-loss exercise. John Wiley & Sons, 1995.

Data-Matter-O–Poetry and Science. O Books, undated.

Celebration of Spring in the Delaware Valley. Three Poets of The Millville Poets, UnLtd (for The National Park Service of the Upper Delaware River Valley), 2004.

Upper Delaware River In Verse And Image, Eastern National (for The National Park Service), 2014.

Over the Banks. The Milanville Poets UnLtd (originally for Stockport Flats (Ithaca), 2017.

Index

NB: An asterisk (*) indicates a peace hero or peace victory. **Peace poems** or **essays** are by the author. An italic '*i*' or '*p*' following a page number indicates an image or poem.

A

Abbasid caliphate 93, 95, 100
Abd-al-Rahman I (Abbasid caliphate) 93
Abkar (Mughal) 38
Abraham (Canaan) 255, 257, 258
Abram (Ur) 255, 259
absolute monarchy 273
Abu Ghraib 194
Acchi 184
Achemenid Empire 34–35
Ackerman, Peter* 183–184, 272
ACLU 158
A Connecticut Yankee in King Arthur's Court (Twain) 145
Act of Supremacy (England) 249
Adab (Mesopotamia) 29, 56
Adams, Byran 217
Addams, Jane* 157–159
administration versus government 156–157
The Adventures of Huckleberry Finn (Twain) 145
The Adventures of Tom Sawyer (Twain) 145
The Adventuresome Simplicissimus (Von Grimmelshausen) 122–123
Advocate of Peace and Universal Brotherhood (American Peace Society) 138
Aethelstan* (England) 94–95
Afghanistan 40, 43, 187, 193, 194, 198, 234, 274
Afghani women 206
Afghan Youth Volunteers 216
Africa 227, 274
   see also Congo; East Africa; Zulus
Against the Crime of Silence (Russell) 165
agriculture. see also community gardens; potato blight (Ireland); Upper
   Paleolithic Period (hunter-gatherers)
   Burma and 74
   Catal Huyuk and 46
   Central Asia and 24
   China and 14, 53, 54
   cooperation and caring and 15, 261, 262, 264, 271–272
   Cucuteni-Trypillian culture and 15, 16
   Egypt and 25
   Ireland and 248, 252
   law codes and 56, 57
   Mexican-American War and 142
   Near East and 255

Index

Neolithic Era and 12, 13, 230, 248
Palestine and Israel and 189, 258
religion and 17
Sri Lanka and 246
Sumerians and 27, 258
trade and 230
US tradition of cooperation and 264
warfare and 45
women and 46, 81
Aha (Egypt) 25, 25–26p
Ahaz (Judea) 66
Ahmad, Eqbal* 184
Ahtisaari, Martti* 184–185
Akhnaten (Egypt) 59
Akiba, Tadatoshi* (Japan) 185
Akkadian Empire 28–30, 50–53, 68, 257, 258
Akreyi, Widad* (Kurd) 185–186
Alameddine, Rabih (Lebanon) .... viii, 259
Al-Andalus (Spain) 37
Albert Einstein Institution 225
Albright, Madeleine (US) 209
ale 231
Alexander III (the Great) 35, 121
Alfred the Great* (England) 93–94
Algeria 20
Alternative Radio 190
Amar-Sin* (Mesopotamia) 57
Amenhotep III* (Egypt) 26, 59
American Peace Society* 138
American Revolutionary War 39, 133–134, 135
"The American Scholar" (Emerson) 137
Americans Who Tell the Truth (AWTT) (series of portraits) 225
Americorp 271
Amnesty International 186
Amorites 29–30
Amster, Randall* (US) 186–187
Analects* (Confucius) 76
anarchism 132, 152, 164, 269
Anatolia. *see* Turkey
Anglicans 196
Anglo-Dutch war 251
Anglo-Irish treaty 253
Anglo-Normans 248
Anglo-Saxons* 95

Index

animals. *see also* horse domestication; pastoralists
    Asian art and 7–8
    aversion to killing and.. 229
    Buddhist beliefs and 219–220
    domesticated... 27
    Essenes* and 67
    Ireland and.. 248
    Minoans and... 62
    Neolithic and.. 5, 12, 13
    stamps and cylinder seals and 19, 20, 20i, 27, 34, 48, 49
An Lushan rebellion (China) 100
Anna Karenina (Tolstoy)... 143
Annot* (Germany/US)... 187
"Anthem for Doomed Youth" (Owen) 168
Anthropocene (peace poem).. iv*p*
Anti-Imperialist League... 146, 149
Antioch... 37
Antipolemus—The Plea of Reason, Religion and Humanity against War (Erasmus)....113
anti-war Constitutional Amendment (US) 174
Antonine Wall 84
Antoninus Pius* (Roman Empire) 89–90
Approaches to the Great Settlement (Balch) 159–160
Aquino, Benigno.. 238
Aquino, Corazon 238
Arab-Israeli War... 218
Arabs 37, 93
    see also Holy Land
Arab Spring (Egypt).. 225
Arafat, Yasser... 218
Arbenz, Jacobo (Guatemala).. 197
arbitration... 170, 222
archaeological record, cooperation and .... ix, 4, 7–10
    see also Narmer palette (Egypt) *and other artifacts*; seals and stamps
    and other artifacts
Arents, Jerica* (US) 187–188
Argentina.. 239, 240
Aristophanes* (Greece)... 69
Arkhipov, Vasili* (USSR)... 181–182
Armenians*... 41, 88, 95–96
Arms and the Man (Shaw) 163
Arms Trade Treaty to Control the Trade in Small Arms and Light Weapons
    (United Nations).. 185
Army Corps of Engineers (US).. 271
Arnaud, Emile*... 188

Index

Arnoldson, Klaus Pontus* (Sweden) 188–189
Arrigoni, Vittorio* (Italy) 189
art. *see also* cave paintings; Kollwitz, Kathe* *and other artists*
    animals and 7–8
    ceremonial places and 17, 25
    Etruscans and 81
    Gudea* and 52
    Minoans* and 61
    US tradition of cooperation and 261
    women and 13
    Xuanzong and 100
Artemis (goddess) 65
The Art of Waging Peace (Chappell) 196
The Art of War (Sun Tzu) 232
Aryans 32, 35
ascetic humanism 71
Ascherman, Arik 189
Ashoka* (the Fierce) (Mauryan Dynasty) 36, 73
Ashot III* (the Merciful) (Armenia) 95–96
Asia. *see* Burma; South Asia; western Asia
Asian pastoralists 23–24
"Asleep" (Owen) 168
Assur (Mesopotamia) 33, 58
Assurbanipal (Assyrian) 33
Assyrians (Near East) 30, 33, 58, 88, 270
astronomy 13, 16, 17, 47, 110, 111
Asvaghosa* (India) 96
Athenian fleet 35, 70
Athenian League 35
atomic bombs and H-Bomb tests 43, 164–165, 194, 195
    see also Hiroshima and Nagasaki bombings; nuclear weapons
Augustus (Roman Empire) 67, 85–86
Aurelius, Marcus (Roman Empire) 85, 89
Australia 195
    see also Caldicott, Helen* *and other Australians*
Austria 151
Austrian Peace Society 151
Aztecs 38

B

Babylon 33, 51, 68, 257
Babylon, First Dynasty of 29–30, 58
Baby Tooth Survey 176, 207
Baez, Joan* 189–190, 221

Index

Baghdad 37
Bagratuni dynasty (Armenia) 95–96
Baha'i faith 204–205
Baker, Russell* 190
Balch, Emily Greene* 159–160
Balkans 37, 42
Ballou, Adin* 139, 140–141
Baltic countries 225
Baltimore (US) 40
Baltimore Four (US) 192
Banker, S. 160–161
banks 174, 180, 202, 265–266
Barsamian, David* 190
Basic Bombs... (peace poem) 155p
Basilikon Doro (James I) 118–119
Basques* (Spain) 80, 81, 83–84
Battle of Ashdown 93
Battle of Bosworth 109
Battle of Cordoba 93
Battle of Ethandun 93
Battle of Flodden 112
Battle of Hastings 37
Battle of Kadesh 30
Battle of Marathon 35
Battle of Mingtiao 31
Battle of Salamis 35, 70
Battle of Spurs 112
Battle of Talas 100
Battle of Teutoberg Forest 85
Battle of the Boyne (Irish-French) 251
Battle of Waterloo 40
Battle Studies (Du Picq) 232
Baxter, Archibald* (New Zealand) 190–191
Bedouins 254, 256–257
Before stylus sticks... (peace poem) 22p
Beikthano (Pyu people) 74
Belgium 146, 197
"The Bells of Rhymney" (Seeger) 225
Benjamin, Medea* 191, 206
Berber tribes (Moors) 37, 38, 92–93, 256
Bermuda 193
Berrigan, Dan* and Philip* (US) 184, 191–193
Bertrand Russell Peace Foundation 165
"Beyond Vietnam: Time to Break Silence" (King, Jr.) 183

Index

Bikini atoll 164, 178
biology. *see* genes and biology
Black Sea 39
Blair, Tony (UK) 212
Blanco, Otilio Ulates (Costa Rica) 180
Blood on our Hands: the American Invasion and Destruction of Iraq (N.J.S. Davies) 201
"Blowback Trilogy" (Johnson) 215
Boer Wars 42, 190
Bolger, Leah* (US) 193
Bolivia 240
The Book of Dreams (Zhou) 64
Book of Kells (Ireland) 248
Book of Songs (Zhou) 63
boredom vi
Born, Max 165
Boston Eight (US) 192
Boudicca (Celt) 84
Boulding, Kenneth E.* 193
Bourne, Randolph* 153–157
Bowles, Samuel 272
Brahe, Tycho 111
Brahmagupta (India) 98
Brahui tribe (Baluchistan) 70
brains .... viii–ix, 4–5, 21p, 32p, 229–230, 260p.
   see also "Second Coming"
Branfman, Fred* (US) 193–194
Brazil 39, 239, 240
Brehon Law (Celts) 248
"Bring Them Home, Bring Them Home" (Seeger) 224
Brinton, Thomas* (England) 108
Britain. *see also* Afghan wars; Brock, Hugh *and other British people*; England; Great Britain; Hundred Years War *and other wars*; New Zealand *and other colonies*; United Kingdom; Wessex*
   Asia and 40
   India and 161
   Iran and 197
   Roman Empire and 87, 88, 167, 248
   Sri Lanka and 246
British Atomic Scientists Association 178
British Columbia (Canada) 20
British Indian government 161
British Navy 38
Brittain, Edward and his friends 166

Index

Brittain, Vera* (Britain) 166–167
Brock, Hugh* (Britain) 194
Bromyard, John* (England) 108
Bronze Age 231, 248, 258–259
Brown, John 142
Bryce, James* 194–195
Buddhism* 72–73, 74, 96, 98, 219–220, 247
    see also Engaged Buddhism; Gautama Buddha; Ikeda, Daisaku*
Buffalo Five (US) 192
Bulgaria 24, 42
Bulgarian-Serbian war (1855) 163
Bully Thistles (peace poem) 268p
Burma* 74
    see also Myanmar
Burritt, Elihu* (US) 138
Bush, George H. W. (US) 215
Bush, George W. (US) 198, 228
Butler, Smedley* (US) 173–174
Byblos (Mediterranean coast) 255
"By Gospel Authority" (Dodge) 134
Byron, Lord (Britain) 40
Byzantines 37, 92, 95, 110

C

Caesar, Julius (Roman Empire) 36, 121
Caldicott, Helen* (Australia) 195–196
California 41
Caligula (Roman Empire) 85
Callinus* (Greece) 66
"A Call to Resist Illegitimate Authority" (Coffin) 198
Cambyses (Achemenid Empire) 34
Camden 28 (US) 192
Cameron, David (Britain) 212
Campaign for Nuclear Disarmament 165
Campaign for Peace and Democracy (US) 205
Canada 20, 39, 217, 274
    see also McTaggart, David Fraser*
Canadian Voice of Women for Peace 204
The Canterbury Tales (Chaucer) 107
Cantonsville Nine (US) 191, 192
capitalism 270
capital punishment 190, 273
Carchemesh (Assyrian Empire) 33
Caribbean 41

Index

Carnley, Peter* (Australia) 196
Carthage 36, 92
Cash, Johnny (US) 224
Caspian-Pontic region 24
Catal Huyuk (Anatolia) 13, 15–17, 47, 254
Catherine II (the Great) (Russia) 39
Catholics 39, 119, 238, 249, 250–252
   see also Nicholas de Cusa (Cusanus) *and other Catholics*
The Catholic Worker (Day) 201–202
cave paintings 7, 8, 22*p*, 229
Cayonu (Anatolia) 13
Cel (goddess) 81
Celts 84, 248
Center for Non-Violence 204
Center for Research and Dialogue (Somalia) 227
Center for Teaching Peace 217
Central America 240
Central American Common Market 180
Central Asia 22–25, 37–38, 99
ceremonial places 17–18, 25
   see also sacrifices
Chadwick, James (England) 177
Chaldeans 33
Chalukya kingdom (India) 98
Chandra Gupta II* (Gupta empire) 97
Chang-an (China) 100
Chappell, Paul K.* (US) 196
Charlemagne 37
Charles I (England) 250
Charles II (England) 123, 124, 125, 250–251
Charles IV (King of Naples) 131
Charles V (Spain) 117
Chaucer, Geoffrey* (England) 105, 107
Chazov, Yvgeniy (Russia) 196
chemical warfare 40, 42
chemistry 4, 178
   see also Hahn, Otto*; Pauling, Linus*
Cheney, Richard (US) 198, 228
Cheng (China) 63
Chenowith, Erica* 197
Chicago Eight (US) 203, 212
Chicago's Voices for Creative Nonviolence (US) 187
children 4, 6, 10, 218, 273
Chile 239, 240

Index

China
    see also Opium War *and other wars*; Sun Tzu *and other Chinese*;
    Tibetan-Chinese Peace Treaty*
    agriculture and 14, 53, 54
    beginning of warfare and 45–46
    Civil War of 43
    fifth century BCE 36
    India and 98
    C. Johnson* and 215
    peace victories* and 52–54, 63–64, 74–80, 98–101
    Tamerlane and 38
    Third Millennium BCE and 30–31
Chomsky, Noam* (US) 184, 197
The Christian Citizen (newspaper) 138
Christianity and Christians
    see also Catholics; Dodge, David L.* *and other Christians*; Holy Land;
    Jesus*; monotheism; Protestants; Quakers
    Burritt* on 138
    Byzantine 37
    Domitian and 87
    England and 249–250
    Erasmus* on 114
    Gower* on 106
    Ireland and 248–250
    Islam and 111
    Native Americans and 116, 126
    Palestine and Israel and 189
    peace heroes* of England and 105–109
    the State and 155
    Tertullian* and 91–92
    Tolstoy* and 143–145
    Twain* and 146
    US tradition of cooperation and 262, 265
Christmas Island 194
CIA (US) 215
Cimmerians 33, 65
cities 27, 49, 54, 153, 254–255, 256, 259, 262, 266
    see also Catal Huuk (Anatolia) *and other cities*; Fourth to Second
    Millennia BCE
Citizen of the World (Burritt) 138
Citizens Committee for Nuclear Information (US) 176
civil disobedience 161, 182, 192, 198, 227
"Civil Disobedience" (Thoreau) 141–142
civilization 12–13

Index

Civilization (peace poem) 44p
civil rights 182, 213–214, 228
   see also Coffin, William Sloane* *and other activists*
Civil Rights Act of 1964 (US) 182
Clare, Richard "Strongbow" de (England) 248
Clark, Ramsey* (US) 197–198
Claudius (Roman Empire) 85
Clearwater Project (US) 224
climate .... xp
   see also environmentalism; Peace Ecology
Clinton, Bill (US) 208
Code de la Paix 188
Code of Hammurabi 30, 57
Code of Lipit-Ishtar of Isin 57
Code of Ur-Nammu 56, 57
Code Pink 191, 206
codes of law. *see* laws and order
Coffin, William Sloane* (US) 198–199
cognition. *see* brains; "Second Coming"
Cold War (US-Russia) 190, 215
Colet, John* 109, 111–112, 115
colonialism 162, 184, 204, 240, 242, 246, 247
Commoner, Barry 176
"Common Sense About the War" (Shaw) 163
communists 179, 180, 224
communities *versus* nations 154–156
community gardens 272
Concert of Europe 128
Confessio Amantis (Gower) 106
conflict, resolutions of. *see also Journal of Conflict Resolution*; treaties
   Ahtisaari* and 184–185
   Indonesia and 240–242
   Ireland and 247–254
   Latin America and 239–240
   methods of 237
   Myanmar and 242–243
   Philippines and 238
   South Korea and 243–244
   Sri Lanka and 246–247
   Taiwan and 244–246
Confucianism 99
Confucius* (Kung Fu Tzu) 76–77, 79
Congo (Africa) 197
The Conquest of Happiness (Russell) 164

Index

conscientious objectors 92, 160, 167, 190–191, 194, 200–201, 202, 207
  see also draft boards
conscription alternatives 149–150, 198
Conservation Corps (US) 271
"Considerations On The True Harmony Of Mankind and How It Is To
  Be Maintained" (Woolman) 129
Constantinople 37
Contra murders (Nicaragua) 216
Convention on the Pacific Settlement of Disputes 151
conversions, religious 116
Cook, Jill 272
Coolidge, Calvin (US) 158, 169
cooperation and caring. *see also* agriculture; archaeological record,
  cooperation and; art; education; genes and biology; hunter-gatherers,
  cooperation and; music; poverty; trade; Upper Paleolithic Period
  (hunter-gatherers)
  Costa Rica and 240
  Cucuteni-Trypillians and 16
  Kropotkin on 152–153
  peace and .... vi–vii
  socio-cultural change and 230, 231–232, 261–274
  tradition of 261–268*p*
  United States and 261–267
  women and .... v, vi–vii, 4, 6
Copernicus 111
Corbyn, Jeremy* (UK) 199
Cordoba* (Spain) 92–93, 101–102, 256
Cornwall (England) 95
corporations .... vi, 169, 174, 202, 208, 265
Corrie, Rachel 189
Corrigan, Mairead (Ireland) 254
Cortes, Hernan 38
Cortright, David* (US) 199
Costa Rica .... vii, 179–180, 240, 271
Council of Basel (1431) 110
Courage of Conscience Award 200, 220
Court of International Justice 170
Cremer, William Randal* (Britain) 145, 222
Crete* 60–62
Crimea 39, 41
Crisis Management Initiative (CMI) (Finland) 184
Croesus (Lydian Kingdom) 34, 68
Cromwell, Oliver (England) 124, 250
Crowe, Frances* (US) 200

Index

Cruce, Emeric* (France) 121–122
Crusades 37, 256
Cuba 41, 116, 158, 180
Cuba Libre 158
Cuban Missile Crisis 181–182
Cucuteni-Trypillians 15–17, 24
culture. *see* social-cultural evolution
Cusa, Nicholas de* (Cusanus) 110–111
Cycladic islanders 61
Cyneas (Greece) 121
The Cyrus Cylinder* 68
Cyrus The Great* (Achemenid Empire) 34, 67–68

D

Danes 37, 93–94
Daniela Dormes (B. von Suttner) 150
Danube 24
Daoism* 75–76
Darius (Achemenid Empire) 34, 35
Dark Tide (Brittain) 166
Darwin, Charles (Britain) 141, 150
Daughters of the American Revolution 158
David, King (Jerusalem) 102
Davies, George Maitland Lloyd* (Wales) 200–201
Davies, Idris (Wales) 225
Davies, Nicolas J.S.* 201
da Vinci, Leonardo (Italy) 111
Davis, Garry* (US) 201
Day, Dorothy* (US) 201–202
DC Nine (US) 192
Death (Kollwitz) 171
Debs, Eugene (US) 158
De Concordiantia Catholica (Cusa) 110
Defend International 186
De jure belli ac pacis (*On the Law of War and Peace*) (Grotius) 120
De jure preadae commentarius (*Commentary on the law of prize and booty*)
  (Grotius) 120
Delian League (Greece) 70
Dellinger, David* (US) 202–203
Deming, Barbara 272
democracy. *see also* Campaign for Peace and Democracy (US); Figueras
  Ferrer, José*; Students for a Democratic Society (SDS)
  Ackerman* on 183–184
  Akreyi* and 186

    Bourne* and 154
    Dellinger* and 202
    Ephesus* and 66
    Gandhi* and 246
    Guatemala and 197
    Ireland and 252–253
    Latin America and 239–240
    Philippines and 239
    Taiwan and 245–246
    war and 270
Democracy Now (TV show) 208, 209
Democratic National Convention (1968) 203, 212
DePaul University 187
"Deranged" (Owen) 168
Los Desaparacidos 239
Dewey, John (US) 153
diamonds 42
Dickinson, Patrick 233
"Disaffection a Virtue" (Gandhi) 160–161
The Disappeared (Argentina) 239
Disasters of War (Goya) 132
"Discours sur la Polysynodie" (Saint Pierre) 127
Divine Right of Kings 273
Dnieper Valley 23–24
"The Doctrine of the Sword" (Gandhi) 161
Dodge, David L.* 134–136
Dolni Vestonice cave paintings 197
Dominican Republic 180
Domitian (Roman Empire) 87
Donne, John (England) 118
draft boards 192
    see also conscription alternatives
"Draft Dodger Rag" (Ochs) 220
Dravidian culture* 70–71
Dravidians 247
Dresden bombings 200
drones 194, 216
Drones Watch 193
Drone Warfare: Killing by Remote Control (Benjamin) 191
Du Bois, W.E.B.* (US) 203–204
"Duce Et Decorum Est" (Owen) 168
Duckworth, Muriel* 204
Dukes of Lancaster and York (Britain) 38
Dulce Bellum Inexpertis (*War is sweet to those who know it not*) (Erasmus) .. 113

Index

Dungen, Peter van den*.. 204
Du Picq, Charles Ardant... 232
the Dutch 240–241, 246, 251
    see also Grotius, Hugo* (Hugo de Groot)
DuVall, Jack.. 272
Dyer, Gwenne.. 233
Dylan, Bob (US)... 190, 224

E

Ea (god)... 255, 259
Eannatum (Legash).. 27–28
Early Dynastic period... 48–49
East Africa... 194
Eastern Europe... 164
Easter Uprising (Ireland)... 253
East Timor 208
The East-West Vision of Peace... 206
Eckstein, Anna B.*... 151–152
economic issues.. 41
    see also agriculture; trade
Ecuador 240
Edicts of Ashoka*... 73
Edo period (Japan)... 274
education. *see also* writing
    Alfred the Great* and 94
    Arnoldson* on 188
    culture of peace and 272
    Duckworth* and 204
    Einstein* on 173
    Figueras Ferrer* and 180, 181
    Galtung* and 207
    Johnson* and.. 215
    More* and 115
    racism and... 203
    Saint Pierre* and 115
    Tolstoy* on.. 144
    US tradition of cooperation and 263
    Vardhana* and 98
The Education of a Christian Prince (Erasmus)............... 113, 118
Edward III (England) 105–106, 107
Edward IV (England)... 109
Effendi, Shoghi* (Baha'i)... 204–205
egalitarian structures.. 6–7, 17
    see also democracy

Index

Egypt. *see also* Arab Spring; peace heroes and peace victories of Egypt
    attacked 33
    beginnings of war and 25–26, 45–46
    expansionism and 62
    Greece and 35
    Isaiah* and 66
    the Levant and 59–60
    Nathan* and 218
    peace victories* and 26–27, 58–59
    Third Millennium BCE and 25–27, 30
Einstein, Albert* 165, 172–173, 210, 218
    see also Russell-Einstein Manifesto
Einstein Peace Prize 179
Ekur temple (Akkadian Empire) 29
Elamites (Near East) 30, 33, 57, 70
Electronic Intifada 189
Elizabeth I (Britain) 38, 118, 249–250
Ellsberg, Daniel* (US) 205, 206
Emergency Committee of Atomic Scientists 176
Emerson, Ralph Waldo* (US) 136–137
The End of War (Chappell) 196
Engaged Buddhism 220
England. *see also* Britain; French and Indian War *and other wars*; Great Britain; Henry VII* *and other English people*; Ireland; Northern Ireland
    peace heroes* of 93–95, 105–110
Enheduanna* (Akkad Empire) 29, 50–51
Enlil (god) 28, 29, 49, 255, 257, 259
"ensi," 48–49
environment 6–7
    see also culture
environmentalism 224, 265
    see also climate; Conservation Corps (US); Peace Ecology
Ephesus* (Anatolia) 65–66
Epistre Au Roi Richart (Mezieres) 108
equality. *see also* matrifocal cultures*
    Dravidian culture and 71
    elimination of war and 270
    Etruscans* and 80
    gender 62, 83, 84, 139, 185
    Haw* and 212
    Seeger* and 223
    Urukagina* and 49
    Yu* and 54
Erasmus, Desiderius* 112, 113–114, 115, 118

Index

Eridu (Mesopotamia) 257
Eshnunna (Mesopotamia) 30, 56
Essays and Addresses In Wartime (Bryce) 195
Essenes* (Judea) 67
Ethelfleda (Denmark) 94
Etruscans* (Italy) 80–81, 82, 83
Eugene Debs Award 228
Eugene IV (pope) 111
Europe, perpetual war and 38–39
   see also World War I (Great War) *and other wars*
Evans, Jodi* (US) 205–206
evil .... vi, 63, 140
evolution 141, 152–153
   see also genes and biology; social-cultural evolution
exploding bullets 158
Exploring Nonviolent Alternatives (Sharp) 225

F

Fabbro, David* 206, 235
Fabian Society 162, 163
Failed States (Chomsky) 197
Farber, Michael 198
Farmer, James 218
Fatah 189
Faustina, Annia Galeria* (Roman Empire) 90
Fawkes, Guy (England) 119, 120
Federation of German Scientists 211
Fellowship of Reconciliation 158, 200, 202, 218
female genital mutilation 273
female images and figurines 8*i*, 15, 17
Ferdinand (Spain) 38
Ferdinand VII (King of Naples) 131
Ferguson, R. Brian* 206
Fertile Crescent 257
   see also Sumerians
Fifth Millennium BCE 23–24
50 Years: Peace and Conflict Perspectives (Galtung) 208
fight or flight 6
Figueras Ferrer, José* 179–181
Finland 43, 184
firing squad member 232
"firmeza permanente" (Latin America) 239
First branch of the family tree... (peace poem) 103*p*
The first flutes... (peace poem) 10*p*

Index

first millennium BCE 34
First they came for the socialists 221*p*
fission 210
Fitzralph, Richard* (England) 108
Five Good Emperors 87
flutes 10*p*
"Following the Equator" (Twain) 146
FOR 186
A Force More Powerful A Century of Nonviolent Conflict (film) 184
Forsberg, Randall Caroline* 206, 235, 272
Fourth to Second Millennia BCE
    Akkadian Empire and 28–30
    Central Asia 22–25
    China and 30–31
    Egypt and 25–27
    India-Pakistan and 31–32
    Sumeria and 27–28
Fox, George* (England) 123–124
France. *see also* Cruce, Emeric* *and other French*; Hundred Years War *and other wars*
    archaeological records and 7, 20
    bomb tests and 195
    James I* and 119
    matrifocal cultures and 80
    militarism and 163
    nuclear testing and 217
    Turks and 41
    Vietnam and 41
Franco, Francisco (Spain) 43, 202
Franco-Prussian War 41
Franklin, Ursula* 206–207
Franks 37
Franz Joseph (Austria) 151
freedom 110, 117, 132
freedom of the press 125
Freedom of the Press Foundation 205
FREEZE 198, 206, 208
French and Indian War (US) 129
French-German War (1870s) 222
French IndoChina 41
French Revolution 39
Friends of Truth* (Society of Friends) 123
Froman, Menachem 189
Fry, Douglas P. 235, 272

Fussell, Paul 233–234, 235, 272
"Futility" (Owen) 168
A Future Without War (Hand) 211

G

Gadfly columns 254–259
Galba (Roman Empire) 87
Galtung, Johan* 207–208
Gandhi, Mohandas K.* ... 139–140, 142, 145, 160–162, 182, 214, 225, 246
Gandhi Peace Awards 191, 198, 199
Ganges Valley (India) 32, 35
Garrison, William Lloyd* 139–140
Gauls 87
Gautama Buddha 71, 72–73, 96
Gaza Strip 189, 216, 257
Gebel el-Arak knife 25
gender. see women and gender
genes and biology. *see* brains; evolution; *Homo sapiens*; killing, aversion to;
    Upper Paleolithic Period (hunter-gatherers) *and other periods*
    activism and 189
    aggression and vi
    aversion to killing and 232
    complex behavior and 20–21
    cooperation and .... ix, xp, 45, 153, 230, 231
    culture versus 25, 32, 231, 274
    great apes and humans and 230
    hunter-gatherers and 5–7, 10, 46
    law codes and 57
    Upper Paleolithic and 25, 229–230
Geneva Conventions viii
genocide 41, 273
GE nuclear plant (US) 192
German-French War (1870s) 222
German League for Human Rights 187
German Peace Society 151
Germany 7, 85, 167, 177–178
    see also Hahn, Otto*; Kollwitz, Kathe* *and other Germans*; Nicholas
    de Cusa (Cusanus); Thirty Years War; World War I (Great War) *and
    other wars*
Gimbutas, Marija 272
Gintis, Herbert 272
Gladstone Bills (England) 252
Glorius Revolution (England) 250
God 133, 255, 259

goddesses 30, 50, 51, 55, 58, 62, 65, 71, 81, 83, 84, 255, 259
gods 28, 29, 49, 50, 52, 57, 65, 81, 119, 255, 257, 259
Godwin, William* (England) 132–133
Goekli Tepe (Anatolia) 13
gold 42, 58
Goldstein, Joshua S. 235, 272
Goldstein, Warren 199
"Good Americans in a Time of Torture" (Branfman) 194
Good Friday agreement (1998) 214, 253–254
Goodman, Amy* (US) 208–209, 241
Goodman, Dorothy (US) 208
Goodman, George (US) 208
Goodman, Mitchell (US) 198
Gorbachev, Mikhail (Russia) 209
Goths 36–37
Gottingen Manifesto (1957) 211
Gournia (Crete) 61
governments. *see also* absolute monarchy; democracy; laws and order;
    "Praise Poem of Urukagina"; war and violent behavior
    administration *versus* 156–157
    collusion and 174
    Confucius* on 76–77
    culture of peace and 272
    killing and 76, 190, 212, 241, 249
    Mo-Tzu* on 77–78
    the State versus 154–157
    Tolstoy* on 143–144
    war and 78–79
    Xunzi* on 79
Gower, John* (England) 105–106
Goya, Francisco* (Spain) 130–132
Granada 43, 198
"The Grand Plan to End the War in Vietnam" (Malkin) 224
graves and burial practices 11, 23, 27–28
great apes 230
Great Britain 17–18, 40, 41, 250
    see also England; Ireland; Scotland
Great Flood 28
Great Turkish War 38
Great War (WW I) 42
Greece and Greeks. *see also* Athenian fleet; Balkan Wars; Cyneas;
    Olympic Games*; Thebes
    Ashoka* and 73
    Babylon and 30

colonies of 66
Etruscan trade and 83
Kant* and 130
Maimonides* and 102
peace heroes* and 68–70
pottery and female figurines and 8*i*, 14
trade and 64
warships of 61
wars with Persia 34–35
war with Troy 30–31
Zoroaster* and 63
Greek alphabet 81
Greek War of Independence 40
Greenham Common Women's Peace Camp* (England) 209–210
Greenpeace International 217
Green Shadow Cabinet (US) 193
The Grieving Parents (Kollwitz) 171
Griffin, David Ray 209
Grossman, Dave 232
Grotius, Hugo* (Hugo de Groot) 120–121
Groves, Leslie 177–178
Guam 158
Guantánamo Bay 41, 187, 216
Guatemala 197, 219, 240
Gudea* (Lagash dynasty) 52
Guernica (Picasso) 132
Guerrilla Radio (blog) 189
Gulf of Tonkin Resolution (US) 205
Gupta Empire* (India) 97
Gustavus Adolphus (Sweden) 38
Guthrie, Woody (US) 223
Guthrum (Anglo-Saxon) 94
Gutian tribes 29, 56, 57, 258

H

H₂O (peace poem) 260*p*
Haas, Jonathan 235, 272
Habitat for Humanity (US) 263
Habsburgs (Europe) 38, 39, 119
Hacilar (Anatolia) 13
Hadrian* (Roman Empire) 88–89
Hadrian's Wall 248
Hague Peace Conferences 145, 151–152, 213, 222
Hahn, Otto* 165, 210–211

Haidt, Jonathan David* 211
Halin (Pyu people) (Burma) 74
Halper, Jeff 189
Hamas Government 189
Hammurabi (Babylon) 30, 57, 58
Hand, Judith* 211
Han Dynasty* (China) 79–80
Hanging Gardens of Babylon 34
Hanh, Thich Nhat* (Vietnam) 219–220
Hannibal 36, 121
Harappa (Indus Valley) 32, 54–55, 70
Harkhuf (Governor Egypt) 26
Harpers Ferry attack (US) 142
Harran (Assyrian Empire) 33
"Harrisburg 7" 184
Hatshepsut* (Egypt) 26, 58–59, 61–62
Hattushilish people 58
Hattusili (Hittite) 60
Haw, Brian* (England) 211–212
Hawaiian Islands 43
Hayden, Tom* (US) 212–213
Heddychwyr Cymu (Wales) 200
Hegetorides* (Thasos) 70
henges 17–18
Henry II (England) 248
Henry IV (England) 106, 107–108
Henry V* (England) 107–108
Henry V (Shakespeare) 233
Henry VI (England) 108, 109
Henry VII* (England) 108, 109–110, 112, 248–249
Henry VIII (England) 112, 114
Hereford, Nicolas* (England) 108
Hericlidus* (Greece) 66
Herod (Jerusalem) 67
Herodotus* (Greece) 35, 66, 68
Hillel, Rabbi* (Jerusalem) 67
Hindus 184
Hippocratic Oath for scientists 178
Hiroshima and Nagasaki bombings 164, 176, 178, 185, 200, 202, 210
History of the Indies (Las Casas) 117
A History of Western Philosophy (Russell) 164
Hittites (Near East) 30, 58, 59–60, 62
Hoccleve, Thomas* (England) 108
Hoffman, Abbie (US) 203

Holocene Epoch 12
Holt, Hamilton* 213
Holy Land 254–259
The Holy Land – The No State Solution (peace essay) 254–258
Homer (Greece) 30
Homo sapiens 3–4, 6, 231
   see also brains; genes and biology; hunter-gatherers; Mesolithic and Neolithic Periods *and other periods*
Honduras 240
Hong Kong 40
Hopewell utopian community* (US) 141
Horgan, John 235, 272
hormones .... vi, 6
horse domestication 23, 24, 75, 84
House of Tudor (England) 109
"How America Spreads Global Chaos" (N.J.S. Davies) 201
How Can Anthropologists Promote Peace? (Ferguson) 206
"How to Establish A Stable Peace" (Boulding) 193
How to Stop the Next War now: Effective Responses to Violence and Terrorism (Benjamin) 191
How wondrous an organ... (peace poem) 32p
Howard, John 196
Hull, Hannah Hallowell Clothier* 213
Hull House 158
humanism 71, 76, 102, 111, 214
human nature v
   see also genes and biology; social-cultural evolution
     aversion to killing and 232
     Godwin on 132
     Xunxi* on 79
human rights 186, 187
human rights, charter of 68
human sacrifice 273
Hume, John* 213–214
Hundred Years War 38, 105–109
hunter-gatherers, cooperation and. *see also* agriculture; Jormon culture (Japan); Paleolithic Period
     archaeological record and ix
     art and 7–9, 12
     cave paintings and 22p
     cooperation and 46, 229
     described 3–6
     egalitarian structures and 6–7, 229
     genes and 6–7

Ireland and 248
Sri Lanka and 246, 247
tool technology and 7, 9–10
women and 3–4, 6, 10, 12, 229
Hurrians (Akkadian Empire) 33
Hutterites (US and Canada) 274

I

"I Ain't Marching Anymore" (Ochs) 220
Iceland .... vii, 193, 274
"I Declare the War Is Over" (Ochs) 220, 221
"If I had a Hammer" (Seeger) 224
Ikeda, Daisaku* 214–215
Ilargia (goddess) 81
imperialism 146, 215, 271
In Praise of Folly (*Encomium Morias*) (Erasmus) 115
Inanna (goddess of love) 50, 51, 255, 259
"Incident in the Philippines" (Twain) 146
India. *see also* Asvaghosa* *and other Indians*; Gupta Empire*; Indus Valley*;
   Mauryan Dynasty *and other dynasties*; Tamerlane *and other conquerors*
   Afghan Wars and 40
   beginning of war and 45–46
   British 161
   cave painting and 8
   China and 98
   peace victories* and 70–73, 96–98
   Sri Lanka and 247
   Third Millennium BCE and 31–32
indigenous populations 195
   see also Native Americans
individualism 265, 267
IndoChinaPeace Campaign (IPC) 212
Indo-Europeans 24
Indonesia 184, 208, 240–242
Indus Valley* 32
   peace and 54–55
Innuit (Canada) 274
"In Praise of Peace" (Gower) 106
Institute for Defense and Disarmament Studies 206
Institutio Principis Christiani (*Education of a Christian Prince*)
   (Erasmus) 113, 114, 118
intellectuals 97, 153–154
   see also Maimonides, Moses* *and other intellectuals*
Intermediate Nuclear Forces Treaty (INF) 209

International Action center 198
International Arbitration and Peace Association* 150, 151
International Arbitration League* 145
International Center on Nonviolent Conflict 183
International Congress of Women 159
International Court of Arbitration 121, 122
International Court of Justice 151, 195
International Parliamentary Union 222
International Peace Congresses of the Friends of Peace* 138
International Peace Research Association 193, 226
International Physicians for the Prevention of Nuclear War 195, 196
International Solidarity Movement 189
International Tribunal 165
Interparliamentary Union (England) 145
Inventory of a Soul (B. von Suttner) 150
IRA (Irish Republican Army) 214
Iran 197
Iraq and Iraq wars 43, 193, 196, 198, 200, 201, 203, 208–209, 216, 219, 228, 234, 254
Ireland 163, 247–254
   see also Great Britain; Northern Ireland
Irish Catholic Confederation 250
Irish Home Rule Acts 252, 253
The Irish League of the Credit Unions 213
Irish Republic 253
Irish Republican Brotherhood 253
Irish Volunteers 253
Isaac (son of Abraham) 255
Isabella (Spain) 38
Isaiah* 66–67, 258
Ishnunna Laws (Near East) 57
Ishtar (goddess) 255
Ishtar Gate 34
Isin (Mesopotamia) 56
Islam* and Muslims 89, 93–94, 111, 184, 247, 256, 259
   see also Abbasid caliphate; Holy Land; monotheism
Islamic forces 92
Israel 165–166, 189
   see also Holy Land; Jerusalem *and other locations*; Nes (Israeli political party)
Istanbul 37
Is your question Love?... (peace poem) 143*p*
Italian-Ethiopian War 43
Italy 7, 80
   see also Arrigoni, Vittorio* *and other Italians*

J

Jacob, Karen 199
Jacobi, Rudolf (Germany/US) 187
Jainism* 71–72, 98
Jallianwala Barg massacre (British India) 161
James, William* (US) 149–150
James I (England) 118–120, 250
James II (England) 251
James VI* (Scotland) 118, 119–120, 250
Japan 38, 193, 215
   see also atomic bombs and H-Bomb tests; Russo-Japanese War *and other wars*
Japanese academics* 215
Japanese Emperor 43
Jarmo (Iraq) 14
Jeannette Rankin Brigade 175
Jeannette Rankin Peace Center 175
Jebel Sahaba site (Egypt-Sudan) 11
Jemdet Nasr period 19–20, 48–49
Jericho 13, 15–16, 254, 257
   peace victories* and 47–48
Jerusalem 37, 87, 256, 257
Jerusalem, Second Temple of 89
Jesus* 90–91, 112, 123, 124, 132, 134, 135, 259
   see also Christianity and Christians
Jews. *see* Judaism and Jews
Jie (China) 31
Jihad, Islamic 189
Joan of Arc (France) 38
Johnson, Chalmers* (US) 215
Jonson, Ben (England) 118
Jormon culture (Japan) 14–15
Journal of Conflict Resolution 193
The Journal of Peace Research 207
Judaism and Jews 68, 87, 89, 210, 256
   see also Holy Land; Isaiah* *and other Jewish peace heroes*; Israel; monotheism
Judea 66, 67
Judelman, Shaul 189
Justinian (Roman Empire) 37

K

Kaiyuan era (China) 100
Kalinga War Of 261 BCE 36, 73
Kaniska* (Kushan empire) 96

Kannada language 70
Kant, Immanuel* (Germany) 102, 128, 129–130
Kaurava clan (India-Pakistan) 31
Keegan, John 233
Kellogg, Frank B.* (US) .... viii, 169–170
Kellogg-Briand Pact (1928) .... viii, 170
Kelly, Kathy* 188, 216–217
Kepler, Johannes 111
Khan, Genghis 37
Khsatriya (South Asia) 35
killing. *see also* Geneva Conventions; peace heroes and peace victories;
   war and violent behavior
    aversion to 229–236
    governments and 76, 190, 212, 241, 249
    laws and 273
    Mesolithic period and 11
    social-cultural evolution and 273
    thrill and vi
kindness (**May First**) 104*p*
King, Jr., Martin Luther* 139–140, 142, 182–183, 214, 218, 219
The Kingdom of God Is Within You (Tolstoy) 143
"King Leopold's Soliloquy" (Twain) 146
King Scorpion (Egypt) 25
Kinsky, Bertha (Austria) 150
Kish (Mesopotamia) 29, 56, 257
Kish, King of 50
Kissinger, Henry (US) 215
Kokhba, Simon bar (Jerusalem) 89
Kollwitz, Kathe* (Germany) 170–171
Korea 38, 42, 43
Korean War 190
Kosovo 184
Kroc Institute for International Peace Studies 199
Kropotkin, Peter* (Pyotr) (Russia) 152–153, 272
Kshatriya warrior class (Aryans) 32
!Kung (Africa) 274
Kung Fu Tzu* (Confucius) 76–77
Kurds 185
Kurgans (early Maikop) (Yamna) 23
Kurukshatra, war at 31
Kushan empire 96

L

Lagash Dynasty (Mesopotamia) 27–28, 49–52, 51*p*, 56

LaGuardia, Fiorello (US) 174
"Lament To the Spirit of War" (Enheduanna).......................29, 50–51p
Langland, William* (England) 108
Laos 193–194
Lao Tzu* 75–76, 79
Larsa (Mesopotamia) 56, 257
Las Casas, Bartolome de* (Spain) 115–118
"The Last Days of John Brown" (Thoreau) 142
Latin America 239–240
   see also Brazil and other countries
Law of Arms (jus in bello) 105
laws and order. see also Code of Ur-Nammu and other codes; Edicts of Ashoka*; Moses*; trial by jury
   Antoninus and 90
   Aryans and 32
   Celts and 248
   Gupta empire and 97
   Hadrian* and 89
   Ireland and 251
   Jewish 101
   killing and 273
   kindness and 104p
   peace victories* and 57–58
   slavery and 117
   Taizong and 99
   women and 58
   Zuanzong and 99
Laws of Larsa 57
Leadbelly (US) 223
League of Nations 195
The League to Enforce Peace 213
Leopold II (Belgium) 146
"Letter to a Hindu" (Gandhi) 145
"Letter to a Non-commissioned Officer" (Tolstoy) 143–144
"Letter to Anthony A Bergis" (Erasmus) 113
Levant* 59–60, 67
Levin, Aryeh 189
Liberation (magazine) 202
libraries 33, 179, 264, 266, 272
Libya 198
life 259p
Life on the Mississippi (Twain) 145
Ligue Internationale de la Paix (France) 188
Li Heng (China) 100

Li Linfu (China) 100
lions 9, 27
Liu Bang (Gaozu) 79
Local Government (Ireland) Act (1898) 252
Lollards* (England) 108
London (England) 266
London School of Economics 162
Lorenz, Konrad vi
"The Lottery" (Jackson) 273
Louis XVI of France 39, 127, 251
love .... *xp*, 71, 77, 106, 143*p*, 145, 205
"Love Me, I'm A Liberal" (Ochs) 220
Lown, Bernard (US) 196
Lugalzagesi (Umma) 28, 29, 49–50
Lumumba, Patrice (Congo) 197
Lutherans 39, 221
Lydgate, John* (England) 108
Lydian Kingdom 34, 68
Lysistrata (Aristophanes) 69

M

maces and mace heads 19, 20, 25, 26
Machiavelli, Niccoló (Italy) 114
The Machine Age (B. von Suttner) 150
Mahabharata epic (India-Pakistan) 31–32
Mahavira* (Great Hero) (Jain) 71, 72
Maikop, early (Kurgans) (Yamna) 23
Maimonides, Moses* 101–103, 256
Mainau Declaration (1957) 165, 176, 210
Malayalam language 70
Malta* (Mediterranean) 55
mammoth ivories 8–9
Manchuria 42
Mandela, Nelson 214, 271
Manhattan Project (US) 176, 177–178
Manifesto of the Peace Pledge Union 173
man-made disasters 218–219
Manning, Bradley (US) 205
Maoris 40
Marchand, Walter 233
Marcos, Ferdinand (Philippines) 238
Mari (goddess) 30, 58, 81, 83, 84
Mars (god) 119
Marshall, S.L.A. 232, 234

Martí, José (Cuba) 158
Mary (England) 251
Mary Elsbernd OSF Social Justice Award 187
Mary I (England) 249
Mary Queen of Scots 118
Massachusetts 200
Massachusetts Peace Society 134
Massacre By Bombing (Brittain) 167
matrifocal cultures* 80–84
matrilinear societies and matriarchies 17, 47, 71, 80–82, 83, 84
Mauryan, Chandragupta 72
Mauryan Dynasty 35–36, 72, 73
Mayer, Peter 272
May First (peace poem) 104p
Mayors for Peace (Japan) 185
McCarthy, Colman* (US) 217
McTaggart, David Fraser* (Canada) 217
Mead, Margaret 235, 271
meat and nicotinamide 4
media .... vi, 265
"The Mediator's Kingdom Not of This World" (Dodge) 134, 135–136
medieval cities 153
Mediterranean 34, 254–255
Mediterranean Sea 39
Mehrgarh (Pakistan) 14, 32, 54
Meitner, Lise 210
men .... v–vi, 4, 270
Mencius* 78–79
Menes (Egypt) 25
"Mental Cases" (Owen) 168
Merenre (Egypt) 26
Mesolithic and Neolithic periods 11–20, 248
Mesopotamia 18, 28, 29, 33, 38, 45–46, 254, 256–257
Mesopotomia 54, 88
   see also Uruk *and other cities*
   peace victories* and 56–57
metal working 13, 24, 27, 31, 49, 54
Metsamor (Armenia) 13
Mexican-American War 141, 142
Mexico 38, 41
Mezieres, Philippe de* (France) 108
Michelangelo (Italy) 111
Middle East 205
   see also Israel; Palestine

peace victories* and 62–63
Middle Path* (Buddhism) 72
Military—Politary (peace poem) 236*p*
Milton, John (England) 3
Milwaukee Fourteen (US) 192
Ming Dynasty (China) 38
Minoans* (Crete) 60–62, 65
The Miracle of Living (Balch) 160
Missouri Peace Planting (US) 216
Mohenjo-daro (Indus Valley) 32, 54
Mongol Empire 37
monotheism 255–256
   see also Christianity and Christians; Islam* and Muslims; Judaism and Jews; religion and religious institutions
Montesinos, Antonio de* (Dominican) 116, 117–118
Moors (Berber tribes) 37, 38, 92–93, 256
"The Moral Equivalent of War" (James) 149, 150
Moravia 7
More, Thomas* 112, 114–115
Moriori culture* 217
Moro Crater Massacre (Philippines) 146
Moses* 60, 259
Mossadegh, Mohammed (Iran) 197
The Most Dangerous Man in America: Daniel Ellsberg and the Pentagon Papers (Evans) 206
Mother with her Dead Son (Kollwitz) 171
Mo-Tzu* 77–78, 79
Mountbatten, Louis (Britain) 253
Mueller, John 235, 272
Mughals 38
Murdoch, Rupert 212
music 27, 71, 100, 136, 261
   see also Seeger, Pete* *and other musicians*
Muslims. see Islam* and Muslims
Muste, A.J.* 158, 202, 217–218, 225
Mutual Aid: A Factor of Evolution (Kropotkin) 152–153
Muwatalli (Hittite) 30, 60
Myanmar 242–243
   see also Burma*
Mycennaeans 30, 62, 65

N

Nairn, Allan 208
Namibia 184

Nanak* (Sikhs) 225–226
Nanda Empire 35
Nanna (Sin) (god) 50, 255
Nanshe (goddess) 52, 255
Nanyue territory (China) 80
Napoleonic wars 39–40, 131
Naram Sin of Akkadian Empire 29
Narmer palette (Egypt) 25
Nathan, Abie* (Persia) 218–219
National Guard (New Zealand) 271
National Liberation Party (PLN) (Costa Rica) 180
Native Americans & indigenous people 40, 116, 117, 125–126, 129, 130, 142
   see also French and Indian War; Peletier, Leonard
NATO 209
Natufian period 15–16
Natural Law 130
The Nature of the Chemical Bond and the Structure of Molecules and Crystals
   (Pauling) 175
naval power 26, 39, 42, 43, 66, 83, 139, 170
   see also Arkhipov, Vasili* (USSR); Athenian fleet
Nazi Germany 177–178
Near East 30, 57, 185, 205, 234, 254–255
Nearing, Scott (US) 158
Nebuchadnezzar (Neo-Babylonia) 34, 68
NeoAssyrian Empire 33–34, 95
Neo-Babylonia 33–34, 95
Neolithic Period. see also Catal Huyuk (Anatolia) *and other cities*;
   Cucuteni-Trypillian Culture; stamp and cylinder seals
   art and 13
   Basque language and 81
   ceremonial places and 17–18
   Ireland and 248
   overview 12–15
   peace victories* and 46–48, 54
   scepters and mace heads and 20
   seals and 18, 48–49
   trade and 230–231, 255
   women and 13
Neolithic period through today 31–44
Nero (Roman Empire) 85, 87
Nerva* (Roman Empire) 87–88
Nes (Israeli political party) 218
Neutral Conference 158
neutrality, permanent 188

The New Cyneas (*Le Nouveau Cynee*) (Cruce) 121
New England Non-Resistance Society 139, 141
Newer Ideals of Peace (Addams) 158
The New Pearl Harbor (Griffin) 209
The New Statesman (journal) 162
New York City 201, 266
New York Peace Society* 136
New Zealand 40, 190–191, 195, 217, 271
"The Next War" (Owen) 168–169
Nicaragua 180, 216, 240
Nicholas V (pope) 111
Niemöller, Martin (Germany) 221
Nigeria 208
9/11 bombing 209
nineteenth century 40–42
Nineveh (Assyrian Empire) 33
Nine Years' War 249, 250
Ningirsu (god) 52
Ninhursag (Nintu) (goddess) 255
Nippur (Mesopotamia) 28, 29, 50, 51, 257
Nobel, Alfred 150, 151
Nobel Prize and winners
    Addams* 159
    Ahtisaari* 184
    Arnoldson* 188
    Balch* 160
    Belo 241
    Caldicott* 196
    Chadwick 179
    Cremer* 145
    Einstein* 173
    Hahn* 210
    Hume and Trimble 214
    International Physicians for the Prevention of Nuclear War 196
    Kellogg* 170
    Kim* 244
    King, Jr.* 182, 183
    Maineau Declaration and 165
    Passy* and Cremer* 222
    Pauling* 176–177
    Richard* 141
    Rotblat* 179
    Schweitzer* 223
    Shaw* 162

Suttner*.. 151
No Conscription Fellowship.. 164
   see also conscription alternatives
"No Cross, No Crown" (Penn)... 125
No More War (Pauling) 176
No More War movement 173, 191
"non-resistance".. 139–141
nonviolence. *see also* civil disobedience; conflict, resolutions of; New England Non-Resistance Society; *Why Civil Resistance Works* (Chenowith)
   Akerman* and.. 183–184
   Arents* and.. 187
   Ballou* and.. 141
   Basques* and... 84
   Cortright* and 199
   Day* and 202
   Gandhi* and 160–162
   Hume* and 214
   Kelly* and 216
   King, Jr.* and.. 182
   Latin America and... 239–240
   McCarthy* and 217
   Moriori culture* (New Zealand) and.............................. 217
   Philippines and... 238
   Sharp* and 225
   Sikhs* and 226
   women and 139
Norman, Mildred Lisette* (US).................................... 222–223
Normans.. 37
Northern Ireland 213–214, 247, 249, 250, 253
Northumbria (England) 95
Norway.. 187, 188
   see also Galtung, Johan*; Vikings
Nubia.. 20, 26
Nuclear Age Peace Foundation 178, 196, 205
nuclear-free zones... 271
Nuclear Peace (Franklin) 207
nuclear power 192, 195–196
   see also fission
nuclear submarines 181
nuclear weapons. *see also* atomic bombs and H-Bomb tests; Baby Tooth Survey; Cuban Missile Crisis; FREEZE; Greenham Common Women's Peace Camp*; radiation effects; SANE; Test Ban Treaties
   Arkhipov* and 181–182
   Baxter* and 191

Berrigan brothers* and 192
Brock* and 194
Caldicott* and..196
Corbyn* and 199
Day* and..202
Du Bois* and 204
Einstein* and 173
Hahn* and 210–211
Ikeda* and..214
Japanese academics* and 215
Kelly* and 216
McTaggart* and...217
Niemöller and 221
Pauling* and...176
Plow Shares and 202
Rotblat* and... 177–179
Russell* and 164–165, 166, 173
Wittner* and..226
number systems 27, 49, 54
Nuremberg International Rights Award...219

O

Occupy Wall Street (US)...190
Ochs, Phil* (US)...190, 220–221
An octopede knows no bones (peace poem)... 21*p*
Olympic Games* 64–65
On Aggression (Lorenz).. vi
On the Beach (Shute)..195
On The Seven Deadly Sins (Wyclif)..107
"An Open Letter to the President of the United States of America" (Shaw)...163
opium 41
Opium Wars (England-China) 40
Orange Order (Northern Ireland) 252
ordinary people ....vii–viii, 189, 227
Orzi (god)..81
Oslo Accords 254
Ostrogoths..36–37
Other Lands Have Dreams (Kelly) 216
Otho (Roman Empire)...87
Ottomans (Turks).. 37, 38, 39, 41, 110
Our Origins in Ancient History (peace essay)..........................258–259
Our Slavic Fellow Citizens (Balch) 159
Owen, Wilfred*...42, 167–169
ownership of goods..45

Oxford Reformers* 112

P

Pacem In Terris Peace and Freedom Award 185–186, 191, 220
"pacifism" 188
Pacificus, Philo 134
Pacifism and Conscience (Franklin) 207
Pacifism as a Map (Franklin) 207
"A Pacifist Epistle" (Woolman) 129
Pact of Paris (1928) .... viii, 170
Padstow church* (England) 95
Pagan Empire (Burma) 74
Pagans 257
Pahlavi, Mohammad Reza 197
Pakistan 31–32, 184, 193, 194
Paleolithic Period 6, 45, 81, 267p
   see also Upper Paleolithic Period (hunter-gatherers)
Palestine 166, 189, 216, 218
   see also Holy Land
Palestinian People's Party 189
Pamplona, Kingdom of 83
Panama 43, 198
Pandava clan (India-Pakistan) 31
Pappe, Ilan 189
Paris Peace accord 205
Parshva* (Jain) 71
Pasenadi of the Kosala region 72
Passy, Frederic* 145, 221–222
pastoralists, Asian 23–24
patriarchal societies 24
Paul III (pope) 117
Pauling, Linus* 165, 173, 175–177, 204, 272
Pauling Appeal 211
Pax Christi Peace Award 191
Pax Romana 85–86
Paxton, Tom (US) 224
PCBs 224
Peace (Aristophanes) 69
peace, culture of 272
Peace, Justice and Conflict Studies Program (DePaul University) 187
peace, peace heroes and peace victories. *see* conflict, resolutions
   of; cooperation and caring; education; Egypt *and other places*;
   Enheduanna* *and other peace heroes*; resolutions of conflict; treaties
"Peace" (Emerson) 137

Peace Abbey Courage of Conscience Award 191, 223, 228
Peace Action 226
Peace and Bread in Time of War (Addams) 158
Peace Bearers (Olympics) 65
Peace by Peaceful Means: Peace and Conflict, Development and Civilization
   (Galtung) 208
Peace Chronicle (newspaper) 186
Peace Corps (US) 271
Peace Ecology 186
Peaceful Revolution (Chappell) 196
"Peaceful Societies: An Introduction" (Fabbro) 206
Peace History Society 226
Peace Information Center 204
"Peace Is Dangerous" (Du Bois) 204
Peace Movement (England) 105–109
Peace News (magazine) 167, 194
"The Peace of Europe and How to Achieve IT" (Shaw) 163
Peace: Peace Research—Education—Action (Galtung) 208
Peace Pilgrim* 222–223
Peace Pledge Union (in New Zealand and Wales) 167, 191, 200
Peace Prize (US) 191
Peace Research Institute 207
Peace Ship 218
Peace Society* (Great Britain) 141
Peace Through Resistance To U.S. Imperialism (Russell) 165
Pearl Harbor 43
Pearson Medal of Peace 207
Peletier, Leonard 198
Peloponnesian Wars 35, 70
Penn, William* 124–127
Pennsylvania 125
Pentagon Papers 205
A People's History of the United States (Zinn) 228
Pepi I (Egypt) 26
Permanent Arbitration Council 128
Permanent Court of Arbitration 151
Perpetual Peace: A Philosophical Sketch (Kant) 128
Persia 34–35, 38
   see also Battle of Salamis; Cyrus The Great* (Achemenid Empire); Elamites
Peru 240
Pfeffer Peace Prize 186
Pharnaces (Pontus) 36
Pharaoh Den (Egypt) 26
Pharaoh the First (peace poem) 26p

Philadelphia (Pennsylvania)...125
Philip II (Spain) 38
Philip of Macedon..35
Philippine-American War 146, 149, 158
Philippines... 41–42, 146, 158, 238
Philippine War of Independence... 42
Phoenicians 64, 80–81
Physicians for Social Responsibility 195, 208
Picasso, Pablo 132
Picts* (Scotland)....................................... 80, 81–82, 84, 88, 248, 268*p*
Pilgrim, Peace*.. 222–223
Pilgrimage of Peace (G.M.L. Davies)..201
Pilgrim of Peace (Llewellyn) 200–201
Pinochet, Augusto (Chile).. 239
Piscitelli, Matthew.. 235, 272
"Pity of War" (Owen) 168
Pizarro, Francisco 38
Plantation system (Northern Ireland).. 250
Plato (Greece) 69
"A Plea For The Poor" (Woolman) 129
Plowshares movement 202
Plowshares Nine 191
poison gas 158
Pole, Michael de la* (England) 108
The Politics of Nonviolent Action (Sharp)..225
polytheism 259
Popular Resistance Committees (Palestine) 189
population densities, larger 12, 74, 254
    see also cities
population densities, smaller...................................3, 5, 6, 229, 231, 262, 266
Port Arthur (Manchuria).. 42
Port Huron Statement.. 212
Portugal 39, 92–93, 246
potato blight (Ireland) 252
pottery 8*i*, 12, 14, 15, 16, 19, 54, 81, 82, 255, 261
    see also female figurines
poverty
    Ahmad* and... 184
    Alfred the Great* and 94
    American tradition and 263
    Balch* and 159
    as cause of war 269
    conquests and 35
    Day* and.. 201–202

Faustina* and 90
Gandhi* and 161
Hadrian* and 88
Irish 151
Kollwitz* and 171
More* and... 114
Nanak* and 226
the Sikhs* and 226
Taizong and 99
war and 271
Woolman* and 129
Zoroaster* and 63
Praetorian Guard (Roman Empire)... 85, 88
"A Praise of Peace" (Lydgate).. 108
"Praise Poem of Urukagina"... 49
Pratt, Hodgson 150
pregnancy 6, 8i
primates.. ix–xp
As primates… (peace poem)... ix$p$
The Prince (Machiavelli) 114
Principles of Mathematics (Russell) 164
prisoners 27
Profits over People (Chomsky) 197
Projet pour Render la Paix Perpetual en Europe (*Project for Creating Perpetual Peace in Europe*) (Saint Pierre) 127–128
Protestants 249–251
Proto-Dynastic era 25
psychopathology.. 233
PTSD (post-traumatic stress disorder)... 234
Public Assistance of the Poor in France (Balch) 159
Puduhepa* (Hittite)... 60
Puerto Rico 41, 158, 187
Pugwash Conference on Science and World Affairs 178
Pugwash Conferences.. 165
Pulakesin II (Chalukya kingdom) 98
Punic Wars 36
Pygmies 274
Pyu* people (Burma) 74

Q

Qaramel (Syria) 13
Qin Dynasty (China) 36, 79, 80
Qin Shi Huangdi (Qin Dynasty) 36
Quakers 123–124, 128–129, 187, 193, 207, 213, 217–218

Querela Pacis (*Complaint of Peace*) (Erasmus) 113
Quincy, Edmund and Maria* 139

R

radiation effects 176, 178–179
Raging Grannies (US) 204
Raleigh, Walter (England) 119, 120
Ramsay, William 210
Ramses II (Egypt) 30, 58, 60
Random Acts of Kindness (US) 264
Rankin, Jeannette* (US) 174–175
rape 56, 73
Raphael (Italy) 111
Raskin, Marcus 198
Reagan, Ronald (US) 209
reason 67, 75, 102
Red Cross (US) 264
"Reflections on Theology and Peace" (Franklin) 207
Reformation 249
Regement of Princes (Hoccleve) 108
"relentless persistence" 239
religion and religious institutions. *see also* Buddhism* *and other religions*;
   ceremonial places; conversions; God; Holy Land; Zoroaster**and other
   religious figures*
   agriculture and 17
   Basque 81
   as cause of war 269
   Etruscan 81
   matrifocal cultures and 81, 82, 83, 84
   Neo-Babylonians and 33–34
   Neolithic Period and 14
   of non-violence 162
   pastoralists and 23
   Philippines and 238
   Sri Lanka* and 247
   tolerance for 226
Religion and Science (Russell) 164
religious freedom 125
Renaissance to the Modern Era 101–138
Renan, Ernest 150
Reno, Janet 216
Resisting the Bomb (Wittner) 226
revolutions 31, 133
Reynolds, Malvina 223

Rhodes, Cecil (Great Britain) 146
Richard, Henry * (Wales) 141
Richard II (England) 107, 108
Richard III (England) 109
Richardson, Lewis Fry 270
The Righteous Mind: Why good people are divided by politics and religion
  (Haidt) 211
Right Livelihood Award 205, 207, 225
Right to Well Being for All 153
Rim-Sin's Laws of Larsa 57
Rishabha* (Jain) 72
Robespierre (France) 39
Rochester, siege of (Britain) 94
Rogers, Will (US) 171–172
Rogge, O. John 204
Roman Empire 36–37, 39, 84, 85–92, 167, 248, 268*p*
  see also Augustus* *and other emperors*; Battle of Teutoberg Forest;
  Seneca* *and other Romans*
Romania 24
Roman Legions 85, 87, 89
Rome 36
Roosevelt, Franklin D. (US) 174
Roosevelt, Theodore (US) 169
Rooted in Peace (film) 206
Rotblat, Joseph* (Josef) 165, 177–179
Rotblat, Tola 177
Rousseau, Jean-Jacques (France) 128
Rowlatt Act (1919) (British India) 161
Roy, Arundhati 184
Russell, Bertrand* 163–166, 173, 179
Russell-Einstein Manifesto 165, 173, 176, 178
Russia and USSR. *see also* Arkhipov, Vasili* *and other Russians*; Russo-
  Japanese War *and other wars*
  archaeological evidence and 7, 23
  Costa Rica and 180, 181
  Einstein* and 164–165
  Johnson, Chalmers* on 215
  Napoleon and 131
  naval warfare and 39
  nuclear weapons and 164, 178
  Ottomans and 39, 41
  Vikings and 37
Russian Civil War 42–43
Russo-Japanese War 42

Rustin, Bayard 202, 218
Rutherford, Ernest 210

S

Sacco and Vanzetti trial (US) 164
Sacred Truce* 65
sacrifices 17, 31, 273
Sage Kings* (China) 52–54, 79
Said, Edward 184
St. Patrick (Ireland) 248
Saint Pierre, Charles Irénée Castel de* 127–128
Sakhalin Island 42
Saladin (Crusades) 37
Samarra 14
Sancho the Great* (Kingdom of Pamplona) 83
SANE 198, 199, 200, 208
Sangam literature (Dravidian culture) 71
Sargon the Great (Kish/Agade) 28–29, 50, 256–257
Sartre, Jean Paul (France) 165
Sasklo (Greece) 14
Sassoon, Siegfried (England) 168
satyagraha 238, 239
Save the Whales 217
Saxons 37
Scandinavia 188
scepters 20
Schell, Jonathan 272
School of the Americas Watch (US) 216
Schweitzer, Albert* 223
Science and World Affairs (J. Rotblat) 178
Scotland 80, 84, 248, 250, 268p
  see also Great Britain; James VI* (Scotland)
Scythians 33, 68
sea creatures 259p
seals, stamps, and cylinders 18i, 18–20, 19i, 20i, 27, 33–34, 48–49, 257
  see also the Cyrus Cylinder*
"Second Coming" 5, 235p
The Second of May (Goya) 131
Seed of Chaos: What Mass Bombing Really Means (Brittain) 167
Seeger, Pete* 190, 220, 221, 223–225
Sein Fein (Ireland) 252, 253
Seleucus I (Macedonia) 35–36
Seljuk Turks 37
Sellon, Jean-Jacques* 136

Semai (Malay Peninsula) ... 274
Semites ... 30, 255, 258
Seneca, Lucius Annaeus* ... 86–87
Seneca Women's Encampment for a Future Peace and Justice (US) ... 210
Serbs ... 42
Serpaj (Uruguay) ... 239
Service for Peace and Justice (Uruguay) ... 239
settlement houses ... 158
Sevrus, Julius (Roman Empire) ... 89
Shakespeare (England) ... 38, 118, 172, 233
Shalom Communities of the United Methodist Church (US) ... 265
Shalom I (plane) ... 218
Shamash (god) ... 57, 259
Shang Dynasty (China) ... 31, 63, 65
Shanghai (China) ... 40
Shar-kali-sharri (Akkadian Empire) ... 29
Sharp, Gene* ... 225, 272
Shaw, George Bernard* ... 162–163
shell shock ... 167
Sherman Anti-Trust Act (US) ... 169
Shetterly, Robert* (US) ... 225
Shift: The Beginning of War, The Ending of War (Hand) ... 211
Shulgi* (Mesopotamia) ... 56
Shun* (China) ... 31, 53
Shu-Sin* (Mesopotamia) ... 57
Shute, Neville ... 195
Siberia ... 152
Sicily ... 66
Sidon (Mediterranean coast) ... 255
Sikhs* ... 225–226
Silver Rule* ... 76
Sinai* ... 60
Singh, Gobind (Sikh) ... 226
Sinhalese (Sri Lanka) ... 246, 247
Sino-Japanese War ... 42, 43
Siriono (Bolivia) ... 274
skeletons ... 229
slate palette (Egypt) ... 25
slavery and abolition. *see also* US Civil War
    Antoninus* ... 90
    Burritt* and ... 138
    de Sellon* and ... 136
    Du Bois* and ... 203
    Emerson* and ... 137

Garrison* and 139, 140
Las Casas* and 116, 117
Penn* and 127
Richard* and 141
Seneca* on 86
slave trade 39
social-cultural evolution and 273
Thoreau* and 141, 142
war and 270
Woolman* and 128–129
"Slave Trade to the United States of America 1638-1870" (Du Bois) 203
"Sleeping Venus" sculpture 55
Sneferu (Egypt) 26
Snow opaque... (peace poem) 259p
social-cultural evolution. *see also* agriculture *and other practices*; Indus Valley* *and other locations*; Neolithic Period *and other periods*
    abolition of war and 273–274
    Arabs and Jews and 257–258
    aversion to killing and 234
    cooperation and caring and 230, 231–232, 261–274
    genes *versus* 25, 32
    Indus Valley and 32
    Ireland and 247
    progress of 272–273
    war and .... vii, 235
social intelligence 5
Social Work profession 158
Société de la Paix* 136
La Société Française Pour l'Arbitration entre Nations 222
Society of United Irishmen 252
Soka Gakkai International 214
A Solemn Review of the Custom of War (Pacificus) 134
Somalia 198
    see also Ali, Abdulkadir Yahya*
So many millennia... (peace poem) 267p
"Some Considerations On The Keeping of Negroes" (Woolman) 129
Songtsan Gambo (Tibet) 101
South Africa 42
    see also Gandhi, Mohandas K.*; Sri Lanka
South America 240
    see also Brazil *and other countries*
South Asia 12, 35
    see also India
Southern Ocean Whale Sanctuary 217

South Korea 243–244
Spain 7, 37, 119, 120, 131
   see also Basques*; Cordoba*; Las Casas, Bartolome de* *and other Spaniards*; Moors (Berber tribes); Philippines; Spanish-American War *and other wars*; Spanish Armada
peace victories* and 92–93, 101–103
Spanish-American War 41–42, 146, 158
Spanish Armada 38
Spanish Civil War 43, 202
Sparks from the Anvil (Burritt) 138
Spartan League 35
Spencer, Herbert (England) 150
Spock, Benjamin 198
sports* 64–65, 265
Sri Ksetra (Pyu people) (Burma) 74
Sri Lanka 246–247
stamp and cylinder seals 18i*i*-19*i*, 18–20, 34, 48, 55, 230–231
Standard Oil 169
"The State" (Bourne) 154–157
Stele of Vultures (Sumeria) 28
"Steps Toward Inner Peace" (Norman) 222
Stockholm International Peace Institute 206
Stockholm Peace Appeal 204
stoicism 86
Stonehenge 17
stoning to death 273
Stop the Next War Now (Evans) 205
Stop Torture Ambassador 186
Strassmann, Fritz 210
Strategic Nonviolent Conflict: the Dynamics of People Power in the Twentieth Century (Ackerman) 183–184
Students for a Democratic Society (SDS) 212
Sufi tradition 184
Sumerians 27–28, 29, 44*p*, 68, 134
   Holy Land and 254, 256–257, 258
   peace victories* and 48–51*p*
Summa Proedicantium (*Notes for Preachers*) (Bromyard) 108
Summersby, Kay 233
Sun Tzu (China) 232
survival 5, 229
Swank, Roy 233
Sweden .... vii, 274
   see also Arnoldson, Klaus Pontus* *and other Swedes*; Vikings
Swedish Peace and Arbitration League 188

Switzerland ... 274
Swynderby, William* (England) ... 108
Syria ... 13, 33, 93

T

T'ai Tsung (Taizong) (China) ... 98–99
Taiwan ... 244–246
Taizong (T'ai Tsung) (China) ... 98–99, 101
Tamanend (Leni Lenapi) ... 126
Tamerlane (Timur) ... 37
Tamil language ... 70
Tamil Tigers (Sri Lanka) ... 246–247
Tang Dynasty* ... 74, 76, 98–101
Taoism* ... 75–76
Tao Te Ching (Lao Tzu) ... 75
Taprock Peace Center ... 200
tax resistance ... 200
Teaching for America ... 271
Tebessa, Maximilian* (Roman Empire) ... 91–92
technologies ... 231
Tel Brak ... 20i
Telugu language ... 70
Ten Commandments ... 259
"Ten Conclusions to Parliament" (Lollards) ... 108
tenth to seventh centuries BCE ... 34
Tepe Sialk (Iran) ... 14
La Terreur (France) ... 39
Tertullian* (Carthage) ... 91–92
Testament of Youth (Brittain) ... 166, 167
Test Ban Treaties ... 176
testosterone ... vi
Texas ... 40–41
Thasos ... 70
Thera (Crete) ... 61
Thich Tri Quang ... 219
Third Millennium BCE ... 22–25
Third Millennium Foundation ... 217
The Third of May (Goya) ... 131–132
Thirty Years' Peace (445) ... 35
Thirty Years War ... 38–39, 119, 122
Thomas, Norman (US) ... 158
Thomas Merton Award ... 228
Thoreau, Henry David* ... 141–142, 225
three eye idols (Tel Brak) ... 20i

Three Mile Island (US) 195–196
Tianbao period 100–101
Tiberius (Roman Empire) 85
Tibetan-Chinese Peace Treaty* 101
Tigris and Euphrates River valley 258
Timur (Tamerlane) 37
Titus* (Roman Empire) 87
Tiye (Egypt) 59
To Dwell in Peace: An Autobiography (D. Berrigan) 192
Tolstoy, Leo* (Russia) 141, 142, 143–144
Tomyris, Scythian Queen 68
tools 9–10, 13, 15, 16
   see also metal working
torture 187, 194, 216, 239, 273
Torturers In the Mirror (Clark) 198
Toward Nuclear Abolition (Wittner) 226
Tower of Mothers (Kollwitz) 171
Toynbee Hall 157–158
trade. *see also* capitalism; corporations
   agriculture and 230
   Asian pastoralists-Cucuteni 23–24
   Catal Huyuk and 47
   China-Tibet and 101
   cities and 27, 49
   Costa Rica and 180
   Cruce on 122
   Cucuteni-Trypillian 16
   Egyptian-Nubian 26
   England and 109
   Etruscans* and 80–81, 82–83
   Hatshepsut* and 58, 61–62
   India and 97
   Indus Valley and 55
   Ireland and 252
   Mesopotamia and 54
   Minoans* and 61
   Neolithic Period and 12–13, 14–15, 230–231, 255
   Phoenicians and 64
   stamps and cylinder seals and 20, 20*i*
   Yao* and 52–53
Trajan (Roman Empire) 88
treaties 30, 60, 80, 109, 119, 130
   see also conflict, resolutions of; specific treaties
treaties, disarmament 271

Treaty of Amity and Friendship 125–126
Treaty of Limerick 251
Treaty of Nanjing 40
Treaty of Paris 146
Treaty of Paris, 2nd 131
Treaty of Utrecht 128
Treaty of Wedmore 94
trial by jury 125
Tritan da Cunha (South Pacific) 274
Trojans 30
Troy Book, the Siege of Thebes (Lydgate) 108
"The True Law of Free Monarchies" (James I) 118
truth force 238, 239
Turan (goddess) 81
Turkey 13, 15, 30
  see also Catal Huyuk (Anatolia); Greek War of Independence;
  Ottomans; Seljuk Turks
Turkish Navy 39
"Turn, Turn, Turn" (Seeger) 224
Twain, Mark* 145–149, 172
Twentieth Century to today 139–223
Two Moons (peace poem) 235p
Two-State Solution (Israel-Palestine) 254
Tyreans* (Mediterranean coast) 64, 255

U

Ukraine 20, 24
Umayyads 93
Umma 29, 56
  see also Lugalzagesi of Umma
Underground Railway (US) 142
Uni (goddess) 81
Union Pacific Railroad 169
Unitarians 133–134
United Kingdom 199, 212
United Nations 185, 186, 214
United States .... vii, 20, 197–198, 227, 238
  see also atomic bombs and H-Bomb tests; Native Americans; nuclear
  weapons; Texas *and other states*; Woolman, John* *and other Americans*;
  World War I (Great War) *and other wars*
    cooperation and caring and 261–267
University of Nalunda (India) 98
Upper Paleolithic Period (hunter-gatherers) 5, 7, 21, 25, 45, 229–230
  see also Cucuteni-Trypillians *and other cultures*; hunter-gatherers

cooperation and 46–47, 230–231
Ur (Euphrates) 255, 257, 258
Ur, royal cemetery and 27–28
Urartu 33, 95
Urban II (Pope) 256
Ur III (Mesopotamia) 29, 56–57, 259
Ur-Nammu of Uruk (Mesopotamia) 29, 56
Uruguay 239
Uruk (Mesopotamia) 28, 29, 49, 50, 56, 257
Urukagina* (Lagash Dynasty) 28, 49–50, 57
Uruk period 19, 48
US Civil War 41, 141
US-Mexican War 41
USSR. see Russia and USSR
Utopia (More) 115
Utu (Samas) (god) 255
Utu-Hegal (Uruk) 29, 56

V

Valitorta rock shelter (Valencia) 8
Valladolid debates 117
Vardhana, Harsha* (India) 97–98
Varuna (Vinnu) (goddess) 71
Varus (Roman Empire) 85
Veddahs (Sri Lanka) 247
Vedism* 98
Venezuela 180, 240
Venus figurines 8i
Verses of a VAD (Brittain) 166
Vespasian* (Roman Empire) 87
Veterans for Peace 193, 205
Veterans March (US) 228
Vienna Appeal 211
Vietnam 41
 see also Hanh, Thich Nhat*
Vietnam: the Logic of Withdrawal (Zinn) 228
Vietnam War
    Ahmad* and 184
    Baker* and 190
    Baxter* and 191
    P. Berrigan* and 192
    Branfman* and 193
    Clark* and 197
    Coffin* and 198

conscientious objectors and 200, 207
Cortright* and 199
cultural slurs and 234
Dellinger and 203
Ellsberg* and 205
Franklin* and 207
Hanh* and 219
Hayden* and 212
King, Jr.*, and 183
Ochs* and 220
Rankin* and 175
Russell* and 165, 166
Seeger* and 224
Twain's "The War Prayer" and 146
Vikings 37, 93–94, 248
The Viking's Kurdish Love—Zoroastrians' Fight for Survival (Akreyi) 186
Vinnu (Varuna) (goddess) 71
Violence, Peace, and Peace Research (Galtung) 208
violent behavior vi
   see also genes and biology; killing; nuclear weapons; social-cultural evolution; war
Visigoths 36–37
The Vision of Piers Plowman (Langland) 108
Vitelllius (Roman Empire) 87
Voice of Peace programs 218, 219
Voice of Women 204, 207
Voices for Creative Nonviolence 216
Voices from the Plain of Jars (Branfman) 193–194
Voices in the Wilderness 216
Voltaire (France) 126, 128
von Suttner, Arthur 150–151
von Suttner, Bertha* 150–152
votetoimpeach (US) 198
Von Grimmelshausen, Hans Jakob Christoffel* 122–123

W

Die Waffen Nieder (*Lay Down Your Arms*) (B. von Suttner) 151
Waging Nonviolent Struggle (Sharp) 225
"Waist Deep In the Big Muddy" (Seeger) 224
Walden Pond (US) 141
Wales 95
   see also Davies, George Maitland Lloyd* *and other Welsh*
War (Kollwitz) 171
"War" (Emerson) 137

War and Peace (Tolstoy)...143
"The War and the Intellectuals" (Bourne)...................... 153–154
war and violent behavior. *see also* conscientious objectors; education *and other cures*; genes and biology; Khan, Genghis *and other conquerors*; killing; naval power; Neolithic Period *and other periods*; social-cultural evolution; United States *and other countries*
    beginnings of 21, 25–26, 46, 237
    causes of.. v–vi, 269–273
    chemical.. 40, 42
    Cucuteni-Trypillian culture and 15
    culture and vii
    first artifact of 27–28
    gender and .... v–vi, 270–271
    just wars 76, 77–78, 105, 106, 107
    Mesolithic Period and 11–12
    perception of... vi–vii
    Sargon and 257
War Crimes .... viii, 165
"War Inconsistent with the Religion of Jesus Christ" (Dodge) ... 134, 136
War Is a Racket (Butler)...174
War of 1812 40
War of Roses 109
War of the Spanish Succession 128
War or Peace: One World or None (Wittner) 226
"The War Prayer" (Twain) 146–149
War Resisters League 187, 200, 202, 218
War Resisters Peace Award 191
Warring State period (China) 36, 77, 78–79
Warsaw Pact 209
Wars of the Roses 38
Washington, George (US) 267
"A Way to Disarm: A Practical Proposal (Holt) 213
weapons. *see also* chemical warfare; maces and mace heads; nuclear weapons
    development of 45
    Dodge* and 134–135
    Lao Tzu* on 75
    Shang Dynasty and 31
    Xunzi* on 79
Weavers (US) 224
Wedmore, peace of (Britain) 94
Welch, Joseph (US) 224
Wen* (Liu Heng) (Han Dynasty) 80
Wen (China) 31
Wen (Zhou Dynasty) 63

Wen Cheng (China) 101
Wen-Han Dynasty* 79–80
Weni (Egyptian commander) 26
"We Shall Overcome" (Seeger) 219
Wessex* (Britain) 93–94
western Asia 15, 34, 35, 85
"Where Have All the Flowers Gone" (Seeger) 224
"Which Side Are You On" (Seeger) 224
Who Rules the World (Chomsky) 197
Why Civil Resistance Works (Chenowith) 197
William of Orange (England) 251
Williams, Betty (Ireland) 254
William Sloan Coffin: A Holy Impatience (Goldstein) 199
William the Conqueror (Norman) 37, 105
Will War Ever End? (Chappell) 196
Wilson, Woodrow 153
Winter Soldier hearing (US) 228
witches 273
Witness Against Torture (US) 187, 216
Wittner, Lawrence S.* 226–227
Women, Power and the Biology of Peace (Hand) 211
Women against War 200
women and gender. *see also* equality; female images and figurines;
    goddesses; Greenham Common Women's Peace Camp* *and
    other organizations*; matrifocal cultures*; matrilinear societies and
    matriarchies; pregnancy; rape; von Suttner, Bertha* *and other women*
    Afghani 206
    agriculture and 46, 81
    art and 13
    Chaucer* on 107
    cooperation and caring and .... v, vi, vi–vii, 4, 6
    Costa Rica and 180
    education and 115
    honor killings and 273
    hunter-gatherers and 3–4, 6, 10, 12, 229
    Jemdet Nasr period and 19
    law codes and 58
    More on 115
    New England Non-Resistance Society and 139, 140
    nonviolence and 139
    opinions on human nature and v
    rights of 140, 157, 185, 195
    US tradition of cooperation and 263
    violence and .... v–vi

war and 84, 270–271
Women at the Hague: The International Congress of Women and its Results
   (Balch) 159
Women's International League for Peace and Freedom (WILPF) 158,
   159, 174, 187, 191, 200, 213
Women's Peace Party 213
women's rights movement 138
Women's Trade Union League of Boston 159
Woodstock Festival (US) 190
Woolman, John* (US) 128–129
Worcester, Noah* (US) 133–134
World Citizen movement 201
World Partisans of Peace 204
World Petition to Prevent War Between Nations 151–152
World War I (Great War). *see also* shell shock; Wilfred Owens* *and other critics*
   Addams* on 158
   aversion to killing and 232
   Balch* and 160
   Bourne* on 153–154
   Brittain* and 166
   Christmas Truce and 232–233
   effect of 237
   Ireland and 253
   Kollwitz* and 171
   overview of 42
   Rankin* and 174
   Russell* and 164, 166
   Shaw* and 162
World War II 43, 164, 174–175, 202, 210, 232, 233–234, 237
   see also Peace Pledge Union (New Zealand)
writing 27, 31, 49, 54, 81
Wu* (China) 31, 63
Wyclif, John* (England) 105, 106–107
Wyndham Land Purchase Act (1903) 252

X

Xerxes (Achemenid Empire) 34, 35
Xia Dynasty 30–31, 54
Xuanzong* (Tang dynasty) 99–101
Xunzi* 79

Y

Yahya, Abdulkadir Ali * 227

Yamna (Kurgans) (early Maikop) 23
Yang Guifei (China) 100
Yankee Nuclear Power Plant 200
Yao* (China) 31, 52–53
Yayoi culture (China) 14
Yellow River floods 53
Yemen 194
Ying Zheng (Qin Dynasty) 36
Yu* (China) 30–31, 54
Yuan, Li (China) 98
Yugoslavia 24
Yu the Great (China) 53

Z

Zarathustra* (Zoroaster) 62–63
Zeeks, Gadfly 106, 237
Zeus (god) 65
Zhao Tuo (China) 80
Zhou dynasty (China) 63–64, 75
Zhou Gong Dan* (Duke of Zhou) (China) 63–64, 79
Ziggurat of Ur 34, 57
Zinn, Howard* 184, 228, 271, 272
Zoroaster* (Persia) 62–63
Zulus (Africa) 42

Also available from Pisgah Press

	Donna Lisle Burton	
From Roots ... to Wings		$14.95
Letting Go: Poems 1983-2003		$14.95
Way Past Time for Reflecting		$17.95

	Michael Amos Cody	
Gabriel's Songbook		$17.95
A Twilight Reel		$17.95

| *Letters of the Lost Children* | **Ron Ferster & Jan Bevan** | $34.95 |

Robin Russell Gaiser

Musical Morphine: Transforming Pain One Note at a Time — $17.95
 Finalist, USA Book Awards—Health: Alternative Medicine, 2017
Open for Lunch — $17.95

Joseph R. Haun

Unbelievable: Faith, Reason, & the Search for Truth — $12.00

| *A Freethinker's Gospel* | **Chris Highland** | $16.95 |

	Michael Hopping	
rhythms on a flaming drum		$16.95
McTiernan's Bottle & other stories		$14.95

| *A Green One for Woody* | **Patrick O'Sullivan** | $15.95 |

Al & Sunny Lockwood

Cruising from Boston to Montreal — $14.95
Cruising the Atlantic — $12.00

| *The Last of the Swindlers* | **Peter Loewer** | $17.95 |

A.D. Reed

Reed's Homophones: A Comprehensive Book of Sound-alike Words — $14.95

Dave Richards

Swords in their Hands: George Washington and the Newburgh Conspiracy — $24.95
 Finalist, USA Book Award—History 2014

| *Trang Sen: A Novel of Vietnam* | **Sarah-Ann Smith** | $19.50 |

Nan Socolow

Invasive Procedures: Earthquakes, Calamities, & poems from the midst of life — $17.95

RF Wilson
THE RICK RYDER MYSTERY SERIES

Deadly Dancing — $15.95
Killer Weed — $14.95
The Pot Professor — $17.95

 Pisgah Press, LLC
PO Box 9663, Asheville, NC 28815-0663
www.pisgahpress.com